Responding to
Student Poems

Responding to Student Poems

Applications of Critical Theory

Patrick Bizzaro
East Carolina University

National Council of Teachers of English
1111 W. Kenyon Road, Urbana, Illinois 61801-1096

This book is written for my children, Jason and Kristin, who have taught me how to teach, and for my students.

Manuscript Editor: Michael E. Himick

Production Editor: Rona S. Smith

Cover Design: Barbara Yale-Read

Interior Book Design: Doug Burnett

NCTE Stock Number 40882-3050

Permission acknowledgments appear on page 236.

Library of Congress Cataloging-in-Publication Data

Bizzaro, Patrick.
    Responding to student poems : applications of critical theory / Patrick Bizzaro.
        p.   cm.
    Includes bibliographical references (p.   ).
    ISBN 0-8141-4088-2 : $19.95 (est.)
    1. English language—Rhetoric—Study and teaching.   2. Poetry—History and criticism—Theory, etc.   3. Poetry—Authorship—Study and teaching.   4. Creative writing—Study and teaching.   5. Poetics. I. Title.
PE1404.B584   1993
808.1—dc20   93-30623
                                                                                          CIP

First, suppose you had a chance to work with someone who would correct your writing into publishability. This person would be efficient, knowing, memorable, valid: an accomplished writer. In the company of this person you could go confidently into the center of current acceptance; you would quickly learn what brings success in the literary scene.

Now suppose another kind of associate. This one would accompany you as you discovered for yourself whatever it is that most satisfyingly links to your own life and writings. You would be living out of your own self into its expression, almost without regard to the slant or expectation or demands of editors and the public.

Let there be no mistake about it: a large and significant, and I believe most significant, group of writers today would prefer the second kind of company.

William Stafford, *Writing the Australian Crawl*

The unsettling fact is that in America the majority of new, "serious" imaginative writing is being produced by writers trained in M.F.A. programs staffed by teachers who themselves are products of M.F.A. programs.

Eve Shelnutt, "Notes from a Cell:
Creative Writing Programs in Isolation"

Most teachers do not share pedagogical strategies; and thus they lack any cohesiveness in their professional interpersonal relationships. By sharing their power and roles, teachers will be in a better position to break through the provincialism and narrow socialization that prevents them from sharing and examining their theory and practice of pedagogy with both students and colleagues.

Henry Giroux, *Teachers as Intellectuals*

Contents

Acknowledgments

First, I would like to thank James W. Kirkland of East Carolina University, who read and reacted to this book in its various incarnations, even as many as ten years ago when portions were being offered as journal articles. He is a true friend and colleague. And by sharing ideas with Nedra Reynolds of the University of Rhode Island and other of my fine colleagues at ECU, including Collett Dilworth and Frank Farmer, I was able to envision and re-envision many of the theoretical elements of this book.

I am also indebted to my colleagues Gay Wilentz and Jo Allen of East Carolina and Rebecca Smith of Barton College, whose advice on how I might approach my chapter on feminist criticism was surpassed only by their encouragement that I continue my work in that area in light of my gender limitations. They are excellent teachers. I would also like to express my appreciation to Resa Crane-Rodger of UNC–Greensboro for helping me better envision the layout of chapter 7.

Naturally, this book would not have been written if it weren't for the many fine students over the years who have found this approach to workshop instruction refreshing, challenging, and sometimes even interesting. Their writing appears with their permission and my appreciation throughout this book.

Still, I want to express my appreciation to East Carolina University, the Department of English, and Dean Keats Sparrow for providing me with time off from teaching early in the process of writing this book. During that time, the basic elements of the book came together in something similar to its current form.

What's more, the depth of Michael Spooner's kindness, encouragement, and patience as I brought this book to completion is unparalleled among the editors with whom I have worked.

My ideas evolved over the years, as some of the earlier efforts I made, published in various journals and collections of essays, will testify. I thus want to thank the following editors and publishers for permission to adapt or reprint materials from my previous publications: David Dillon for an article published in *Language Arts*, Alex Albright and Luke Whisnant for "Tobacco Fields," first published as "Collard Fields" in *Leaves of Green*, and Peter Makuck for "Imagining the Bees," first published in *Tar River Poetry*, all of which I make use of in chapter 2; Charles R. Duke and Sally A. Jacobsen, editors of *Poets' Perspectives: Reading, Writing, and Teaching Poetry*, and their publisher, Boynton/Cook, for material adapted for use in chapters 3, 5, and 8; Donald A. Daiker and Max Morenberg, editors of *The Writing Teacher as Researcher*, and their publisher, Boynton/Cook, for material used in chapter 8; and Nell Ann Pickett for material from *Teaching English in the Two-Year College* also used in chapter 8.

Finally, I cannot adequately express my gratitude to my wife, Susan, and our children, Jason and Kristin, without whom the courage to put a word on the page might never have come.

Introduction

If he is worth a damn, any poet teaching poetry writing constantly and often without knowing it is saying to the student, "Write the way I do. That's the best sound you can make." The student who shakes this, who goes on to his auditory obsessions and who writes the way the teacher never told him, may become a poet.

Richard Hugo, *The Triggering Town*

Perhaps no course in writing is more difficult to teach than poetry writing, and no task in that course more challenging than reading and evaluating poems written by student-writers. In spite of this fact, little scholarship has been published in recent years concerning how to teach students to write poems. At one extreme, this dearth of scholarship reflects our profession's lack of curiosity concerning what happens when teachers read and evaluate student poetry. At the other, it reflects simple acceptance of traditional but untested methods of instruction. Joseph M. Moxley (1989) essentially summarizes this predicament when he writes, "At present, no debate rages in professional journals as to whether creative writing programs are providing students with the necessary skills, knowledge of the composing process, or background in literature to write well" (xi). Wendy Bishop (1990) adds, "It is my belief that academic creative writing has not been responsive enough to theoretical and pedagogical changes now going on in literature studies and composition studies (not to mention cultural studies, feminist studies, and linguistics)" (xvi). She argues that "we need to move beyond critique and begin to institute more productive practices" (xvi).

Because no one has yet scrutinized methods of reading and evaluating student poems, we have had to rely for guidance upon the anecdotal reports and insights of expert-practitioners (see Moxley 1989, Turner 1980, Hugo 1979, Packard 1974 and 1987, and Stafford 1978). While no doubt valuable contributions to the teaching of poetry writing classes, these statements nonetheless leave us with a string of untested opinions. As a result, "no debate rages," and instructors must plan and teach their courses without access to a body of literature that would enable them to participate in what Sharon Crowley (1989) calls the "interrogation of the strategies used to teach reading and writing" (48).

Building a Foundational Understanding

This book attempts to "interrogate" a strategy teachers might employ in reading and evaluating student poems. It begins by encouraging teachers to better understand themselves as writers and readers; it ends by showing how teachers might use various literary-critical methodologies to evaluate student poems in a way that helps students shorten their apprenticeship to their master-teachers. There is little doubt that such apprenticeships exist, even among renowned literary figures. There is also little doubt that such apprenticeships can have ill effects, as Richard Hugo's (1979) discussion of Theodore Roethke's dominance over his students makes clear:

> Roethke, through his fierce love of kinds of verbal music, could be overly influential. David Wagoner, who was quite young when he studied under Roethke at Penn State, told me once of the long painful time he had breaking Roethke's hold on him. (29)

In fact, those who have considered the problems inherent in writing teachers' authority over their students wonder how writers ever manage to set themselves free. According to William Stafford (1978), "You can become a lost soul in literature just as surely as you can in any activity where you abandon yourself to the decisions of others" (78). This book confronts the problem of authority in the poetry writing course in the belief that teachers can do a great deal to shorten their students' apprenticeships by becoming what Stafford calls "the second kind of company."

The confrontation here begins by bringing together the concerns and strategies of the composition theorist and the literary critic in an effort to deal with matters not satisfactorily handled by "received" methods of instruction, which, for lack of a better name, I will call the traditional workshop approach (see chapter 7). Such matters include how the stated or unstated strategies teachers employ as writers, readers, and critics of their own writing influence the way they read, interpret, and evaluate their students' poems. Only if teachers recognize their reliance on received methods of instruction and evaluation will they be able to determine when methods employed "naturally" or "unknowingly" in examining their own writing will be helpful in evaluating their students' poems—and when evaluation through other critical lenses might be more beneficial. In the words of Bishop (1990), a pioneer in such inquiry, "By looking at our own processes and by studying current writing research, we can build a foundational understanding of composing that will help us choose and evaluate our own pedagogy" (15). To reinforce this view—that additional tools are necessary if we hope to institute more productive practices in evaluating student poems—recent commentary on reading and evaluating writing will be surveyed to show that methods of literary criticism are well suited to the goal of reading and interpreting student writing.

The best possible justification for a study such as this one seems uniquely related to the profession's reliance on untested methods of instruction in poetry writing classes. As Moxley (1989) notes, "Despite the rapid growth and popularity of courses and programs in creative writing, pedagogical techniques have not evolved all that much. In fact, perhaps because they studied at Iowa or were trained by graduates of the Iowa Writers Workshop, most creative writing teachers at the undergraduate and graduate levels follow the same studio method established at Oregon and Iowa over ninety years ago" (xiii). Such techniques need to be tested, especially since they rely upon the teacher's authority in all course-related matters, from selecting texts to judging student poems. And in testing this method of instruction, we must pay particular attention to the methods of reading and writing supported by traditional pedagogy, methods which "have not evolved all that much." For if we do not question this pedagogy now, the problem we must ultimately confront is, as Eve Shelnutt (1989) describes it, "the unsettling fact . . . that in America the majority of new, 'serious' imaginative writing is being produced by writers trained in M.F.A. programs staffed by teachers who themselves are products of M.F.A. programs" (4). Thus, the evolution of genre and potential for self-expression will be effectively checked.

Making Necessary Interrogations

This book does not attack or indict the workshop or studio method of instruction. Rather, its purpose is, first, to simply acknowledge the existence of a pedagogy long accepted in the teaching of poetry writing, and second, by bringing together recent findings concerning the interrelatedness of literary-critical theory and composition theory, to offer some new insights into how a teacher of poetry writing (and writers in most workshop situations) might most effectively approach the task of reading and evaluating student poems. The advice of teacher-writers as authorities, as usually echoed in workshops, is invaluable in guiding students in the making of poems. But many teachers are concerned that students be able to scrutinize, read, and

comment on poems from perspectives other than the narrow one offered through the power of tradition and privilege.

Questioning accepted pedagogy requires that we acknowledge
and name the critical lens through which an individual teacher reads
and evaluates poems, since only by doing so can teachers render
alternative readings. Thus, to read student texts differently, we must
first determine how individual teachers—including well-known expert-practitioners—use their experiences as writers in teaching students to write poems. Then we must accept the crucial challenge of
determining how other methods of reading might be employed in
commenting on student writing. Our ultimate goal from this perspective on reading and writing is to help students become more capable
and knowledgeable critics of poems, both their own and others'.

The problem, then, that must eventually be dealt with is not only
what Stephen Minot (1989) describes as placing "a student in the
context of a literary heritage" (89). An effort must also be made to help
both students and their teachers see that this "context" reveals itself to
teachers from certain cultural vantage points, perspectives learned
and subsequently perpetuated often without any conscious decision
by the teacher to do so, as is discussed in chapter 1. My examination
in chapter 2 of the critical perspective I employ in reading and writing
my own poems gives me reason to believe that the critical stance from
which teachers read and evaluate students' poems—especially in poetry writing classes, where no one seems to be certain what constitutes
a poem anyway—is determined by biases about what is meaning-
making in various drafts of a text. In short, then, this book's inquiry
into methods of reading and evaluating student poetry writing begins
where it should: with the self.

Most universities wisely hire "expert-practitioners" to teach poetry writing courses. But they do so not simply to bring esteem to the
university. Rather, well-published poets are hired to teach what they
do in the belief that their experiences as writers will fill the pedagogical void that has resulted, at least in part, from our reluctance as a
profession to explore, evaluate, and alter long-accepted approaches to
teaching poetry writing.

Applying Literary-Critical Methodology to Student Poems

The central effort of this book is to model in chapters 3–7 the way
various literary-critical theories—including the New Criticism, reader-
response criticism, deconstruction, and feminist criticism—can be

used both by the teacher in reading and evaluating student poems and by students during workshops in commenting on their peers' work. No doubt other critical methods are applicable to evaluating student poems. These four methods, however, offer a range of possible readings that I have tested, found most useful for students at various levels, and continue to use. What's more, they represent the range of possible relationships between student and teacher. As will be demonstrated in subsequent chapters, these methods offer teachers a way out of the predicament created by an exclusive reliance on received pedagogy, a predicament stated excellently, though unknowingly, by Alberta T. Turner in *Poets Teaching* (1980). In her overview of what she has discovered about the way expert-practitioners approach the teaching of their poetry writing courses, Turner notes that poets go about the task of commenting on drafts of student poems in a manner that reveals not only something of their personalities, but also what they value as writers, readers, and rewriters of their own poems. As Turner concludes, "To the student-poet as artificer the teacher-poets give (or rather offer) advice from their own experience as artificers" (15). That experience may include a wide range of activities, some beneficial to students, others not, but almost all of them unexamined as tools of instruction. And there is a good reason why they are unexplored.

Generally, we have left determination of how to safely enter, return from, and lead others back into the realm of poetry in the hands of a very few. Such territory has long been seen as sacred, and therefore beyond the scrutiny of any except the acknowledged experts. There are, for certain, no mapmakers among us to ease our anxiety over this journey. Even the reports of esteemed poets in various craft interviews as well as in Turner's excellent book are filled with guesswork and uncertainty. One thing we can be certain of, however, is that though expert-practitioners have not always enjoyed the respect they deserve in English departments, the writing of poems as an activity has been so elevated by other writers and teachers of writing that outsiders (that is, those who have not published poems widely) have been hesitant to inquire seriously into how students should be taught in a poetry writing course, even while they inquire further and further into the pedagogy of other writing courses. Moxley (1989) writes, "While many creative writing teachers and artists have tended to enshrine and mystify the creative process, composition theorists have been charting common patterns of how writers generate and refine material by studying the planning, prewriting, revising, and editing practices of professional and student writers" (27). But the information that composition theorists offer on composing has not, in general, enabled us to progress much beyond the early stages in answering basic questions about what ought to go on in poetry writing courses: What makes for good instruction in the making of poems? What kinds of influences might affect the way teachers read and evaluate student poems? And, most important for my purposes, does a connection exist between the way teachers read and evaluate drafts of their own poems, the way they comment on their students' drafts, and the activities (including the selection and discussion of anthologized poems) employed in their courses?

It may take years to satisfactorily answer any of these questions. After all, while teachers of composition are encouraged to continue interrogating the way they teach reading and writing, only recently has this responsibility applied to teachers of poetry writing. Naturally, many poets who teach students to write do not want to demystify the process of making a poem, which is not to say that they do not want their students to write well. Rather, they do not trust the language of pedagogy; the use of "methods" or "procedures" in helping students write poems might seem to many practicing poets as contradictory at best and dishonest at worst. Who would deny that poetry arises from some mysterious source? No doubt most teachers of writing would agree that the most difficult gift from nature to duplicate through artificial means is talent. Still, Shelnutt (1989) cautions against letting poetry writing's mystery blind our efforts to teach it:

> I have never been interested in the question that has plagued M.F.A. programs since their inception, namely, *can* creative writing be taught? The question puts teachers of writing immediately on the defensive and seems of little practical value— M.F.A. programs will doubtless continue to exist. Indeed, a number of English departments owe their fiscal security to writing programs. And since student demand for space in these programs grows yearly, the relevant questions seem to me to be, *what* are we teaching students who come to us wanting to learn how to write fiction, poetry, and nonfiction? And how does what we teach or fail to teach affect contemporary literature? (7–8)

Acknowledging the unique and special nature of poetry writing should not prevent us from making the necessary inquiries into what results in the most effective teaching of it.

Recommending Changes

Moxley (1989) notes that "taken as a whole," the authors who wrote essays for his book "make the following recommendations: (1) student writers must be readers—a background in literature and criticism enables student writers to identify and produce creative work; (2) academic training in writing must be rigorous and diverse; (3) student writers must have an understanding of the composing process and a knowledge of a variety of composing strategies; and (4) student writers must master the fundamentals of craft" (xvi). These four recommendations give rise to questions taken up in this book.

First, what influences the way students learn to read if not the reading habits of their teachers? This is perhaps a question that should be asked of teachers in all writing courses, but it is especially pertinent when asked about students learning to read poems. No doubt a corollary question is critical as well: Do teachers' habits of reading, when employed in reading and evaluating drafts of their own writing, influence the way they read, evaluate, and eventually grade drafts of their students' writing? Further, since teachers author the course syllabus and select model pieces to be read for and discussed in class, do they assign poems that satisfy their biases not only as readers, but also as writers? And, in the end, is there any harm in doing so? Is it more harmful to practice such modeling with advanced students than with beginning ones? Finally, is received pedagogy such as the workshop designed to reinforce the way an individual teacher determines meaning in a text? That is, do methods of instruction in poetry writing classes reflect a teacher's stated or unstated emphases and values as a reader and evaluator of poetry writing?

Second, if instruction in writing must be rigorous and diverse, as Moxley suggests, how do we make it so if teachers of writing—even expert-practitioners—do not determine for themselves how they approach the reading of poems and model their reading and writing processes for their students? To do otherwise is to employ a pedagogy that is both confusing and illogical, especially since teachers may find themselves talking about student writing by employing one set of critical tools and discussing anthologized works by employing another. The result? A student may receive mixed messages about what teachers value as meaning-making in a text—and, therefore, mixed messages about what they reward. Very little rigor and even less diversity of a pedagogically productive sort will occur in such a poetry writing class.

Third, if students are to have an understanding of the composing process and a knowledge of a variety of composing strategies, teachers must be conscious of the variety of ways a single text can be read. Of course, such consciousness means nothing if it is not communicated to students. Not only must students be introduced to current literary-critical theories, they must also be shown how to employ those theories in reading and evaluating poems written by students and professionals alike. For "if students in M.F.A. programs are not presented with the means by which to ask searching questions about imaginative forms, how will universities continue to make a distinction between the kind of education provided in a university setting and that provided by commercial schools of writing" (Shelnutt 1989, 10)? This means, of course, that in addition to the received methods of instruction used in reading drafts of their own poems, teachers must be adept at employing a variety of alternative methods for reading and evaluating poems written by their students. In the end, a pedagogy suited to the teaching of poetry writing must connect literary-critical methodology to reading strategies. The hybrid that results must, in turn, enable us to overcome limitations imposed on us by the very habits we employ naturally or unknowingly in reading our own texts, for those habits influence and limit our perceptions of and responses to our students' writings. Alterations to the current pedagogy must inevitably have as their goal "showing students how to revise and edit their manuscripts" (Moxley 1989, xvii), and they must show students how to do this in as many ways as possible.

And fourth, if students are to learn the fundamentals of craft and overcome what Shelnutt (1989) calls "the writing students' intellectual isolation," we must broaden our notions of craft to include not only the craft of writing, researching, and submitting manuscripts, but also the craft of reading and understanding literature. Only then will students be able to find where their writings fit into the larger and ongoing efforts of other writers. An explanation missing in the little commentary available concerning reading and evaluating student poetry writing is one that addresses the value of helping students comment on their peers' work during workshops by employing various methods of literary analysis—including the use of the New Critical, reader-response, deconstructive, and feminist critical lenses employed in chapters 3–6—that are usually reserved for commenting on literary texts. And we need another explanation to assess the value of employing different literary-critical strategies in the workshop situation, as in chapter 7, and in grading student poems, as in chapter 8. From this perspective, Moxley's (1989) insights are prophetic: "Engaging students' imaginations requires an interdisciplinary approach, one which brings together creative writing, literature, criticism, and composition" (25).

And there is little doubt that literary theory has been employed in interpreting student texts all along. All available evidence suggests that the task of reading, interpreting, and evaluating student poetry writing in most workshop situations typically requires the use of New Critical assessments—whether applied consciously or not—of the sort advocated by Alan Ziegler (1981 and 1984) in his popular guides to teaching creative writing *The Writing Workshop, Vol. 1* and *The Writing Workshop, Vol. 2*. Ziegler (1981) writes:

> Mechanically, most revisions are additions, subtractions, or replacements. I offer students the following metaphor for approaching revision.
> Imagine that you are the boss of a factory or company, and the words you have written are your employees. You are an extremely tough, demanding boss, but a fair one. If the workers are productive, they stay; if not, they go.
> Some words get fired because they don't do their jobs well and need to be replaced, as in "The meal set before him was unappetizing."
> The word "unappetizing" gets the pink slip, perhaps being replaced by "greasy, with a faint odor of ammonia." (80)

Without citing more of Ziegler's advice than this on how to be a good "word boss," it should be clear that revision to Ziegler and many others influenced by received pedagogy is a matter of text manipulation, as will be shown in chapters 1 and 2. Though Ziegler and others (see Tsujimoto 1988, Johnson 1985, and Bishop 1990) offer some excellent advice concerning how and when to make such manipulations, the fact that the New Criticism dominates discussions of student writing reflects, I think, our limited scrutiny and inquiry into what we do and what works best in teaching students to write poems. With such limited vision, we often end up enforcing certain kinds of authoritative readings in the poetry writing classroom, not all of which benefit our students.

1 Literary Theory, Composition Theory, and the Reading of Poetry Writing

John Crowe Ransom was to visit Workshop one week, and a ludicrous thing happened. Our poems were submitted and then multigraphed in the office, and my poems for that week . . . got shaken down to two, and these for reasons of economy were pushed close together on one page. Mr. Ransom kindly fished my page out and began an analysis with so much finesse and care that I began to realize that I was the only one present who knew that the page was supposed to be two poems. That afternoon the New Criticism welded my poems brilliantly together, and I was too gratified, and too timid, to pull them apart.

William Stafford, *Writing the Australian Crawl*

In the poetry writing workshop (as in most other courses in writing), students' texts are most often read and evaluated through methods influenced by the New Criticism. There is little reason to be surprised at this, though. Indeed, the graduate education that prepared an entire generation of teachers to be experts in the analysis of literary texts makes the New Criticism's dominance in the affairs of the writing workshop inevitable. As a result, literary theory, composition theory, and the evaluation of student poetry writing have always been intertwined for many teachers, perhaps unknowingly and without question. The fact is, they had never been taught that the theories were different, especially on a matter so basic to evaluation as where the authority for finding meaning in a poem can be placed.

Nonetheless, in undergraduate poetry writing classes and graduate workshops alike, an increasing number of teachers argue for poststructuralist methods of reading literary texts, calling into question long-held assumptions about where meaning resides. Many of these same teachers, however, continue to model New Critical meth-

---

This chapter is based on a paper presented at CCCC in Chicago, 1990.

ods and assumptions in their in-draft evaluations of student poems. While in recent years the field of literary theory has exploded with alternative ways of approaching texts and raging debates over where meaning resides, these teachers, often unconsciously, continue to read and evaluate student writing, including student poems, within the tenets of the New Criticism, ensuring that this conventional approach and its ideology will persist.

Turner's *Poets Teaching: The Creative Process* (1980) offers a case in point. Turner's introduction—in which she gives an overview of the teaching methods used by thirty-two well-known poets—suggests wide use of exactly this traditional perspective on reading and writing as text manipulation:

> Studying writing [is] a process of sharpening perception: awareness of all the connotations of a word, of all the rhythms of an emotion, of all the possible clashes among images, awareness of clichés and how to avoid them or use them so that they become effective allusion. . . . (1)

For Turner and many of the poets whose observations about student poems appear in her book, meaning seems to be something that begins inside the student and, if it is brought outside the student at all, comes to exist in the word, the rhythms, the allusions—in short, in the text.

By contrast, in *Creative Writing in America* (1989), a more recent endeavor at determining what should be taught in a creative writing course, Moxley includes the complex skill of reading like a writer. On the one hand, Moxley notes that "writing students need to become active readers—to study the point of view, the tone, the plotting and other techniques that the authors employ" (259), suggesting that students need to perceive meaning as technique, as text manipulation. But, addressing what recent critical commentators such as those cited later in this chapter have urged, Moxley goes on to say that "writers need to question what effect the writer's personal and social history has had on that writer's choice of subject matter and treatment" (259), suggesting that meaning is also determined by matters outside the text.

The messages of Moxley and other recent commentators—notably Wendy Bishop, who in *Released into Language* (1990) identifies recent efforts to merge composition studies with critical theory—have been clear: we need to be conscious of what we are doing when we respond to all student writing, especially student poetry, because in many cases we are sending our students conflicting messages about what we value as meaning-making in discourse, poetic and otherwise.

To this end, we need to unravel some of the ambiguity that abounds in much of our discourse with students, first by noticing the prevalence of New Criticism in current theories of writing and then by examining recent developments concerning the interrelatedness of literary theories and composition theories. The question we must ask is, Does literary theory provide a viable means for reading and evaluating student poems?

Examining the Text for Meaning

In recent years, we have become increasingly conscious of critical theories and their relation to our reading and interpretation of a wide range of texts. Even as you read this chapter, agreeing with what is said or disagreeing, you will receive or re-create or deconstruct the text, depending, of course, on where for you, consciously or unconsciously, the authority for meaning resides: in the text, in the receiver of the text, or outside the text, in what, in effect, has not been written. Clearly, the meaning of this chapter may be influenced by a wide range of matters in addition to (or because of) the language it offers: some in its structure, some in its ideology, and some outside its ideology. In any case, teachers of poetry writing must be clear on the way they determine meaning when confronted by a text. Otherwise, we risk sending students the conflicting message that we apply one set of values and attitudes toward meaning to literary texts and quite another to their productions.

For nearly forty years, the New Criticism alone has had a place of unquestioned authority in its relationship to the reading and evaluation not only of canonical literature, but of student texts as well. Undoubtedly because so many of the students who received advanced degrees between the Second World War and the end of the Vietnam Era have backgrounds as literary specialists, the New Critical methodology taught in the graduate schools of that time still persists in methods of reading and evaluating. Well known is the theory that in the post–World War II period, when university professors were anxious about having their political preferences called into question, the New Criticism, by virtue of its elevation of the text as the authority for meaning, made the study of literature apolitical and, as a result, safer than innocent membership in certain social clubs. But, as William E. Cain (1984) notes, "Politics cannot be avoided in literary study, and we should not pretend otherwise" (xiv). We might add to this that politics cannot be avoided in the classroom, and we should not pretend otherwise. For surely the politics of the classroom make teachers, as exemplary readers, authorities for determining meaning, not only in literary texts, but in student texts as well.

To permit themselves this privilege, teachers give assignments, offer observations, and employ teaching strategies that make New Critical estimations possible. For example, the looming question at a recent meeting of the National Testing Network in Writing was "How in assessing writing do we build into writing prompts the stimuli that evoke what we desire from students?" (quoted in Wolcott 1987, 41). By and large, we continue to view writing as a text-centered discourse, and we continue to assign tasks that can be evaluated as though meaning exists in the text itself. Again, to cite Cain in *The Crisis in Criticism* (1984):

> What we have is a curious phenomenon. The New Criticism appears powerless, lacking in supporters, declining, dead or on the verge of being so. No one speaks on behalf of the New Criticism as such today, and it figures in critical discourse as the embodiment of foolish ideas and misconceived techniques. But the truth is that the New Criticism survives and is prospering, and it seems to be powerless only because its power is so pervasive that we are ordinarily not even aware of it. (10)

Describing the Text: New Criticism and Composition Theory

Many of us have attempted in recent years to keep the New Criticism out of our systems for evaluation, but with little success. One reason for this resistance to change is that most of the currently fashionable methods for evaluating writing begin with the premise that meaning exists in the text. In this vein, it is interesting and enlightening to juxtapose the language of current theories for evaluating student writing with language expressing New Critical values and emphases. Take this brief excerpt from Charles Cooper's "Holistic Evaluation of Writing" (1977):

> Procedures to follow in developing an analytic scale are simple though time-consuming. Since the features that make up the scale must be *derived inductively from pieces of writing in the mode* for which the scale is being constructed, the first requirement is for *large amounts of writing.* . . . (14, emphasis mine)

Now compare Cooper's explanation with the following excerpt from Rene Wellek's *Theory of Literature* (1949):

> The real poem must be conceived as a structure of norms. . . .
> The norms we have in mind are *implicit norms* which have to be
> *extracted from every individual experience of a work of art* and to-
> gether make up the genuine work of art as a whole. (150–51,
> emphasis mine)

Cooper may not have intended to so clearly echo Wellek's insistence
that the measure of a text's value comes from norms that are implicit
to the kind of text it is and extracted from all other texts of its kind. Of
course, while we might say that a reader, and not a textbase, is being
built from all these "poems" and "papers," the reader built is, as W.
John Harker (1987) points out, one who "insist[s] on the external
verification of [reading] by direct reference to the text" (244). Clearly,
continues Harker, "while it may at first seem that the affective fallacy
dismissed the reader entirely, this is not so. Rather, the New Criticism
clearly established the reader's role and set out the arena of critical
activity within which the reader could legitimately function" (244).

Such a close correspondence in theory between Cooper and
Wellek suggests that the attitudes, values, and emphases of the New
Criticism are, as Cain (1984) so convincingly argues, "so deeply ingrained in English studies . . . that we do not even perceive them as the
legacy of a particular movement" (105). And the reading and evaluating of student poems are no less influenced by the New Criticism than
the reading and evaluating of student essays in a composition class.
Even those expert-practitioners who have not received advanced degrees have likely been influenced in learning to read and write—even
in the elementary and middle grades—from teachers who had similarly been taught to find meaning among the marks on the page; a
teacher is not required to know what the New Criticism is to unconsciously or naturally employ it in examining texts, whether canonical
or noncanonical.

The politics of the New Criticism permeate the classroom. After
all, few arenas offer the power of privilege so totally unchecked by a
second or third party than the classroom, especially in the poetry
writing course. If a teacher devises the plan for teaching the material,
offers the authoritative reading of assigned texts, stipulates specific
requirements for student writings, suggests revisions, and offers
grades and justifications for grades, then the teacher is not only doing
most of the writing in the course, as Crowley (1989) asserts, but is
setting rigorous laws for students to abide by. Crowley offers this:

> . . . teachers do most of the writing in composition classes. . . .
> Students, on the other hand, spend most of their time reading:

they read the teacher, to determine what he "wants"; they read
the textbooks or anthologies he has assigned to find out what
he wants them to know; they read his assignments to determine
what he wants them to do. When they "write" in response to his
assignments, they tell him what they think he wants to see
realized in their papers. Almost never do they envision themselves as having something to teach their teachers. (35–36)

If Crowley's remarks are true about the composition class, no doubt
they apply to classes in other kinds of writing as well, including those
in poetry writing.

Decentralizing Authority

Before we consider employing literary-critical methods in evaluating
student poems, we should consider several questions that will influence not only the kinds of comments students receive from us, but also
the way we teach our classes.

First, what will happen to our authority as evaluators if we
employ methods of analysis that undermine what students have been
taught by previous teachers to expect? If we do not always employ the
New Criticism when we read canonical literature—"real" literature—
but do employ it when we confront students' literature, we are encountering student texts, as Edward White (1985) says, "as if our
confusion about evaluation is somehow bound up with a confusion
about the nature of the student text, an odd form of literature created
for the sole purpose of being criticized" (95). More than that, if we treat
student texts with the respect usually reserved for "real" literature, we
as teachers somehow diminish our importance in the classroom. We
need to consider the critical issue at stake here, the issue of privilege:
What if the usual authority for meaning (i.e., the text)—and, therefore,
the guidelines for reading and the advice to students about revising
(i.e., manipulating the text)—exists somewhere else, as it does when
we employ alternative literary-critical methods (e.g., reader-response
criticism, deconstruction, feminist criticism)? If it does exist somewhere else, the traditional argument for authority in the classroom—
by virtue of tradition and privilege—will no longer apply, and
authority will inevitably become decentralized.

Second, what will happen to texts written in our classes if we do
not require students to make them conform to certain norms or contain
within them certain rhetorical features? Clearly, the evaluation of texts
poses a problem in reading. Among other things, we will be required
in writing courses to teach our students, and in some cases ourselves,

how to be better readers, to empower them to see texts—their own and others'—differently, to devise a plan for their own writing not just from the perspective of author, but also from the point of view of a first reader who can see the text better by having been shown how to view it through various critical lenses.

Third, what then will be the teacher's responsibility in evaluating student texts? Teachers should serve as model readers, employing various critical methods both in analyzing literature in class and in evaluating and commenting on student writing. The commentary that results from these methods will at first seem unusual, as I show in chapters 4, 5, and 6. And it will be substantially different from commentary made only from a text-centered perspective, relying not on intertextual comments but, for example, on the writing of "parallel" or "detached" texts. Still, one obvious benefit of employing literary-critical methods is that teachers will no longer send the mixed message to their students that in canonical literature meaning can be determined through a variety of rich and interesting methods, while in student literature it can only be measured in terms of the text.

Clearly, the decision to employ literary-critical methodology in evaluating student writing, poetry or otherwise, is a commitment to make changes in the classroom. After all, if meaning in student texts is no longer seen from one perspective only—that is, from the perspective of the New Criticism—we will no longer be able to say to students, as we seem to have said, whether implicitly or explicitly, for so long, "I, the teacher, am an exemplary reader. Your job as student is to please *me*. If I can't be moved by your text, you better take my advice on *how* to move me." In short, we may need to become authorities on how to disperse authority. Of course, to some extent, our early efforts at decentralizing authority in the classroom will be problematic.

Any solution we offer to these problems will alter not only the tools of evaluation, but methods of pedagogy as well, since pedagogical concerns in the teaching of reading and writing increasingly seem to be driven by how we locate meaning in a text. If we determine meaning in student texts using the same critical methods that we apply to literary texts, we will be forced to rearrange our classrooms to accommodate the decentralized authority. But at least we will no longer offer our students contradictory evidence concerning what we value as discourse or employ a pedagogy that, by its very nature, is illogical and confusing.

One method for overcoming the confusion that often arises from the use of traditional pedagogy in the poetry workshop—and it is the method advocated here—requires teachers to begin with self-analysis. By this I mean that we must first ask ourselves where meaning resides in both canonical texts as well as our own. Once we do this, we will be better able to help our students consciously find meaning there and understand the implications of the approach we use. Then we must do the hard work of determining if and when those same principles can be profitably put to use in examining student writing. In the process, we must overcome the tendency to give in to time-worn and out-moded arguments of authority-by-privilege, since the most effective approach to a student text will probably require us to employ critical methods we do not ordinarily apply to our own works. There are, however, no models for this hard work. As a result, models and justi-fications for the application of reader-response criticism, deconstruc-tion, and feminist criticism in examining student poems are offered in chapters 4, 5, and 6. Still, we are at the beginning, in some ways at the mercy of established tools of assessment that we have received, often with other purposes such as literary analysis and protection from political persecution in mind.

To move forward, we must answer several questions that are answered entirely or in part in the chapters that follow. What can we learn about our hidden biases as critics by examining our own processes of writing? What are the limits of the New Criticism as a method for commenting on student poems? How can we profitably employ other literary-critical methods, such as reader-response criticism, deconstruc-tion, or feminist criticism, as tools for reading and evaluating student poems? Can we teach students to employ these methods during work-shops in commenting on each other's works? What kinds of revisions are students apt to make in response to comments from these various critical perspectives? And, finally, can an entire curriculum be devised for use in a poetry writing workshop that takes as its aim commenting on student writing by using various critical methodologies?

These "interrogations of the strategies used to teach reading and writing" will be far-reaching, influencing not only the way we evalu-ate writing, but also the way we assign writing tasks and the strategies we provide students with as they attempt to "read" our assignments.

Relating Literary Theory to Composition Theory: Some Recent Commentary

Fortunately, some interrogations have already begun. A great deal of recent commentary suggests that the time is right for us to rethink not only the relationship between literary and composition theory, but to rethink pedagogy if we find such a link. In effect, the question now being asked is, Should we read student texts as we read literary texts? John Clifford and John Schlib (1985) note that "efforts to synthesize the two pedagogies seem refreshing, not only because they promise to unify a curriculum that has suffered too long from fragmentation but also because they proceed from sophisticated understandings of what writing and literary interpretation can involve" (45). Tilly Warnock (1983) advances this same notion when she suggests that we juxtapose what writing theorists know and do with what, "for example, a specialist in Renaissance drama knows and does with language" (176). And Patricia Bizzell (1987) takes us one step further when she writes in her review of Edward White's *Teaching and Assessing Writing* that "although he doesn't quite say so, White seems to be arguing that student essays should be treated like literary texts, both in the sense that each student by virtue of being human deserves the sort of respectful reading that we are accustomed to give canonical authors, and in the sense that the same reading techniques English teachers use on literature can be used on student writing" (578). These views have made virtually inevitable the language of Patricia Donahue and Ellen Quandahl (1989). They write, "As the new work in composition demonstrates, critical theory offers us a voice that lets us hear ourselves: a way to interpret and revise our own practices" (6).

One of the barriers to proceeding from here is that the model for evaluation we currently have to work with—a model whose source is so basic to the way we think that we hardly ever seek it—is based on New Critical emphases, no matter how we manipulate them. What's more, such models are chiefly useful, like the New Criticism itself, in evaluating texts that solve writing problems devised with New Critical values in mind. Herein lies the source of confusion for many of our students in our discourse with them: students, both like their teachers and because of them, are steeped in New Critical methodology and need to become aware of how they have been taught to make meaning in a text before discussions of writing or comments written on their papers will make any sense. One way for teachers to confront this problem is to study their habits of reading their own writing, determine how they make meaning as they revise their texts, and then learn to discuss with their classes what they have discovered. Many introspective teachers have come to see that pedagogy is driven by their stated or unstated need to emphasize and reinforce what they believe to be meaning-making in a text. And many composition theorists, impatient with the persistence of New Critical emphases, are already revamping their views of reading, interpreting, and evaluating student writing.

Nonetheless, we must consider at least two other matters: first, that most of our thinking about the relationship between literary-critical methodologies and the evaluation of student writing is theoretical, and second, that we have far fewer models for employing poststructural developments in critical theory in the evaluation of writing than we do for employing the New Criticism. If critical theory and composition theory "interact," new models for reading and evaluating (and perhaps even intruding upon or construing) student writing, such as those offered in chapters 3–6, will need to be developed to reflect our current understanding of discursive authority.

In one helpful study, Lester Faigley (1989) "examines assumptions about selves in writing evaluation" (396). His starting point— that "writing teachers have been as much or more interested in *who* they want their students to be than in *what* they want their students to write" (396)—seems to reinforce a broader belief: that "each judgment of value is made from some notion of value, usually a notion that is widely shared within a culture" (395). Faigley's effort at finding "a description of the selves that writing teachers now privilege in 'good' writing" takes us outside the boundaries of New Critical methodology and into what we would have to tentatively call reader response, precisely because the "selves" found in the good writing analyzed are not found *in* the text. Rather, they are found in the *reader's reconstruction* of the text. Faigley remarks at one point, without reaching a formal conclusion, "I'm struck by how similar student and teacher sound" (408).

But this view of pedagogy is also "tentative" because some of these reconstructed selves, these personas, are ideologically constructed. "It's no wonder, then," writes Faigley a bit later in his essay, "that the selves many students try to appropriate in their writing are voices of authority" (410). We need to remember that how we teach is what we teach. Or, to say this with a slightly different pedagogical emphasis, nonetheless ideological, what the profession often seeks as the critical element in evaluating discourse is its adherence to and reinforcement of certain unstated premises about social relations in the classroom, relations such as writer to reader and student to teacher. In short, if we believe the authority for meaning resides in the reader, we must recognize the potential influence of ideology on what is reconstructed and see that Faigley's study reflects a growing awareness in our profession that subtle changes are underway in the way we interpret student writing.

Clearly, if reader-response and ideologically based methods, values, and emphases have come to influence current approaches to evaluating student writing, we must examine these approaches and name them. Until then, we must wonder how to honestly discuss with students what we value and reward in their writing. It would be foolish, even unethical, to tell students the little we seem to know right now about how we evaluate writing: that we reward writing that states our personal ideologies in a voice which, when reconstructed, echoes a self we associate with good writers, one honest, humble, and on the path to self-discovery, but admittedly not quite there. We should keep in mind Donahue and Quandahl's reminder in *Reclaiming Pedagogy* (1989) that "in teaching cultural critique, we must not become blind to the ideology of our own position" (4).

How may this changing perspective on evaluating student writing influence our classrooms? John Trimbur (1989) contributes to the growing understanding of this problem—especially as it may affect the poetry workshop—from the perspective that pedagogy is reinforced by ideology and, as a result, reflects certain values that may hinder our efforts at making needed adjustments to accommodate our changing perspectives on meaning in texts and authority in the classroom. Trimbur argues that "pedagogies that take the individual as the irreducible, inviolate starting point of education—whether through individualized instruction, cultivation of personal voice, or an emphasis on creativity and self-actualization—inscribe a deeply contradictory ideology of individualism in classroom practice" (604). By advocating collaborative learning, Trimbur does not advocate simply locating the authority for meaning in what Stanley Fish calls "interpretative communities." Rather, the contradictions he refers to result from the conflict between a pedagogy such as the traditional poetry workshop, which seems to give authority to the group, and a method of evaluation that thunders in the authority of the teacher. As a result, Trimbur takes a position very near to the one advocated here "by asking why interpretation has become the unquestioned goal of literary studies and what other kinds of readings thereby have been *excluded* and *devalued*" (613, emphasis mine). He writes, "We might begin the conversation in literature classes by talking not about how to read a literary text but rather about how the students in the course have been trained to read literature and how their schooled reading differs from the way they read outside of school" (613). Trimbur does more than offer insight into the contradictions that abound in many class-rooms; he also provides the basis for a model of instruction through which we can transfer authority from the teacher-as-reader to other members of the classroom community as readers, a model ideal for use in workshops. To enable this transfer, the teacher in a poetry writing class might begin by talking not about how a poem may be written, but about how a poem may be read and what identity a student asserts in offering a particular reading.

The poetry workshop does offer us an opportunity to enable our students to assume and assert identity in the classroom. As Robert E. Brooke (1991) argues, teachers must become increasingly conscious of the possible roles offered to students in a writing course, since students are more apt to improve as writers in a workshop situation if a teacher focuses on the students' efforts to better understand themselves. "Rather than focus directly on students' writing," says Brooke, "I suggest that we see writing as part of a much larger and more basic activity: the development and negotiation of individual identity in a complex social environment" (5). Brooke argues convincingly that "because students in workshops are able to explore writers' roles outside the narrow context of the classroom, they can begin to use writing as a means of addressing other roles they face" (28). But we must not forget that students can, and must, make the same explorations of identity with reading in a workshop if they are provided with instruction in reading methods and with an opportunity to play various roles as readers in responding to their peers' writing.

Ultimately, however, since students, like teachers, read according to the models they have learned, we—in a dialogue that includes our students—must consider what exactly would constitute good teaching of reading and writing. Let's start with three central premises that can influence the way we read, evaluate, and comment on student poems:

> 1. Though the most thoroughly developed pedagogy of reading and writing involves either the New Critical apparatus or the manipulation of that apparatus, we should *not* teach exclusively from the perspective that the final authority for determining meaning resides in the text.
>
> 2. A growing number of classroom teachers feel comfortable using alternative literary-critical methods for discussing literature. Still, the hard work of developing these methods into useful tools for reading, evaluating, and commenting on student

writing has just begun. What's more, good teaching of reading and writing will do more to develop an entire pedagogy based on these critical approaches, including not only their application in the evaluation of student writing, but also the design of assignments, instructional materials, and methods of intervention.

3. Recent scholarly endeavors—including Faigley's, Trimbur's, and Brooke's—ask questions that any good teacher of writing and reading should ask. For one, what self is privileged as belonging to good writers? For another, how do we disperse for students the authority for meaning in a text so that they will see both reading and writing as meaning-making activities, the writer making meaning by reading and the reader by rewriting the text? And third, how can the workshop enable students to explore identity by adopting various reading strategies?

What remains to be made is an effort to take theory and move it into the realm of practice, an effort that must involve these three steps.

First, we must see that the chief purpose for a class in writing, poetry or otherwise, is to enable students to determine meaning as readers and writers (including as readers of their own writing) in various ways. Without advocating the teaching of theory per se any more than touting any single theory, we must nonetheless reassess the ways we teach reading and writing. This reassessment may require us to respond to what seems to be our students' underlying request: that we spend less time telling them what they should do when they write and more time showing them who they can be.

Second, teachers must become more conscious of the critical methodologies they use both when they talk with students about literature and when they evaluate student writing. There is no substitute for examining how and why we teach reading and writing as we do. And the results of this examination should be shared with students, perhaps through the process of self-examination modeled in the next chapter.

Finally, we must devise assignments, instructional materials, and pedagogy, not just instruments of evaluation, compatible with the way we approach literary texts in classroom discussions. Simply put, how we teach is what we teach. Thus, what students learn in our classrooms about reading comes by and large from how we read, and guide them in reading, their own texts, a process modeled in chapters 3–7.

2 The Teacher as Writer, Reader, and Editor

More than two years of telephone calls, meetings in Georgia, Virginia, New York, and Vermont, and prolonged debate have not allowed us to articulate any better that initial standard: We wanted poems we liked.

Dave Smith and David Bottoms, "The Anthology in Our Heads" (introduction to *The Morrow Anthology of Younger American Poets*)

Methods teachers employ in the teaching of writing are influenced by a wide range of matters, many of which can be traced to the teacher's habits of writing, reading, and revising. The effort to trace such influences inevitably leads us back to the self, for one of the most important sources of information worth exploring prior to teaching courses in poetry writing is in teachers' examinations of their own habits of writing, reading, and revising. Of course, Moxley (1989) is correct when he states that "theorizing that things ought to be done is much easier than explaining how these things can be accomplished" (xvii). But the related question that this chapter addresses is why things often get done as they do in the teaching, reading, and evaluating of student poems, especially since teachers' biases influence not only what the teacher believes is good poetry—or what poetry is at all for that matter—but also how a teacher guides students in revising their poems.

To better understand what they are attempting to impart to their students, then, teachers of poetry writing should begin by examining their own writing habits. Clearly, students must be taught the two ways that writers read, one way in examining their own texts and the other in examining others' texts. But to perform such teaching, teachers must have written some poems of their own and learned how they read drafts of those poems. This might not be a problem in M.F.A. programs where poetry writing courses are taught by expert-practitioners, but poetry writing classes elsewhere are often taught by people who have achieved advanced degrees in the study of poetry but never

---

Some portions of this chapter first appeared in *Language Arts* (October 1983). Other portions are based on a paper presented at SCETC, Jackson, Mississippi, 1989.

written a poem (see Bishop 1990, 1). Instruction by these teachers will inevitably be off the mark, since their lack of appropriate experience will prevent them from developing what David St. John (1989) calls "apprenticeship relationships" with their students. As St. John explains, "It is crucial that the students sense their teacher's excitement and involvement not only with their writing but also with his or her *own* writing as well" (189).

Certainly, teachers of poetry writing classes who do not write *should*; there is no substitute for experience. For teachers who do not write, no one's advice about how to teach poetry writing to students will do much good. But teachers should take the risk of writing a poem keeping in mind that the point is not necessarily to produce an excellent poem, which is a difficult task under any circumstances. Rather, their aim should be to experience firsthand what their students will experience in the belief that the best teachers of writing are most often writers themselves. They should not, however, buy the argument that the best writers are the best teachers of writing, no matter how vigorously or insistently that argument is made. But we must nonetheless confront what Shelnutt (1989) writes about the status of the creative writing teacher, namely, that "a 'star' can give a student's manuscript to an agent or editor to be heard, while a writing teacher whose national reputation is modest may simply ask the student to consider a variety of revisions" (16). The message offered in such an observation should be obvious: while the goal for both the "star" and the teacher with the modest national reputation is to get students to write excellent poems, the prominent poet offers students a greater chance to publish that excellent poem. Nonetheless, both kinds of poets teach poetry writing classes, and the goal of this book is to help both accomplish their primary goal by exploring methods of reading and evaluating that will enable students to write excellent poems.

We should remember that if it were true that only the best writers should teach writing, only the boldest and most shameless among us would show up to teach any writing course, let alone a course as difficult to teach as poetry writing. So, without arguing for the worth of my own approach to writing—or of my own writing—I want to show why I became interested in monitoring my writing process and to examine drafts of two of my poems, first to reveal something of my hidden biases toward writing poems and then to determine how my habits of reading drafts of my own writing influence the way I read drafts of both my students' writing and of finished texts submitted to me as poetry editor of a journal. For surely not all (if any) of my methods of teaching and evaluating student poetry writing come from outside sources, in part because so few of these sources exist. What's more, I, like many who teach poetry writing without ever having taken a writing workshop, am conscious of what portion of my teaching is received and what is "invented." Nonetheless, I do not argue for better or worse methods of teaching students to write poetry, only for more informed methods. And we certainly are not informed teachers of poetry writing classes if we do not write poetry or if we are not clear on how we go about the task of revising drafts of the poems we do write.

From this perspective it should be clear that craft interviews, such as those in the *New York Quarterly* (see Packard 1974 and 1987) where "expert-practitioners" are asked (presumably because they are expert practitioners and not necessarily because they are expert teachers) to examine how they teach their students, tend to benefit the expert-practitioner more than the reader. The same might be said of a collection of essays such as Turner's *Fifty Contemporary Poets: The Creative Process* (1977), for which poets are asked to discuss the making of one of their poems (but without the useful reference to what this tells them about how they teach students to write poetry). While these texts serve to some extent to demystify the making of poems, the kind of examination they offer can do teachers of poetry writing more good if viewed as models for the self-examination teacher-writers should employ prior to teaching a course in poetry writing. Such models provide a way out of the trap of teaching students to write poems by emphasizing, consciously or unconsciously, the mystery of the creative process. As Moxley (1989) writes:

> Though some elements of the creative process are indeed mysterious and though some creators are geniuses, emphasizing the mysterious nature of creativity erects walls around our writing classrooms. With a dismissive wave of a hand, we should not foster the myth that writers are born, that you cannot teach someone to be a talented writer. The price of our lack of pedagogical and theoretical inquiry is isolation and divestment: many students don't enroll in writing courses because they've been trained to think they're neither creative nor gifted. Still others avoid writing (and literature) courses because they perceive English and writing to be an esoteric discipline, an artistic (or even magical) activity depending solely on divine inspiration. (28)

Unless teachers become conscious of the way personal habits of writing, reading, and revising influence the way they teach, their teaching may be more a matter of guesswork than of planned, flexible, and therefore revisable behavior. This is especially true of the writing of poetry, which, as I have argued in "Poetry and Audience" (1988), is basically the teaching of what one believes poetry to be. But what Moxley (1989) says of teaching students to write stories is true of teaching students to write poems as well:

> Our goal should not be to defend the tower—a particular code of aesthetics—but to help students write the kind of story [or poem] they want to write and to expose students to a variety of literary forms. (260)

After all, what is "the tower" where poetry writing is concerned if not what the teacher (or the editor) believes it to be? And what teacher teaches from greater isolation than the teacher of poetry writing? As Bishop (1990) warns, "Before undertaking ambitious classroom agendas . . . , it is important, first, to see that prejudices, myths, models, and culturally determined practices drive us *and* our students" (3). Among those prejudices, myths, models, and culturally determined practices, Bishop places "years of New Critical reading instruction" (3). Teachers who are interested in offsetting these influences must start with an examination of their own practices as teachers, readers, and writers of poetry.

Teaching, Writing, and Risk-taking: The Poetry Dilemma

Nearly eight years ago, after teaching a three-week poetry writing course to a group of fourth, fifth, and sixth graders identified as gifted by the local school system, I was struck by two specific course evaluations. One student wrote, "Once a day kids should have a chance to write what they want." Another wrote, "The exercises were fun, but there were lots of other things I wanted to write about."

Like most teachers, I thought I had, all along, given the children an opportunity to write what they wanted. Like most teachers, I clutched both my yellowed *Wishes, Lies, and Dreams* (Koch 1970) and my belief that students need some prodding to write anything, let alone poetry. And, like many of my colleagues, I was forced to begin asking questions that ultimately led me to an examination of my own habits of reading and writing.

My first stop, however, was the library. What I discovered there is almost too obvious to say: though there were a variety of books, all geared in one way or another to the teaching of poetry writing, little serious scrutiny of what does and should go on in poetry writing classes was available. Nonetheless, I did run across an article that classifies the approaches used most often in teaching poetry writing. The author, Lucky Jacobs (1977), attempts only to provide "teachers with a conceptual framework for teaching writing" (161). Jacobs does not evaluate these methods, argue that they are the only methods, or assert the superiority of one approach over another. What he did for me, though, was provide a point from which I might depart in exploring the dilemma of teaching students to write poems.

Jacobs highlights three methods for teaching poetry writing: the models approach, the activities approach, and the models-and-activities approach. Unlike Jacobs, I chose to evaluate the three approaches in terms of my own experiences.

According to Jacobs, the models approach attempts to stimulate writing by asking students to read a poem. Isn't this the approach I used, after all, in asking my students to read Williams's "Red Wheelbarrow" and then to write a poem of their own beginning "So much / depends upon"? Certainly. Then I have to ask myself what the benefits of this models approach are, a question Jacobs safely, and perhaps wisely, opted not to ask.

It seems to me that if I want to show students a sample of the kind of writing they could do, I would want to show them a good sample, a "model." Clearly, a student who has never read a poem will have trouble writing one. But it also occurs to me that a fourth-grade student (or an adult, for that matter) might see the single, finished draft of the model and assume that the poem always looked that way, that the poet never moved lines or stanzas around, never worried over a word. What's more, my experience with models tells me that students seldom spend time revising them. I think that's because the poems are derivative; no ownership is established. It would make more sense to show students several drafts of a poem and ask them to model the process of revision they see there. This way students would see writing as process and still have a standard against which they might measure their own writing.

Still, the greatest drawback to the models approach is that it presents the student with a product-oriented and therefore static view of composing. The second and third approaches Jacobs writes about—activities and models-and-activities—improve upon the models approach by involving students in revision rather than in simply producing a text.

In using the activities approach, teachers stimulate students to write by providing either a suggestion or an actual activity. For instance, a teacher might suggest that students write about a childhood experience, such as the feelings associated with spending a night away from parents and home. Or, a teacher might ask students to write about some "poetic" object, such as a horseshoe, a leaf, or a crumpled soda can brought into the classroom.

Students seem to enjoy such activities, often reporting how much fun the "writing games" were. Another clear benefit of the activities approach is that it engages students in the process of generating the initial impulses for writing from personal feelings and idiosyncratic responses. Exercises such as those found in Kenneth Koch's work, for instance, especially *Wishes, Lies, and Dreams,* involve students in "meditation" prior to the actual writing.

Koch also provides models of other student writing, if teachers choose to use them. This combination of models and activities seems to come closest to the process contemporary writers rely on to generate writing. According to Turner (1977):

> At one extreme the poet has no idea [how the poem starts]; at the other he can give you everything he saw, heard, or read that in any way affected the poem. More often he can give you a date, place, bit of experience that started him putting pencil to paper. . . . Behind those [poems] lie preconceptions, often lifelong, which the poet only recognizes later, if at all, as the source of the poem. . . . (3)

The suggestion here is that most poets see poetry writing as a process leading to newer and greater awareness. Unlike the activities approach, which children enjoy because it leads to an immediate reward—a written product—most poets view a poem as a series of concentric circles moving outward and away from the initial impulse to write. Revision then comes, as Turner (1977) says, "only if [the poem] has surprised—and continues to surprise—him or her" (5). For revision to take place, the poet must feel an ownership, sense an urgency or promise of discovery, or else the poem will be abandoned.

Theory of the kind offered by expert-practitioners is useful provided it remains theory and the teacher tosses it aside once classroom experiences or individual student needs require a more specific response. I believe I enter the classroom predisposed to certain feelings about teaching writing, not all of which derive from the articles and books I have read about it. So for a period of six months, give or take a few days, I closely monitored my own process of writing. I did this first to uncover for myself the hidden theory that resides in my experiences as a writer. But I also did it to see if I could put into words certain procedures of writing and revision that I felt existed, despite the fact that I could not at the time describe them or find their description in any source on the teaching of writing.

One of my own poems that I studied, "Imagining the Bees," is shown below in three stages, not to suggest that the poem was written in three drafts (between the three stages shown here were dozens of drafts), but to suggest the kind of work any piece of writing entails from start to finish.

Imagining the Bees [1]

"No one lives in this room without going
through a crisis"
—Adrienne Rich

I have never kept anything
long enough to be stung by it.
When tears roll they keep going
down the street in small schools.
These are not cheeks of sponge.   5
I like to forget.

When I enter a room, my first
few steps give me away.
I have watched how the others
shake water from their hair.   10
I try always to be dry
among the soggy carpets.

But once, and this is it,
I followed a bee keeper
to a back room of a barn.   15
I watched him duck into
a small screened room.
He wore a tent over his head,
gloves on his hands.

There were thousands, maybe   20
millions of bees hugging the queen
like wool. Small bees, the size
of a tear. When he pulled
a screen from the hive
the bees clung tightly to their queen.   25
There is no mistake in holding hard
to your life. I know this.

"Imagining the Bees" is reprinted with the permission of *Tar River Poetry,* where the poem originally appeared (Fall 1981).

Then the man dropped the screen
and the bees leaped like a bearded
man's chin, direct to the bee keeper's   30
tented face. I watched a dozen,
maybe more, bees rise humming
beneath the net and to the man's
eyes. I stepped back. The man's
arms rose to push the bees away.   35
There's no pain like stinging eyes.
He had already told me.

He ran past me, slamming the door
behind him, to the hose hanging
beside the barn. He ran water over   40
his eyes, pushing the bees away.
His eyes were already closing
when he told me it wasn't so bad.
The bees would die now for stinging him.

Sometimes it comes down to this.   45
We hold something so closely
it breaks through our skin.
Then we want to wash it away,
bring tears to our eyes, let
water flood our eyes while   50
no one's looking. There are people
who I would hold this closely.

When I am stung around the eyes
I will know they are leaving
and enter this room of bees   55
where pain rises quickly,
where my wooden eyelids
will learn how to dance.

Imagining the Bees [2]

I have never kept anything
long enough to be stung by it.
When tears roll they keep going
down the street in small schools.
These are not cheeks of sponge.   5
I like to forget.

But once I followed a bee keeper
to the back of his barn
and watched him duck into
a small screened room.   10
He wore a tent over his head,
gloves on his hands.

There were thousands, maybe

millions of bees hugging their queen
like wool. Small bees,   15
the size of a tear. When he pulled
a screen from the hive
the bees clung tightly to their queen.
There is no mistake in holding
hard to your life. I know this.   20

But then the screen slipped to the floor
and bees leaped like a bearded
man's chin, direct to the keeper's
tented face. I watched a dozen
bees rise humming beneath the net   25
and to the man's eyes. I stepped back.
The man's arms rose to push the bees
away. He had already told me:
there's no pain like stinging eyes.

He ran past me, slamming the door   30
behind him, to a hose hanging
beside the barn. He ran water over
his eyes, washing the bees away.
His eyes were already closing
when he told me. This is nothing,   35
not real tears, nothing at all.

Sometimes it comes down to this.
We hold something so closely
it breaks through our skin.
Then we want to wash it away, letting   40
water flood our eyes while
no one's looking. There are people
I would hold this closely.
When I am stung around the eyes
because they are leaving, I enter   45
this room of bees, where pain rises
quickly and my wooden eyelids
learn how to dance.

Imagining the Bees [3]

for Charley and Debbie Gordon

I have never held anything
long enough to be stung by it.
But once I followed a bee keeper
to the back of his barn
and watched him duck into   5
a small screened room.
He wore a tent over his head,
gloves on his hands.

There were thousands, maybe
millions of bees, small bees   10
the size of tears, hugging
their queen like wool.

When the keeper reached for the comb,
it slipped to the floor.
Hundreds of bees leaped to his face,   15
maybe a dozen danced beneath the net
and to the man's eyes.
I stepped back.
The keeper's arms swung to his face.
He had already said   20
there's no pain like stinging eyes.

He ran past me, slamming the door
behind him, to a hose hanging
beside the barn. He ran water over
his eyes, washing the bees away.   25
His eyes were closing when he told me.
This is nothing. Not real tears.
Nothing at all.

Still, I know it comes down to this:
we hold something so closely   30
it breaks through our skin.

There are people I would hold this way.
And when I'm stung around the eyes
because they are leaving,
I enter this room of bees   35
where pain shows beneath the net
of my smile and my wooden eyelids
learn how to dance.

What I discovered as I analyzed my own process of writing is that, while it is possible to teach from Jacobs' three approaches, I teach poetry writing in a manner clearly influenced by the way I compose. What follow are some general observations concerning what might be called my personal biases:

1. **Prewriting is an essential activity.** My process of writing, I discovered, begins long before anything is put on paper. What my experience tells me is that "prewriting" should not be misconstrued to refer to only those activities immediately preceding writing. Rather, prewriting in a poem such as "Imagining the Bees" is a scattered process that only begins to gain focus as the poem takes shape on the page. The immediate experience of reading, for instance, a poem by Adrienne Rich or of talking to

a beekeeper actually encourages me to consider other, some-times long-forgotten, personal experiences. Those personal ex-periences then become the subjects for writing.

2. **The poem talks.** My students enjoy hearing about how my poems talk to me. "Imagining the Bees" is perhaps my best example. In the poem's first stage, the words "and this is it" in line 13 and "Sometimes it comes down to this" in line 45 were words I recognized in revision as reminders of what the poem was about. Those two lines in particular served as cues helping me to revise lines 14 and 46.

3. **"Language bridges" can connect two strong sections of a piece of writing.** Before I kept a journal about my writing proc-ess, I could not find language to describe what I knew to be true about the composing process: that writers often compose so quickly that they use language—inexact or incorrect words, weak lines, sentence fragments, misplaced modifiers—to con-nect one strong portion of a piece of writing with another. These obviously revisable portions of writing permit a writer to con-tinue on with the flow of language even though he or she recog-nizes, even as the words are put on the page, that they will need to be changed. Let's call this use of language—since until I discovered it in my own writing I didn't really call it anything at all—a "language bridge." Then we can encourage students to use these bridges both in making a first draft and during their first revision. Lines 28–30 in the first stage of "Imagining" are an example of a language bridge.

4. **The subject suggests itself.** My original impulse in "Imagin-ing" was to write a poem suggested by a line from Adrienne Rich. Once the poem progressed midway down the page, though, I realized that it was not about a room in which a crisis takes place, not about being stung by bees, not even about the loss the poem goes on to recount. Rather, the poem arose from an ongoing sense in me of having difficulty accepting hurt in my life. I came to understand this as the subject before the second stage of the poem. As I said before, there were at least a dozen drafts between stage one and stage two, and by the time stage two was written, the artificial structure of the Rich quotation fell away and the poem began to take on more directly the subject it suggested. This reinforced for me the importance of what Rich-ard Hugo calls "the triggering town."

5. **Revision is a recursive activity.** While only three drafts of my poem are given here, its revision involved looking at several drafts to decide, first, what I understood the poem to be about, and second, what the proper tone for the poem should be. Early revision, that is, revision prior to stage two, involved a constant moving back and forth from draft to draft in an attempt to make the content as full and as organized as possible. My journal tells me that I have always worked this way. I have, in all the pieces written while I analyzed my process of writing, focused first on saying something. Only after something is satisfactorily expressed do I begin to worry about correctness, about punctuation, spelling, and sentence construction.

Did these five discoveries about my own process of writing translate immediately into teaching methods? Not directly. By studying my own process of writing several things did happen, though.

First, I uncovered long-hidden biases about writing that had crept into my teaching strategies. I didn't realize, for instance, how important reading is to my writing until my journal told me that nearly seventy percent of my writing sessions were preceded by sessions in which I had been reading material that engaged me in my personal conflicts. Since those times were also sessions during which music—usually without singing—coexisted with reading, I came to understand why I placed more emphasis on prewriting than my teachers ever did and why I enjoyed bringing activities into the classroom.

But I also came to better understand how static the usual notion of prewriting is. I have discovered that I write because I am engaged in an emotion that brings to mind specific images. For me, this rarely happens the other way around; that is, images rarely give rise to emotion, at least not as a component of my writing process. As a result, I generally do not use observations of paintings as a prewriting activity. Nonetheless, I still might show a large variety of prints to my students and ask them to begin writing when a specific painting helps them feel something that reminds them of other experiences. Or, rather than the usual exercise of asking students to read a poem as a model, I might match a poem with a painting (since many such matches are available in literature throughout the ages) and help students see how an emotional connection has been made through these two media. But the lesson I have learned from studying my own writing is that writing should not be a response to a prewriting activity. Rather, the activity should help students see their own experiences as subject matter suited to writing, poetic or otherwise.

I also discovered that my real purpose as a teacher is to model what Donald Murray (1982) calls an "ideal other self." When I write, I am aware of a voice—most often inside me, though sometimes, as in "Imagining," on the page—that guides the making of the poem. I think of the self that writes as one self; the self that guides is the "other" self. As a teacher, my role is to serve as the students' other self until they are ready to perform in that role by themselves.

I can model this other self in at least two ways. First, I can bring in an unfinished piece of my own writing—something suited to the reading level of my students—and revise it in front of them, talking through my thoughts so that they can hear the vocabulary of revision that a writer uses (e.g., "language bridge") and intervene in my process to ask why one change was made and not another. Or, I can ask questions of them that I ask myself as a writer to reinforce my revision practices, most of which focus on text manipulation: "Is that the best, most exact word?" "Do these two lines work together?" "Is there another, less usual way to say this?" "What do you think the poem is telling you about your subject?"

In any case, my examination of how I wrote "Imagining" has helped me to clarify what I value as a writer and why I offer students the instruction and advice that I do. Only by understanding the pedagogy I begin with—that is, the teaching methods that arise "naturally" or "unconsciously" from years of reading and writing practice—can I add to my teaching repertoire strategies that will enable me to more effectively aid my students.

But my inquiry into "Imagining the Bees" only touches the surface of what I need to know about myself, offering some insights into how I write poems. I also have to ask myself how I read others' poems and how I go about selecting poems for inclusion in a journal I edit. Indeed, the role of teacher in a poetry writing class and of editor in selecting work for publication are closely bound. I need to allow myself the opportunity to study further what I value and emphasize as meaning-making in reading and evaluating drafts of my own poetry and consciously determine how much of that method of reading should be employed when I comment on drafts of poems by others.

Viewing Teachers as First Readers:
Is There Meaning in the Drafts of This Poem?

Most universities hire expert-practitioners to teach poetry writing courses. But even these professionals run into the problem of where to begin in helping students read and evaluate poetry. This problem is especially present when students have done little or no reading appropriate to the course. For many teachers of poetry writing, more perhaps than for teachers of composition, methods of instruction tend to reflect the way they read and revise their own poems. As Turner (1980) puts it, teachers often tend to offer "advice from their own experience as artificers" (15). Since that experience includes the way they serve as first readers of their own poems, examining the way teachers read drafts of their poems—in addition to how they write them—will go far in helping us understand how and why they respond as they do to drafts of their students' writing.

Another of my poems will serve to model a method for discovering the habits I have developed in reading the early drafts of my own writing. It seems axiomatic to me that the reading habits of writing teachers, developed as a method for reading their own poems, will, if left unexplored (and, as a result, used unconsciously), influence the way teachers read and evaluate their students' drafts, if not the way they approach the teaching of their courses. What teachers need then is a systematic analysis that will enable them to recognize their own reading habits, determine when such habits can be useful pedagogical tools, and empower them to let such readings go (and to perhaps offer more appropriate readings) when the readings threaten to be ill-advised or ineffective.

Why should teachers of poetry writing study their composing processes and the methods they employ in reading drafts of their writing? More than teachers of any other genre, those who teach poetry writing must confront with some uncertainty the task of reading and evaluating their students' efforts. That no one can determine what, exactly, constitutes poetry—let alone "good" poetry—is well known (see Bizzaro, "Poetry and Audience"). But teachers of poetry and poetry writing are called upon to examine texts and to act out the role of authoritative reader nonetheless. And they will perform this task more effectively after they have noted what they value as readers of their own poems, after they have discovered how they employ what they believe to be "standards of excellence" as guidelines for moving from draft to draft of their own writing. What's more, by modeling this procedure in front of their classes, teachers can use their self-examination as a starting point in discussing standards with students who have done little prior reading appropriate to the course. In a perfect world, who could disagree with John D. MacDonald (1989), who writes, "The only students who belong in advanced undergraduate or graduate creative writing courses are those who have been compulsive and omnivorous readers all their lives, and who have thereby acquired some sense of the excruciating complexity of the history and existence of humanity" (83). Many creative writing teachers can handpick their students; most, however, cannot.

As a way of modeling how teachers of poetry writing might become more conscious of themselves as both readers and writers of their own poems, let me examine three drafts of a poem of mine originally entitled "Collard Fields." My intention is not to offer a definitive reading of my poem or to suggest that the methods I employ in reading it are the ones any teacher, including myself, should use in reading student poems. Rather, I hope to identify a starting place from which we can move in examining the connections that teachers must make between composition theory, literary-critical theory, and the reading and evaluating of student writing.

"Collard Fields" has a unique history. Shortly after having moved south in 1983 to eastern North Carolina, and prior to having seen much of the farmland, I was asked to write a poem for the Collard Festival held annually in Ayden, North Carolina, several miles from my home. Having never seen collards—let alone tasted the green, broccoli-like plant—I set out to do my best. Naturally, like anyone else, I could only write and serve as the first reader of a poem based on my experiences. My lack of knowledge about collards notwithstanding, I wrote the following draft:

Collard Fields

Once each year we wonder
how the Tar River survives
the heat, the quenching
sun along its banks
slim as water snakes through branches   5
and as quick to take from you
something once yours, once
belonging to someone far away;
forgotten as rain, as grass
unfolded. Collard season   10
and we are long drawn and thin

Before being remade into "Tobacco Fields," "Collard Fields" was published in *Leaves of Green: The Collard Poems,* edited by Alex Albright and Luke Whisnant (Ayden, North Carolina, Collard Festival, 1984). Copyright © 1984 by Alex Albright and Luke Whisnant. Reprinted with their permission.

this year as last, remembering
thin strands of collards waving
through our teeth. It is collard
time and we dream of narrow paths   15
through rows and rows
we think of children discovering
in these fields
their own reflections
their own slim dreams of a future   20
that waves out in front of them
in the sunshine, in the Carolina heat.
And we remember a puberty come at last
so thick we smell it in the summertime,
so thick we know its presence   25
in our children's eyes,
in their smiles,
collard smiles,
and the strings that wave
when they speak,   30
smelling slightly of earth,
slightly of youth,
entirely of this season
that has come, without warning,
into our fields, into our lives.   35

Admittedly, this is not a strong draft. Nonetheless, I am interested, as I read the draft nearly eight years after its invention, not in its quality, but in the stereotyping I had done as an outsider lacking appropriate experiences upon which to construct this poem. I imagined the Tar River evaporating into something "slim as water snakes." I imagined collard season making us into something like a cigarette, "long drawn and thin." I even pretended that people who ate collards would walk around with "thin strands of collards waving through" their teeth. Only after these observations, based on faulty imaginings rather than on real experiences, did I discover what I wanted to write about: something (like my move to eastern North Carolina?) "that has come, without warning, / into our fields, into our lives."

The second phase of the poem—perhaps ten or twelve drafts from the draft cited above—is an improvement made possible solely because of my prior experiences as a reader and evaluator of similar texts, and not because of any great insight I had had between drafts about collards:

Collard Fields

Once a year we wonder
how the Tar River survives

the heat, how sun
along its banks passes
slim as water snakes through branches   5
despite the forgotten rain,
unfolded grass.

This is collard season
when we are long drawn and thin
this year as last,   10
remembering thin lines of collards
waving in the fields,
stuck between our teeth.
It is collard time and we dream
of narrow paths   15
through rows and rows,
remembering how children discover
in these fields
their own reflections,
their own slim dreams   20
of a future that waves out in front of them
in the sunshine,
in the Carolina heat.

And we remember a puberty come at last
so thick we smell it in the summertime,   25
so thick we know its presence
in our children's eyes,
in their smiles,
collard smiles,
and in the strings that wave   30
when they speak,
smelling slightly of earth,
slightly of youth, entirely of this season
that has come, without warning,
into our fields, into our lives.   35

Students I have discussed this poem with have been quick to point out a certain kind of improvement, improvement in word choice, lineation, and imagery, though certainly not in my understanding of collards and how they grow. I seem to have attended here to sounds within lines and even to the rhythm of this open form poem, but not necessarily to lines of collards and the condition of the land.

More specifically, I read this poem as though poems render their meanings through a reader's text-based activity. The changes I made thus result from my past experiences as a reader of similar texts and, as such, were clearly influenced by my own history as a student of the New Criticism. Now I approach reading more consciously and revise my own texts using different critical lenses than I was able to use eight years ago. But from draft one of "Collard Fields" to draft two, the most significant changes are those that attend to the language of the text. Deleting "quenching" from the original version (line 3) seems to me to be suggested by the image. And adding a second "how" in line 3 of the revision enabled me to rework the image by selecting a better verb, "passes," to show the movement through trees of sun along the banks of the Tar. Since I was determined to focus on the text, I was likewise determined to make images do the work of conveying meaning (an ironic determination, since I now feel certain that I must trust my reader to re-create that meaning in rewriting my text). The original lines 6–8, besides striking me as prosaic given my past experiences with poems, seemed unrelated to the subject of the poem I believed I was rewriting. Finally, I see some intent on my part to work on the rhythm of the poem by restructuring line breaks, most clearly at lines 20, 21, 22, and 33 of the revised version.

When I show this process of revision to my students, they generally are able to see that what I valued as meaning-making in this poem—what I read for as it was revised—was what I could manipulate in the text. To put it another way, my reading and revision of "Collard Fields" arose from my familiarity as a reader with the norms implicit to the kind of text it is, extracted, as the New Critics say they should be, from my experiences with other texts of its kind. What I thus show my students about myself as a reader of "Collard Fields" is that the attitudes, values, and emphases of the New Criticism were and are so deeply ingrained in my system for reading and evaluating early drafts of this poem that an examination such as this is required for me to recognize how I read the poem, determine when such a reading can be beneficial, and empower me to examine other poems through alternative interpretive lenses when it seems sensible to do so.

Nonetheless, what is revealed about my reading of the second phase of "Collard Fields"—and my reason for discussing this particular poem, both in this chapter and before classes of students—might be noticed in the changes I made prior to re-entitling it "Tobacco Fields":

Tobacco Fields

Once each year we wonder
how Tar River survives
the heat, how sun
along its banks passes
slim as water
snakes through branches

to startle life
despite forgotten rain,
unfolded grass.

This is tobacco season
and we are long drawn and thin
this year as last,
recalling lines
of tobacco,
hunched and silent.
In the shallow pools of our dreams
we envision narrow
paths through rows and rows,
recalling children discovering
in these fields
their own shiny reflections,
their own slim dreams
of futures that wave
out in front of them
in the sunshine,
in the Carolina heat.

And we recall a harvest
come at last
so thick we smell
it in the summertime,
so thick we know its presence
in our children's eyes,
in their smiles,
tobacco juice running
when they speak,
smelling slightly of earth,
slightly of youth,
entirely of this season
that has come without warning
into our fields,
into our lives.

Since I wrote from my experience, impoverished for never having seen collards grow, I ended up describing not how collards grow in the fields, but something nearer to the way tobacco grows. As one student pointed out, collards are not grown in lines or rows, no matter how "thin" I imagined them to be. An entire row of collards would be enough to feed all the world's collard-eating people. Only then was I able to understand why my poem gave rise to hilarity at the Collard Festival. This additional information, that what I was "really" describing was "tobacco season," enabled me to make several other changes that brought the poem into focus. In fact, at one point, in acknowledging my silliness in calling the poem "Collard Fields," it occurred to me that what I had *really* written about, after having lived much of my life in the Midwest, was neither collards nor tobacco. If I ever publish this poem again, I might have to entitle it "Corn Fields."

Thus, I am able to reveal to my students not only my occasional foolishness, but also what I valued as meaning-making in the process of revising "Collard Fields." I offer this reading of my poem not because I think only the changes that I make result in something I would call a "good" poem, but because such analysis enables me to determine the kind of reader I am of early drafts of both my own poems and my students'. It enables me to verbalize for both the students and myself the guidelines or "standards of excellence" we will study further in reading and writing assignments throughout the semester. And to be honest, I must admit as well that, as the class syllabus-maker, I have tended to instruct students in the reading of poems that are written by others who value what I value in poetry and whose poems withstand the kind of analysis I offer. After all, this authority is a privilege that is self-perpetuating. If in composition classes teachers give assignments, offer observations, and employ teaching strategies that make New Critical estimations possible, why not in poetry writing classes as well?

I do not want to suggest by my analysis of "Collard Fields" that such close readings are without their own kind of usefulness. But the kind of reading that should be offered students—if it respects the student-writer as well as a poem's integrity—should be commensurate with the amount of prior experience and the depth of background with subject and genre students bring to their poems as readers of poetry, both in the text and in the world around them. In fact, I believe the less experience a student-writer brings to his or her poem, the more intrusive the teacher needs to be. Naturally, a text-based criticism, where it might be essential to comment on the appropriateness of images, word choice, line breaks, and rhythm, could benefit the student-poet who has not read much, who does not know that what might not be a cliché in common discourse just might be in poetic discourse. On the other hand, a more advanced reader and writer of poetry might benefit from interacting with the teacher in discussing what, exactly, constitutes the kind of poetry that the student-poet is attempting to write. And less intrusive yet, commentary on the poems of advanced writers might address the poem as a whole, providing the student-poet with a kind of reading unique to that particular poem.

But by addressing the teacher as writer and reader we have not addressed the other problem so perplexing, in the end, to teachers of poetry writing classes: How do editors decide what a good poem is, anyway?

Making Decisions about Other Writers' Poems: Teachers as Editors

By invitation several years ago, I offered attendees at the Southeastern Conference on English in the Two-Year College (SCETC) some advice on how to get poems published in *Teaching English in the Two-Year College*, for which I then served as poetry editor. This speaking opportunity forced me, in light of my ongoing examinations of how I read and write my own poems, to study poems I chose for publication in an effort to provide my audience with a theoretical framework for understanding the supposed workings of editors' minds. Though this task involved some self-examination and guesswork, my job was nonetheless easier for having examined my own reading and writing habits.

I started with the premise that editors, like myself at the time, hardly ever attempt to sabotage their journals by publishing poems they do not like or, in any event, poems they deem *unworthy* of being made public. This seemed a safe enough starting place, though it failed to offer any insight at all into how to determine what a contemporary poem is. In short, what we really need to know is perhaps what we will never discover: How does an editor determine what constitutes a poem these days, particularly one others might agree to be "good"?

I began my study of the way I read as an editor by positing several theories. First, I believe that poetry is not one thing, but many, and that editors, like myself, have personal, though discernible, biases about what poetry is. This hypothesis certainly does not seem to be an issue of debate among editors; in fact, where statements clarifying an editor's values and emphases are available, editors tend either to avoid the issue completely or to state their opinions with surprising frankness and candor, as do many of the editors who have stated their preferences in Judson Jerome's *1990 Poet's Market*.

Jerome's carefully edited book advertises itself by claiming that it will tell you "what you want to know about each publisher" (back cover). If you ask yourself as a writer what you want to know about a magazine, you will probably decide it is important to know what "kind" of poems the various magazines accept for publication. Simply put, this concern might be expressed in these questions: What are the editorial biases? Or, what do the editors envision as poems worthy of publication? Or, more succinctly, what kinds of texts will be acceptable as poems in these contemporary literary magazines?

Some editors brush off these questions and others of their type, perhaps wisely. For example, the editors of the *Partisan Review* simply state that they want "poems of high quality" (Jerome 1990, 262). About poems acceptable to the editors of the highly regarded *Iowa Review*, David Hamilton offers, almost as vaguely, "We simply look for poems that at the time we read and choose, we admire" (Jerome 1990, 173). The word "admire" interests me in this context, and I will return to it later. For now, let's look at comments by editors who write at greater length about what they believe constitutes a poem they would deem worthy of publication in their journals.

The excellent and perhaps underrated *Raccoon* publishes "tightly crafted work dealing with the dark image" (Jerome 1990, 172). From this we might surmise that David Spicer seeks "image" poems rather than "language" poems, two broad categories that teachers of poetry writing like to discuss. With considerably greater feeling than Spicer, the editors of *Spoon River Anthology* write, "We want interesting and compelling poetry that operates above and beyond the ho-hum, so-what level, in any form or style about anything; poetry that is fresh, energetic, committed, filled with some strong voice of authority that grabs the reader in the first line and never lets go" (Jerome 1990, 355). The editors are as frank about what they don't want: "Do not want to see insipid, dull, boring poems, especially those that I cannot ascertain why they're in lines and not paragraphs; poetry which, if you were to put it into paragraphs, would become bad prose" (Jerome 1990, 355).

In short, I contend, at least for purposes of getting someone to engage in a raging debate with me, as Moxley suggests we should, that what editors really want are poems they wish they had written, or to return to the words of David Hamilton, poems they "admire." By pointing this out, I do not wish to criticize any of these editors. Rather, I am trying to determine what I should teach my students to do as they write and rewrite their poems. After all, I know firsthand that editing a poetry journal is a time-consuming and thankless job, requiring that the editor read hundreds or even thousands of "insipid, dull, boring poems" just to select a handful of "good" ones for publication. But the description of poems as "insipid, dull, boring" does not carry the slightest aura of objectivity. So the question that must, of necessity, follow is this: Are the judgments of editors purely subjective? Probably not. But such judgments, in the absence of an agreed-upon notion of what constitutes poetry, can hope to do little more than reflect personal biases, biases naturally developed by the extensive reading, composing, and studying of writing in various genres. What's more, not only can it be said that every editor has such biases, but I believe that editors want to be, as Harold Bloom might insist, entirely "ravished" by a poem, so much so that the experience of reading the poem may even cost the editors poems of their own. What conscientious writer does not fear exactly this loss? What conscientious editor does not hope for it?

I believe as well that editors have "perfect" and "unblemished" poems in their minds, poems that are perfect and unblemished by virtue of being unwritten. But let me add that the search for such a poem is never-ending, and editors will publish—and wish to have written—poems they find to possess qualities as near to those of their "perfect" poem as possible. Such texts, then, will be "above and beyond the ho-hum, so-what level" poems that approximate the "perfect" poems editors use as standards in judging poems for publication.

It seems clear to me, as it must for anyone who reads Jerome's *Poet's Market* (including, apparently, Jerome, who quotes several lines of poetry typical of what gets accepted for publication in each magazine), that many editors cannot state exactly what they believe constitutes a good poem. This is not to say that editors simply do not know one until they see one, any more than the need for a book on reading and evaluating student poetry writing is meant to indict teachers. No doubt many editors can point out what they believe to be a good poem and can pick one out of a batch of poems on the desk. But asking them to describe it so that someone else can write one—as we must do when we read and evaluate student poems—creates a situation both irritating and, without some self-examination, impossible.

Nonetheless, I hypothesize that most judgments resulting in the rejection of a poet's work must signify that the poems involved failed to appeal to the editors' biases about poetry. And I believe that poets—and teachers—will not be able to adequately explain to someone how to write the "perfect" poem until they analyze their own poems. In fact, examining my own poems against the list of biases I prepared for my talk several years ago suggests that such biases deeply affect my methods of reading, interpreting, and evaluating poems, both my own and others'.

Mind you, these are just theories, theories based upon self-explorations that I test in chapters 3–6. But we have to begin someplace in determining what we are evaluating when we evaluate student poetry writing. And when it comes to evaluations of matters as private as "preferences" and "tastes" in writing, the self is an excellent place to start. Still, I must also stress that it is a place to begin, not end, our search. The list of "Bizzaro's Biases" that follows, a list that will not surprise anyone who has read the first two sections of this chapter, is only a list of *one* person's biases. By returning to this list four years after writing it, I can see that my descriptions of what a poem should do reveal the same New Critical background so apparent in the decisions I made while reading drafts of my own poems. If my teaching has changed over the years, it has done so only because I performed a search that enabled me to identify how my biases influence and intrude upon the way I teach.

Bizzaro's Biases

A poem should

- show control of language and focus of vision: "a moment's monument"
- convey some feeling, but avoid sentimentality: "recollected in tranquility"
- use sound to underscore meaning: "similitude in dissimilitude"
- rely on metaphor that is unique but conveys more similarities than differences
- possess regular rhythm, using irregularity for surprise
- rely on free verse or unemphatic rhyme
- appeal to the senses: "no ideas but in things"
- avoid cliché
- possess more than a "private" meaning: at some point consider audience
- avoid expressions that are too easy, especially between subject and verb
- match accomplishment with intention
- be understandable, but not easy: invite more than one reading
- develop an attitude toward the subject and suggest something beyond the literal meaning
- rely on imagery, visualness, and figurative language: "show rather than tell"
- concern itself with lineation
- surprise the reader

I am not happy to note that this list reinforces an almost authoritarian perspective on teaching poetry writing. Yet knowing I am so inclined helps me to temper this approach when it seems appropriate to do so. Nonetheless, as I will show in the next chapter, the New Criticism does sometimes provide a useful lens for interpreting, reading, and evaluating poems.

3 The Authority of the Text: Some Applications of the New Criticism

. . . whatever relation poetry bears to experience, it is to the reader an experience in itself, a little world of words that does or does not take hold of our imaginations.

David Young

What I would do now is pretend the poem is mine and let the student watch me rewrite it while I talked aloud about what I was thinking while revising.

Stuart Friebert

In spite of efforts to use alternative methods, most teachers and students continue to employ the New Criticism. Indeed, as Jane Tompkins (1990) might argue, it is the method of reading and evaluating that "everyone still carries around in their heads, whether they've been studying post-structuralism for twenty years or have only begun to study it today" (21). Despite the fact that we can declare, as Charles Moran and Elizabeth F. Penfield (1990) do, that "the text is dethroned, New Criticism is not 'true' or 'false,' but is a culturally situated set of assumptions about the nature of texts, readers, and the transactions between the two" (2), the New Critical view of reading and evaluating as text-based activities persists. Many of us thus share Tilly Warnock's (1989) wonder:

> While we may seem to have turned our attention from product, a New Critical approach, to process, perhaps biographical, historical, developmental, intentionalist, we wonder. Our practices in responding to texts still seem tied to New Criticism's concern for unity and intensity of words-on-the-page. . . . (67)

Portions of this chapter first appeared in "Some Applications of Literary Critical Theory to the Reading and Evaluation of Student Poetry Writing," in *Poets' Perspectives: Reading, Writing, and Teaching Poetry*, ed. Charles R. Duke and Sally A. Jacobsen (Portsmouth, NH: Boynton/Cook, 1992), 154–74. Reprinted by permission of the publisher.

I have already shown that my practices often lend support to War-nock's observation, as do the practices of most of the poets who comment on student texts in Turner's *Poets Teaching* (1980). And the fact that I did not recognize the New Criticism's role in the development of pieces of my own writing until I examined the way I revised drafts of my poems further reinforces William E. Cain's (1984) conclusion: New Critical values are "so deeply ingrained in English studies . . . that we do not even perceive them as the legacy of a particular movement" (105).

Adaptations of the New Criticism to the classroom situation, both in teachers' reactions to words on the page and in their insistence that revision entail manipulations of the text, reflect efforts to employ methods of reading and evaluation that at least appear to be fair and objective. And when viewed from a particular cultural standpoint, they often are. As Warnock (1989) concludes, "We tell ourselves that the world values order, coherence, and unity, and so should we to prepare our students for future work in the world" (67). Yet we must grapple with our orientation to student writing in an effort to better understand the boundaries within which we respond to our students' texts. If our reliance on New Criticism shows a discrepancy between what we know we should do and what we do in actuality, then we need to explore new and more fruitful models for evaluating student writing.

Finding New Criticism in the Writing Classroom: What Teachers Should Know

Among the various methods advocated by our profession for the evaluation of writing, text-based commentary—including New Criticism and its adaptations, the Analytic Scale and Primary Trait Scoring—is perhaps the most influential. The New Criticism approaches literary texts as finished products, products that can be analyzed for the relationship among their parts without regard to the author's intentions, the reader's responses, or the biographical and historical backdrop. Its goal is to determine a text's meaning by offering a close analysis of the text itself, which is seen as the final authority for such determinations. Current methods of evaluation, especially those advocated in Cooper and Odell's important *Evaluating Writing* (1977), differ from the New Criticism primarily on what might be done to the text, as student texts, unlike literary ones, are viewed as incomplete and often in need of correction. In fact, according to Edward White (1985), the prevailing perception of student texts is that they "exist in general in order to be criticized" (291), especially when held alongside what Nancy Sommers (1982) calls an "ideal text."

This major difference aside, the New Criticism and current thinking about evaluating student writing hold a great many elements in common. First, at the epistemological center of both systems is the belief that meaning arises not from ideology or logic, but from analyzing the structure of norms that direct—in fact, *are*—the reader's experience of the text. Using New Critical values in evaluating student writing thus requires students to believe that the teacher's reading of the text, as the meaning rendered by an exemplary reader, is the text as it really exists. Second, both systems derive their standards for evaluation from reading numerous other texts of the kind under examination. The New Critics refer to these standards as "norms," which, according to Lynn (1990), enable us to focus on the poem itself "rather than the author, the reader, the historical context" (102). Composition theorists refer to such standards as "features": "the separate elements, devices, and mechanisms of language" which enable us to make "judgments about the quality of writing" (Lloyd-Jones 1977, 33). Third, by appealing to their familiarity with other texts, commentators in both systems can claim to be able to remain objective and scientific, basing analysis on their experience of the text rather than on personal opinion. As White (1985) notes, the positive side of this sort of analysis is that evaluators are urged "to attend to the texts that the student produced, rather than to the student's social class, appearance, or moral predispositions" (286). Nevertheless, a classroom driven by the New Criticism places emphasis on the teacher's authority, which, as Bishop (1990) says, arises because teachers are "much more widely read in the conventions and history of literature" than are their students (141). Finally, meaning arises in both systems from "close reading," which reveals how the formal elements of the text work together and whether a piece of writing has the characteristics "crucial to success with a given rhetorical task" (Cooper and Odell 1977, 32). As Mark Schorer writes in "Technique as Discovery," "Technique is the only means [the writer] has of discovering, exploring, developing his subject, of conveying its meaning, and, finally, of evaluating it" (quoted in White 1985, 286).

All this said, what is it that I hope to accomplish by adapting New Critical methods to the evaluation of my students' poems? Moxley (1989) writes, "Ultimately, our goal is to teach students to adopt the critical role writers assume when they ask questions about their work"

(40). So it is for me. When I use the New Criticism to evaluate my students' poems, I do so in an effort to model for my students the critical role *I* assume when I ask questions about my work, as I did with "Imagining the Bees" and "Collard Fields" in chapter 2.

Applying the New Criticism to Three Student Poems

From all available evidence, the New Criticism plays an important role in current methods of evaluation, whether or not it reflects the values currently advocated by composition theorists. For while the theory itself has not been translated verbatim into the writing classroom (after all, it was not designed to assist us in evaluating student writing), its values are the values expressed in most teachers' interpretations of their students' texts. As Turner says in the introduction to *Poets Teaching* (1980), "I am impressed again and again by the poets' recurrent agreement on the fundamentals of teaching method and poetic theory" (15). And it doesn't take an in-depth reading of the poets' commentaries to see that what most urge is more often text-based than an outgrowth of any other concern.

With most of the poet-teachers in Turner's book, adaptations of the New Criticism's values take two dominant forms. First, as Young (1980) suggests, teachers tend to view the poem as an entity in isolation, "a little world of words" (22), which either engages the reader and is deemed a success or fails to engage the reader and, as a result, needs to be revised. And second, teachers tend to assert the authority of the exemplary reader when they model a teacher-centered method for teaching revision skills. Friebert (1980), for instance, takes the student poem as his own and verbalizes changes he would make to the text if the poem were his (29). In both of these adaptations of New Critical values, the teacher's authority arises from reading a large number of other poems in a wide range of forms and styles. In Turner's (1980) words, the poets "have read widely, not only other poets, but also what these other poets have said about the craft" (6).

These are fine generalizations about evaluation. But what kinds of comments are produced when these New Critical values are put into practice with student writing? Nancy Sommers (1982) found that teachers employ many of the same kinds of comments when responding to student writing from the New Critical perspective, that there is "an accepted, albeit unwritten canon for commenting on student texts" (152). These comments tend to perform two important tasks. First, they respond primarily to textual matters. Second, they tend to encourage a view of revision as text manipulation. Naturally, if misused (or used at the wrong place in the writing process), such comments can easily enable a teacher to appropriate a student's text, since only one text exists, the one the teacher reads and thus rewrites.

Wendy Bishop (1990) notes, "M.F.A. graduate students I have worked with indicate they are used to giving and receiving copious on-text responses. But no one has really analyzed the type, focus, or effectiveness of the responses made by creative writing teachers" (158). Indeed, no one has thought to do the work with creative writing teachers that Sommers has done with composition teachers. We might begin such work by examining the type, focus, and effectiveness of our own responses to student poems. To that end, let's look at poems by three of my students: John, Kim, and Jonathan.

Type and Focus of Comments

For each of the three student-writers, I have included the first draft they showed me (below) and that same draft with my comments on it (see figures 1–3). My comments were made entirely on the page; that is, I did not hold conferences with these students or interact with them in any way over these poems except through my comments in, around, and over their texts, and perhaps through informal discussion if they needed some clarification.

> There is a warm breeze blowing through
>   the sad faced oaks
> that surround the fountain like
> the walls of a church.
>
> Green azaleas wish to bloom again
>   as they are gently brushed
>   and slickened by the wayward
>   tears of the fountain on the breeze
>
> A squirrel dances among the flowers
>   to silent music carried on the gentle breeze,
>   sung by sad faced oaks
>
> All that is heard is the patient
>   brush of fully dressed trees
>   and the casual rippling of
>   the fountains, airborne tears
>   straying from the pool are stranded
>   on the surrounding pavement.
>
>   —John

An Apology

While driving down this lonely road
I think of Grandpa
taking me fishing
in a comfortable lake somewhere, someplace
near Muncie.

"Good fish bite here," he used to say
while casting his line
all the way to the other side
of the placid lake.

Fishing is not a game;
It's a sport.
There is a winner,
and unfortunately
there is a loser.

I cast out my line now
as I think of the white gown
I wore only months ago,
and the veil
that hung over my face,
over my eyes.

Those pieces of my life
are stored in a viewing box
upstairs in the attic.
The effulgence of the garments
once visible through the plastic window
now cannot be seen.

I sit here,
my line dangling
waiting to see
who is going to win
this time.

My line feels heavy.
My eyes are straining,
burning,
as they always do
when I cry.

He won't bite.
I don't want to hold
the line anymore.
I'm tired.
I can't see my gown.
I'm sorry Grandpa.

                                        —Kim

Marian Ave.

A sandy lot
remains.

The old house
sat across my street.
Day after day
her framework weathered
blue. Latex skin cracked, flaking

monument to age removed in a day.

grandma would sit
seemingly empty
within, like the house.
untouched, not giving and
not really partaking
of peas or conversation.

Balanced on the nose,
her shaky windows simply
reflected. no one home.
Who knew? Her address
no longer received.

I saw potential across the street
I began to unnotice her.

—Jonathan

Because of my experience examining essays in composition classes, it seemed natural to me to make the three kinds of comments most teachers make: intertextual comments, marginalia, and summative statements.

Intertextual Comments. My intertextual comments, which do the poetic equivalent to the poem that editing does to a student essay, tend to serve three functions: to condense lines, to refocus images, and to avoid redundancies. First, while I do not work with spelling or punctuation and did not have to help any of these three writers with grammar, I have crossed out certain words in an effort to condense. For instance, John's lines 3–4 read "that surround the fountain like / the walls of a church." I changed those lines to read "surrounding the fountain / like church walls." Yet many times I cross out not only to condense the language, but also to bring the intended image (that is, what seems to me as reader to be the intended image) into sharper focus. By dropping the opening word in "An Apology," "While," Kim can suggest an entirely different perspective on time in the poem. The poem is more immediate, more spontaneously unfolding. The speaker is actively driving, not simply recalling a time when "while" she drove

There is a <u>warm breeze blowing through</u> *can the breeze be described in some less usual way?*
the sad faced oaks
that surround the fountain like
~~the walls of a~~ church. **walls.**

lots of articles here that interfere with your poem's rhythm: a, the, the, the

can you show this by cutting an image here?

Green azaleas [wish to bloom] again
as they are gently brushed
and slickened by the wayward
tears of the fountain on the breeze

three bumping prepositional phrases make this hard to follow and very slow.

A squirrel dances among the flowers
to silent music carried on the gentle breeze,
sung by the sad faced oaks

All that is heard is the patient
brush of fully dressed trees
and the casual rippling of
the fountains, airborne tears
straying from the pool are stranded
on the surrounding pavement.

nice enjambment? *good ideas through here!*

John — This is a good start. You seem to have *in mind* some subject. In some ways having a subject in mind requires that you write something about it in some predictable fashion. Remember Hugo's notion of "the triggering town." Let the chosen subject lead you to the subject you just can't avoid.

Here I've made three suggestions: ① watch for a tendency to describe things in their usual ways — surprise the reader ② watch out for telling where you should be showing and ③ be alert to overreliance here on articles and prepositional phrases. This is an outstanding start. More to do!
PB

Figure 1. John's poem (untitled) and my comments.

she had these thoughts. The same effect is achieved in the second stanza by ridding its second line of the word "while." Finally, as in stanza 2, line 3 of Kim's poem, I use intertextual commentary to help students reduce redundancy. As with many beginning poets, Kim feels compelled to explain the image rather than let the image stand by itself. Simply put, Kim's image is this: her grandfather talks as he casts his line "to the other side / of the placid lake." A reader can understand without being told that if the line hits the other side of the lake, it went "all the way" there. A similar effect is achieved in stanza 5, line 3. We do not need to be told that the attic is "upstairs." And in

An Apology

While driving down this lonely road
I think of Grandpa
taking me fishing
in a comfortable lake somewhere, someplace
near Muncie.

"Good fish bite here," he used to say
while casting his line
all the way to the other side
of the placid lake.

Fishing is not a game;
It's a sport.
There's a winner ~~and~~ *and*
~~and unfortunately~~
~~there is a~~ loser.

I cast out my line now
as I think of the white gown   *nice transition*
I wore only months ago,
and the veil
that hung over my face,
over my eyes.

Those pieces of my life
are stored in a viewing box   *can you see here a tendency*
~~upstairs~~ in the attic.   *to repeat what is already*
The effulgence of the garments   *clear or at least implied?*
once visible through the plastic window
now cannot be seen.

I sit here,
my line dangling
waiting to see
~~who is going to win~~
~~this time.~~

My line feels heavy.
My eyes are straining,   *Kim — The two subjects come together*
burning,   *poignantly. Now you should work toward*
as they always do   *making the two scenes leap forward*
when I cry.   *more vividly. One thing I urge is to*
     avoid repeating by telling what you've
He won't bite.   *already shown in an image. The next*
I don't want to hold   *is to go back to those images and*
the line anymore.   *make certain they say/suggest every-*
I'm tired.   *thing you want them to.*
I can't see my gown.   *PB*
I'm sorry Grandpa.

Figure 2. Kim's poem and my comments.

Marian Ave.

A sandy lot
~~remains.~~ *needed? or should this be suggested*
                    by the context?
The ⊙old house
sat across my street. — *make an image*
Day after day
her framework weathered
blue. Latex skin cracked, flaking

monument to age removed in a day.

grandma would sit
[seemingly empty   — *this too seems that it*
within] ~~like the house~~.   *should be suggested in the*
untouched, not giving and *comparison with the house —*
not really partaking   *do you see why I think so?*
of peas or conversation.
                            — *nice combination*
Balanced on the nose,
her shaky windows simply
reflected. no one home.
Who knew? Her address
no longer received.

I saw potential across the street
I began to unnotice her. ——— *good ending*

Jon — Nice job here. You've made a powerful
connection between your grandmother and her old
house on Marian Ave, often through images that
enable me to see what you mean. Work primarily
on letting your images do their work without
prosaic explanations. Also, make certain to use
images to show what you mean rather than rely
on language that tells!

Figure 3. Jonathan's poem and my comments.

Jonathan's poem, I cross out "like the house" in stanza 4, line 3, since
the comparison Jonathan wants to make already suggests the connect-
edness between his grandmother and her house. In short, by simply
crossing out such unnecessary elements, I can help young poets overcome the need to write prosaic explanations and get more directly to
the poetry they have written.

Marginalia. My comments in the margins are generally used
to reinforce what I've done within the text. To this end, I often use

underlining to draw writers' attention to lines in their poems that I comment on in the margins. For instance, in line 1 of John's poem, I underline "warm breeze blowing through" and ask in the margin, "Can the breeze be described in some less usual way?," thus objecting to the common notion of breeze blowing. Similarly, I bracket "wish to bloom" in line 5 and ask, "Can you show this by cutting an image here?," indicating that my ideal poem will rely more on image, that it will show rather than tell. Lines 7–8 of John's text—"slickened by the wayward / tears of the fountain on the breeze"—struck me as slow-moving and hard to read. I wrote in the margin, "Bumping prepositional phrases make this hard to follow and very slow reading."

My estimation that the poem improves in stanzas 3 and 4 is indicated by both my comments in the margin that say so and the fact that I do not clutter John's text with my intertextual markings. While there are some of the same problems in stanza 3 as in the first two stanzas, most notably, "gentle breeze," I resist pointing out more than can be revised. There is, of course, some point at which students cannot attend to all that we suggest they should. Stanza 4 is the strongest in the poem, as though John is now beginning to find his subject. My comment, "good ideas here," is meant to reinforce his work in that stanza.

My marginal notes to the writers tend to ask questions more than give directives, and they generally attend to matters found in the lines directly beside them. A major concern of mine about Kim's poem is addressed by the question "Can you see here a tendency to repeat what is already clear or at least implied?" In Jonathan's poem, I ask about the opening two-line stanza, "Needed? or should this be suggested by the context?" At his fourth stanza, lines 2–3, I write, "This, too, seems that it should be suggested in the comparison with the house—do you see why I think so?" In Jonathan's poem, I also find myself reinforcing much that he has already done, from individual images, to word combinations, to the way his poem ends.

Summative Comments. My summary comments begin with some form of praise and then point out two or three kinds of changes the writer should attend to when revising. In my summary to John's poem, for instance, I note that John has made a good start. But, in keeping with my observation about the fourth stanza, I write, "You seem to have *in mind* some subject," and urge John to take the advice of Richard Hugo (whose *The Triggering Town* was required reading for the course): "Let the chosen subject lead you to the subject you just can't avoid." I also attempt to encourage John to do three specific things in revision, a number I believe most students can handle:

> Here I've made three suggestions: (1) watch for a tendency to describe things in their usual ways—surprise the reader; (2) watch out for telling where you should be showing; and (3) be alert to overreliance here on articles and prepositional phrases.

Of course, the three things I urge John to do reflect my own values and biases as a reviser of my own poems.

In my summary reaction to Kim's poem, I similarly begin with praise: "The two subjects here come together poignantly." In Kim's case, I offer only two general areas to work on: "One thing I urge is to avoid repeating by telling what you've already shown in an image. The next is to go back to those images and make certain they say/suggest everything you want them to."

Finally, I tell Jonathan that he has "made a powerful connection between [his] grandmother and her old house on Marian Ave., often through images that enable me to see what [he] means." Though Jonathan's poem is near completion, it is not finished. I reinforce my comments in the margins by writing, "Work primarily on letting your images do their work without prosaic explanations. Also, make certain to use images to show what you mean rather than rely on language that tells."

Overall, my summary comments seem to reinforce and generalize upon questions I ask in the margins of students' texts. In turn, the questions in the margins direct the writer's attention to the more specific elements I am responding to in the text of the poem. Since the basis for each of these kinds of comments is the text, the New Critical biases are apparent. But how effective are such comments in provoking students to revise?

Effectiveness of Comments

The final revision of each student's poem follows:

> There is a patient breeze blowing through
> the sad faced oaks
> surrounding the fountain like church walls
>
> Green azaleas peer through sadly closing eyes
> as they are gently brushed
> and slickened by the fountain's wayward tears.
>
> All that is heard is the patient

brush of fully dressed trees
and the casual rippling of the fountains,
airborne tears straying from the pool
and stranded on the surrounding pavement.

—John

An Apology

Driving down this
lonely road,
I think of Grandpa
taking me fishing
in a comfortable lake somewhere,
someplace near Muncie.

"Good fish bite here,"
he used to say
casting his line
to the other side
of the placid lake.

Fishing is not a game;
It's a sport.
There is a winner
and a loser.

I cast out my line now
as I think of the white gown
I wore only months ago,
and the veil of illusion
that hung over my face,
over my eyes.

Those pieces of my life
stored in a viewing box
in the attic
the effulgence of the garments
once visible
cannot be seen.

I sit here,
my line dangling,
waiting.

My line feels heavy.
My eyes strain,
burn,
as they always do
when I cry.

He won't bite.
I don't want to hold
the line anymore.
I'm tired.

I can't see my gown.
I'm sorry Grandpa.

—Kim

A Sandy Lot on Marian Avenue

Her framework weathered
blue, the house empty
sat across my street.
grandma would sit
day after day
latex skin cracking, flaking
untouched, not giving and
not really partaking
of peas or conversation.

Balanced on her nose,
the shaky windows simply
reflected
no one home.
I saw potential across the street.
I began to unnotice her

a monument to age
a sandy lot in a day.

—Jonathan

John's revision shows his willingness to make whatever changes I propose, but that willingness proves the ineffectiveness of my commentary. For John, revision is simply a matter of making the corrections I have indicated in my comments on his earlier draft. He has made very few of the choices, opting instead for the easy way out, a way made possible by the type of commentary I offered. His change of "warm breeze blowing" to "patient breeze blowing" in response to my request that he describe the breeze in "some less usual way" substitutes one cliché for another and entirely misses the fact that part of the problem with his description of the breeze is that he describes it as "blowing." And while he has managed to work his poem free of the large number of articles that interfere with the rhythm, his revision in stanza 2 is minimal, changing "wish to bloom" to "peer through sadly closing eyes" in response to my question in the margin "Can you show this by cutting an image here?" I'm not satisfied that John has figured out yet what an image is, if the revision he has offered is indeed an effort to demonstrate that use of language.

Kim's poem, in my estimation, is superior to John's in its reliance on imagery, concise language, and metaphor, as well as in the author's effort at making rather complicated connections. As with

Penney's poem, to be discussed next, Kim's early draft might have benefited more from a different kind of criticism, one my instincts told me to make, but my methods would not permit. As a result, most of my suggestions to Kim came in the form of crossouts in which I attempted to help her achieve conciseness, focus, and at the same time avoid redundancy. But, like John, Kim made very few of the choices in her revision. Some of their reluctance, of course, arises from the fact that these poems were among the first both writers had ever written and, having read little, they tended to trust me in my efforts to help them revise. But there is more than trust motivating their revisions. Perhaps they made very few changes of their own out of fear that they would receive a lower grade by challenging the authority of my commentary on their texts.

Jonathan's revision stands at the other extreme of the three poems studied here. Perhaps because my comments on his poem are relatively vague and general (I made few crossouts and intertextual changes), Jonathan took seriously the task of revision. He succeeds in part at making the images do the work, though I suspect the syntax of line 2 ("the house empty" rather than "the empty house") is an effort to present the image differently.

This brief look at my comments on three student poems leads me to the conclusion that the New Critical emphasis on the text required me to use my energies to make intertextual comments. In fact, my comments in the margins asked questions intended to reinforce intertextual comments, and my summaries in turn reinforced those questions. The result of these kinds of comments, however, is that students can simply make the adjustments I urge and resubmit the poem as finished. This outcome might have been expected given the New Criticism's original goal: to interpret finished texts. Through the kinds and quantity of comments made on these poems, I tended to do much of the work for these students, perhaps in the hope that they would learn from making such changes and apply what they learned to the revision of other poems. Nonetheless, this method of evaluation offers only one reading of the student text and, as a result, does not "grant to the student possible intentions or insights not yet present on the page" (White 1985, 289).

Inquiring Further into the Effective Use of the New Criticism

From these efforts at analyzing student texts, it is clear that the New Criticism and the methods commonly employed in reading student writing have qualities in common. Regardless of whether it is employed in response to compositions or in response to poetry, a teacher might still use text-based commentary in a way that is ultimately ineffective, or even hurtful, to students. In an ineffective adaptation of the New Criticism, a teacher might inadvertently require students to write in a narrow range of poetic styles, thereby imposing, as Petrosky (1989) says, "stylistic limits that act to seal off . . . students' writing, to keep it within the boundaries of academic expectations" (218). On the other hand, it seems to me that the New Criticism might be profitably adapted to the evaluation of student poems if students are involved in the process of identifying the boundaries within which the teacher evaluates their texts. As Young (1980) urges, student poems could be submitted not to an authoritative reading, but to "a mutual finding out of subject, theme, intention, strengths, and weaknesses." New Criticism can be an effective tool in the evaluation of student poems if it helps students better understand what they want their poems to do and, at the same time, enables the teacher to stay involved in the students' writing processes.

By consciously making such adaptations of the New Criticism in evaluations of my students' work, I felt satisfied, on the one hand, that I was reading their poems in the way I might read other literature and, on the other, that I was employing methods of evaluation used successfully in my other writing courses, from freshman composition to technical writing. And what I set out to accomplish in using text-based commentary—to help students better understand what I valued as reader, evaluator, and eventual grader of their poems—was praiseworthy enough.

Nonetheless, in the process of clarifying what would eventually be rewarded in their poems, I seem to have required my students to write one kind of poem—the kind I write—in spite of the fact that I could see a much wider range of texts called poems in recently published magazines than I was willing to permit my students to write. I've even written about the trend. The cause of this narrowness of vision was a desire to be, above all else, objective and fair in commenting on my students' poems. It is apparent to me now, however, that had I done nothing more than model my methods for evaluation after the methods of expert-practitioners who voiced their biases in Turner's *Poets Teaching*, I would have done exactly what I did for years by telling students what I believed to constitute that kind of text called a poem and then enforcing this view during evaluation. Perhaps Richard Hugo's (1979) words best describe this still-popular method of evaluation: "If I can, I talk as if I'd written the poem myself and try to find out why and where it went wrong" (xii).

Finding Out Why and Where I Went Wrong: An Examination of Penney's Poem

Penney, whose early draft of "Chasm" appears below, was a high school English teacher and an M.A. candidate who wrote her poem as one of the writing requirements of the four-week summer institute of the Coastal Plains Writing Project (a site of the National Writing Project) at East Carolina University. Because of her lack of experience as a writer of poetry and her relative unfamiliarity with contemporary poets, poetry, and poetics, I would classify Penney as a beginning poet in spite of the fact that she taught high school English and studied literature in graduate school. Moreover, the amount of instruction at the summer institute concerning the writing of poetry amounted to roughly one hour, though I did encourage Penney to write poems once she expressed an interest in doing so, and I did confer with her at various times at her request.

Here is the first draft that Penney permitted me to see of her poem:

Chasm

Faded photograph, 1944
The daughter is the mother, revisited.
One black and white image
Explains it all . . .

Tears spent in angry frustration—
Both desperately seeking her place
In the world,
A bridge across the pain.
No one listens
When both talk at once.
Too many feelings
Bleed
Into shades of gray.

The girl is caught
Between her present and her future;
The woman caught
Between her future and her past.
They clash with the violent
Force
Of pent-up sameness.
They scream into a black void
Of misunderstanding.

At last,
The three-by-five impression
Sheds light into the darkness
Which lies between . . .

In conference with Penney, I pointed out that this draft was very good, especially for a first effort at writing poetry. I was not surprised, however, to see such a competently written draft, because Penney, who was an excellent student and effective teacher, had read a great deal in her classes, most notably in one of her favorite areas, English Romanticism, and was a strong writer of other kinds of texts. But as Petrosky (1989) notes, "Students who are unfamiliar with modern poetry . . . have very different models in their heads of what poems are, and they also have very different senses of how to use language" (210). So, drawing on my experience as a reader, I pointed out (as my checklist of biases indicates I might) that the best lines in her poem were those which offered new perceptions or perceptions that were entirely hers, such as "No one listens / When both talk at once" and "They clash with the violent / Force / Of pent-up sameness."

Since we did not have a common body of literature to which we might refer for examples, I found my comments on Penney's first draft rather general. As a result, I marked up her poem to provide more specific guidelines for her (see figure 4). According to these guidelines, Penney was to attend to the following list of features in revising her poem. Of course, these features figure prominently in "Bizzaro's Biases":

1. Remember: lines that are not clichés in normal conversation or, for that matter, even in other kinds of written discourse, are sometimes clichés in poetic discourse. Naturally, only a considerable amount of reading will solve that problem. The underlinings in your draft indicate where I believe you will need to rethink how you have expressed yourself to avoid "poetic clichés."

2. An additional area you need to work on is your verbs. Verbs should make "unusual" connections with their subjects. Avoid "tired" verbs whenever you can. I've bracketed verbs most in need of revision in your draft.

3. I think your poem does a good job of "showing" what you mean rather than "telling," at least most of the time. But on occasion, I think an image would help you along. I've indicated where.

By interacting with Penney in conference and by identifying three general kinds of changes that she might make in her poem, I

Chasm

Faded photograph, 1944
The daughter[is]the mother, revisited.
<u>One black and white image</u>
Explains it all . . .

Tears[spent]in angry frustration—
Both <u>desperately seeking her place</u>
<u>In the world,</u>
<u>A bridge across the pain.</u>
No one listens
When both talk at once.
Too many feelings
Bleed
Into shades of gray.

The girl[is caught]
Between her present and her future;
The woman[caught]
Between her future and her past.
They clash with the violent
Force
Of pent-up sameness.
They scream into a black void
Of misunderstanding.

At last,
The three-by-five impression
[Sheds light]into the darkness
Which lies between . . .

[handwritten annotations:]
nice image - can you clarify? develop further?
instead of summarizing here, please let an image show- what is in the photo? Be specific.
can you show this?
] nice
nice contrast, but can you make an image to show this better?
excellent - well said

Figure 4. Penney's poem and my comments.

essentially told her how the poem should be revised. The revision, however, indicates some new trouble areas, since Penney has hyper-corrected in certain places, attempting to write the poem she believed I wanted her to write, the poem she might have believed I would have written had this been my first draft. Her revision follows:

Chasm

Faded photograph, 1944
The daughter stands
In unfamiliar shoes on
Undeniable feet
Beneath unquestionable knees.
A solitary figure,
Reflected
In yellow black and white,
Transcends ambiguity.

Tears lost in angry frustration—
Femininity,
Innocence and experience
Both incomplete, unfulfilled—
Reaching for truth
Grasping for light
Clawing for comfort.
No one listens
When both talk at once.
Too many feelings
Bleed
Into a moist gray fog.

The girl crouches
On the precipice of her future
As stones of her present
Give way
To uncertainty.
The woman waits,
Poised on the selfsame brink,
Her footing eroded
By the past.
They clash with the violent
Force
Of pent-up sameness.
They scream into a black void
Of misunderstanding.
At last,
The three-by-five impression
Warms the darkness
Which lies between . . .

In this revision, Penney has attempted to conscientiously attend to the three features I identified for her. Let me examine her new version of the poem, one feature at a time:

1. **Clichés.** Penney has done a great deal to rid her poem of clichés, and she should be commended for her efforts. However, the remedy to one problem is the cause of another. In attempting to be more specific about what she meant by "Explains it all," Penney has introduced language more abstract than that of the first draft; "Transcends ambiguity" is a concept in need of development. And while Penney has managed to solve the problem of "A bridge across pain," which bothered me in her first draft, her alternative description of that pain (lines 2–7 of the second stanza) is also vague.

Penney has attended to the features identified within her earlier draft, but in doing so, she has introduced new problems. For her next draft, I might ask her to focus on the invention of a scene which suggests the ideas she wants to convey. I might also ask her to attempt to go back to the first draft and salvage it by developing further the line "The daughter is the mother, revisited" as a way of solving the problem of abstraction in stanza 1. In retrospect, I see that this is a strong line of poetry and that my comments should have more directly noted this fact.

2. **Verbs.** Of the three necessary revisions to her poem, Penney has done the most to improve the verbs. In stanza 1, the decision to change the "to be" verb into an action verb leads to an image instead of the interesting but undeveloped (and therefore dropped?) "The daughter is the mother, revisited." The new verb, "stands," seems to suggest to Penney the image of a woman standing in a certain way. But Penney takes this image too far and ends up again in the unproductive abstract of "undeniable feet" and "unquestionable knees." Again, a solution might be to reintroduce the paradox of daughter as mother (and in this case, reading Carolyn Kizer's wonderful "The Blessing" might help), developing that particular image further by referring back to the photograph.

3. **Imagery.** Imagery is still the strongest element in the poem. But in stanza 1, yet another problem is introduced, one that might be listed in a taxonomy of difficulties beginning poets often confront: the tendency to explain the image (as students are often taught to do in composition classes) instead of permitting the image to suggest its meaning to the reader.

In stanza 2, the original version is more concrete than the revision, and the stanza's last five lines as retained are five of the stronger lines in her earlier draft. In the third stanza, Penney does a good job of staying with the visual, of permitting the image to do the work it should.

In commenting on Penney's poem, I have attempted to offer an analysis specific to the poem written, commentary that would measure Penney's relative success with "Chasm" against predetermined, text-based criteria and permit me to move from observations about poetry in general to more specific observations about elements of her text. Yet my observation of Penney's response to my comments helped me reach three tentative conclusions about using this kind of evaluation.

First, teachers of poetry writing know quite well that in commenting on the poems of beginning student-writers, they always run the risk that the revision will make the poem less effective. In some ways, this is true of Penney's poem. But in using the New Criticism to comment on poems by beginning writers, we should aim at something higher: we should aim at the writer's increased fluency with the elements of poetic writing.

Second, for beginning poets the solution to one set of problems is often the cause of another. As a result, I believe beginning poets should work hard on numerous drafts of a small number of poems. That the process is recursive, as it must seem to Penney when she is asked to return to her first draft to find help in writing her third, simply reinforces what we already know to be true about writing in general. If the process were linear, it would be considerably easier to write an acceptable poem. Unfortunately, poetry writing just isn't that kind of process. The writing of poems, like the writing of other kinds of texts, inevitably involves some guesswork, both for the writer and for those offering solutions to the problems writers, especially beginning writers, must confront.

Finally, something I feared even as I commented on her poem: in using the New Criticism to read and evaluate, I felt I had appropriated Penney's poem. This disappointed me since I made a conscious effort in conference not to. With disarming honesty in her comments attached to the third draft of "Chasm," Penney wrote:

> I am pleased for now with what I have done in draft three. I hope that you can see some improvement, too. The most important thing that I hope you will take into consideration when evaluating this particular poem is how well I have attempted to "reclaim" my poem. I did allow you to take it over at first, perhaps because I thought that that was what I was supposed to do. I believe that draft three is closer to what I wanted to say in the beginning. Draft three is certainly somewhat better poetry (I hope!).

Here is Penney's most recent draft:

Chasm

Faded photograph, 1944.
The daughter is the mother
revisited,
their ambiguity
reflected

in yellowed
black and white.

Tears
spent in angry frustration;
no one listens
when both talk at once.
Too many feelings
bleed
into a moist gray fog.

The girl crouches on
the precipice of her becoming as
stones of her being, now
give
way
to
uncertainty.

The woman waits, poised
on that selfsame brink, her
footing
eroded
by
a vacant past.

They clash with the violent
force
of pent-up sameness.

They scream into
the black
void

until, at last,
a three-by-five impression
illuminates
the darkness in between.

Appropriations, such as mine of Penney's poem, often take place, in poems as well as in essays. As Nancy Sommers warns us in "Responding to Student Writing" (1982), student texts are apt to be appropriated when teachers confuse their purposes in commenting on the text with the student's purposes in writing it. Additionally, a teacher runs the risk of further alienating students from their texts by making comments that are interchangeable—"rubber-stamped"— from poem to poem. With the New Criticism, we run the risk of both of these problems; clearly, both arose in my efforts to respond to Penney's poem.

Our concern must surely double when we realize that one of the side effects of the methods employed in commenting on students' texts is that they will use these very same methods in commenting on each other's poems during workshop. As Richard Beach (1989) notes, "One way of teaching students to assess their writing is simply to tell them what their problems are and how to remedy those problems. Of course, by mimicking our commands, students won't learn to assess on their own" (127).

But more important, Penney, if not Penney's poem, demanded something more than the perceptions I was afforded through the New Critical lens. The very reason why so many of us adhere to the New Criticism in commenting on student texts—its dispassionate and objective methods—now seem to me to have been entirely inappropriate to Penney's passionate poem, a poem in which she seems to explore her relationship with her mother. I have come to realize that some poems demand certain types of readings. In reviewing and contemplating my appropriation of Penney's poem, I can see that her text calls for a feminist reading (see chapter 6) rather than a line-by-line close reading of the sort the New Criticism requires.

In any case, proof that something went awry in Penney's revision can be found in the hypercorrections of her second draft. She has, it seems to me, interpreted my comments and applied them where they were not intended to be applied. It might be argued, given the authority with which advice is given, that hypercorrections are "natural" or logical responses to New Critical commentary. In the case of Penney's revision, hypercorrection in response to my text-based criticism was a product of confusion from being given so much to respond to in revising her poem, no more unusual perhaps than hypercorrections made by students learning a second language. Alan Ziegler's (1989) analogy seems appropriate: "Feedback can be compared to time-release pills: if all the medication goes into the bloodstream at once, the cure can be worse than the disease. A teacher/editor needs to consider how large and frequent the dosages of criticism should be" (217).

For me, my experience with Penney's poem reinforces and broadens Petrosky's (1989) observation about his responses to student writing: "If I give students ways to revise, or if I tell them how I might revise a particular moment in an essay or poem, they almost always follow my directions and the revision is mine not theirs" (214). My authoritative evaluation of Penney's work, though I intended it to be helpful, was, in the end, judgmental and anxiety-provoking. The difficulties I ran into in analyzing Penney's poem simply reinforced misgivings I had had all along about evaluating every poem by every student similarly, through the same adaptations of the New Criticism that I have used to evaluate writing in my other courses.

As a result, I was forced to consider other questions. Aren't poems different from essays in some basic ways that my list of biases does not and perhaps cannot account for? Don't students develop from their reading (before, during, and after the course) some sense of what a poem is, in general, and what their poems should accomplish, in particular? Isn't there some way to involve students in the development of such a list of criteria so that they might aid me in making a more accurate statement of what they should attempt to produce in revising their texts into acceptable poems? Finally, isn't there something basically wrong with telling students, in effect, that their grades will be determined by how nearly they make *their* poems conform to *my* biases? Shouldn't I strive to achieve the high ideal described by Knoblauch and Brannon (1981) over a decade ago: "The teacher's role is to attract a writer's attention to the relationship between intention and effect, enabling a recognition of discrepancies, but finally leaving decisions about alternative choices to the writer, not the teacher" (4)?

The decision to employ New Critical values in evaluating my students' writing was, by and large, an unconscious and natural decision for me, as it must be for most teachers of my generation. Applying these values when evaluating student poems, as my experience commenting on Penney's poem suggests, has both drawbacks and benefits. But what does a conscious application of the New Criticism entail, and how much theory must a teacher of poetry writing know to employ it? Most teachers already know a great deal about the New Criticism, whether or not they have actually read Wellek, Brooks, or Penn Warren.

Re-establishing the Reader's Responsibility to the Text: Some Tentative Conclusions

Reconsidering my response to Penney's poem gives rise to two concerns. First, how can I best involve students in the process of establishing criteria by which their poems will be evaluated? I felt that only by including students in decisions regarding what their texts will be would I be able to avoid the problem of text appropriation. And second, can I do more in a text-based analysis of student poems to treat each poem as a piece of writing with its own integrity? Clearly, it would be as foolish to use a single set of criteria, such as "Bizzaro's Biases," in examining all poems as it would be to treat writing in all genres as the same.

I hoped to find a method of evaluation that would deal primarily with the text while enabling students to better understand which elements in the text would be crucial in my evaluative judgments. In an effort to explore these matters, I attempted to employ a specific adaptation of the New Criticism, Primary Trait Scoring, in combination with interactive teaching methods, such as individual conferences, peer workshops, and interactive journals. One of the results of such a method of evaluation, as demonstrated in chapter 8, is the development of a list of criteria unique to each poem for purposes of grading.

The process of evaluating any piece of writing should parallel the process of writing. This procedure is even more crucial when students are asked to write in a genre as foreign to most students and as difficult for all writers as poetry. While we may ask such questions of any kind of discourse we hope our students will generate, we must especially ask of student poetry writing, among other things, what, after all, is a poem? What in a poem can or even must be evaluated? How can evaluation procedures encourage students to revise? How can an evaluator possibly justify grades? And finally, how can all of this be done in such a way that the student will be encouraged to write poems in the future?

In its adaptation as Primary Trait Scoring (see chapter 8), text-based criticism provides a model for a kind of evaluation that serves teachers best by evaluating the text the student has written and not the text the reader expects. Nonetheless, some applications of reader-response criticism to the evaluation of student poems seem the logical extension of my findings. Perhaps such a method will permit us to reach a compromise about how students' poems should be evaluated and revised.

4 Interaction and Assessment: Some Applications of Reader-Response Criticism

Knowledge of poetry, which is gained, as in science or other areas, by induction and deduction, is likely to remain provisional by falling short in one of two ways: either it is too specific, too narrow and definite, to be widely applicable—that is, the principles suggested by a single poem are not likely to apply in the same number or kind in another poem—or, the knowledge is too general, too abstract and speculative, to fit precisely the potentialities of any given poem.

A. R. Ammons, "A Poem Is a Walk"

One drawback in my adaptation of the New Criticism to the reading and evaluating of student poems was text appropriation. An unwanted though mostly unavoidable by-product of using text-based methodology, appropriation results when teachers do what seems instinctive in the traditional classroom: quickly provide students who have not had adequate reading experiences with the information they need to write poetry. Composition theorists, including Sommers (1982) and Brannon and Knoblauch (1982), have argued that such appropriation is undesirable because it takes the power of writing away from students and subordinates them to the authority of their teachers.

But most students enter poetry writing courses without relevant reading and writing skills. With this in mind, text appropriation seems a natural consequence of conscientious teaching. Teachers have the opportunity—as plumbers might with their apprentices—to say, "Move over and let me show you how I would do it." Appropriation of the text—or of the pipewrench—might thus offer two distinct advantages. First, it gives primary consideration to experience in making the needed repairs; that is, it assumes that the expert-practitioner is handier than the apprentice because of superior experience. And second, since such a view suggests that beginners merely lack information that, once obtained, will enable them to perform like their teachers, many expert-practitioners believe that students will carry the skills learned by observing the teacher into subsequent tasks. Now, though writing and plumbing are hardly the same kind of activity, they do offer similar problems to the novice: an inexperienced writer will have no more luck writing something called a poem than an inexperienced repairperson, who is unfamiliar with the "rules" (if, indeed, any exist), would have repairing a dishwasher. For this reason, most students willingly relinquish control of their texts to teachers who, if they do not actually know rules, are at least believed by students to possess special information.

Yet despite the inclination to do so when confronted by under-prepared students, most teachers do not intentionally take over their students' texts, as evidenced by the comments of many of the expert-practitioners in Turner's *Poets Teaching*. In fact, an increasing number of teachers are convinced that appropriation, whether intentional or not, results in students' loss of control over their texts and apprehensive hypercorrection of the kind Penney made in an effort to salvage at least something of her original idea, if not her grade (see chapter 3). My experience, however, suggests what many teachers still believe: learning of some kind can result from modeling, especially for inexperienced writers who seem to prefer focusing on what the teacher does rather than to revise for themselves, who make changes to their poems principally on the basis of guesswork anyway. Many conscientious poet-teachers who teach by modeling revision practices for their students will openly agree with Dave Smith (1980): "We must try to be what we would have our students emulate and surpass" (190).

In the absence of models for employing alternative critical methods in commenting on student poems, such teaching-by-showing has been and continues to be the primary mode of instruction in poetry workshops. Nonetheless, many teachers have attempted to decentralize authority in their classes by working in peer groups, through interactive journals, or in student-oriented workshop situations. Such efforts, reflecting a change from product pedagogy to process pedagogy, have resulted in increased awareness among many teachers that meaning arises not from the text alone, as the New Critics would insist, but from an interaction between reader, writer, and text.

Lawson and Ryan (1989) reach certain crucial conclusions that serve to distinguish New Critical estimations of student texts from the reader-response evaluations made in this chapter. For instance, the New Criticism views the teacher as exemplary reader:

> If we believe that the locus of interpretation is in the student paper, then we must also believe that there is determinate meaning, something the student intended from the outset to say. This notion assumes that teachers can recognize . . . the thoughts their students are trying to express and assist them in improving ideas or communication. (xiii)

By contrast, reader-response criticism is based on the belief that meaning is determined by the reader's re-creation of the text:

> If one looks to the reader as the locus of interpretation, then the teacher becomes the significant creator of student texts, a "writerly" reader who makes meaning of texts in light of personal experience. (xiii)

The adaptations of the New Criticism in chapter 3 focus on the text in the belief that meaning is a matter of technique, of what Warnock (1989) calls the "intensity of words-on-the-page." In a writing course, the final judge of the success of such technical efforts is the teacher—the exemplary reader who recognizes what students are attempting to impart. Revision, then, reflects a student's efforts to more effectively produce the text the teacher has in mind. But as Cynthia Onore (1989) writes, "As long as judgments of what may be 'better' or 'worse'—that is, of what constitutes improvement in writing—remain the province of teachers alone, then the writer cannot fully and authentically engage in choice making and problem solving" (232).

If properly adapted to the classroom situation, reader-response methodologies will require that students determine who they want their texts to address and that teachers relinquish some power in examining those texts. Rather than enforcing their readings of student poems as definitive, teachers must willingly submit to the text, participating in the development of the reader summoned by the text and evoked, knowingly or unknowingly, by the author. Certainly, the teacher need not *be* that reader. But the teacher must reflect back to the author not what the poem, as a collection of literary devices, means, but how the poem's meaning is reassembled by an individual reader. The use of reader-response methods in evaluating student poems thus does not undermine the student's responsibility, as Onore writes, to "fully and authentically engage in choice making and problem solving." Since the writer makes choices that dictate who the reader will be, the problem a student must solve in revision is how to make certain that the text will be read as he or she intended. As Edward White

(1985) insists, "The writer is not relieved of responsibility by this process, but rather now must assume a new responsibility: to create the kind of reader he or she needs for the text being produced" (92). This chapter will offer models for commenting on student writing from a reader-response perspective.

Incorporating Reader-Response Criticism in the Writing Classroom: What Teachers Should Know

To incorporate reader-response critical tools into our strategies for evaluating student writing, we must begin to view revision less as the application of certain rules and procedures to a nearly finished text and more as an effort to unfold meaning in a manner that somehow makes possible a similar unfolding for the reader. As White (1985) argues, "Recent theories of reading differ most sharply from the old New Criticism in their underlying assumption that meaning is not necessarily identical with expression" (94). The teacher-reader must thus make an effort to envision the audience that the writer's text produces. And the student-writer must revise the text to more effectively address (and thereby create) that audience.

But this changed orientation to meaning necessitates another more difficult adjustment. For reader-response criticism to be employed with any success, students and teachers must be willing to revise the roles they traditionally play in the unfolding drama of classroom relations. For students, the task of creating a poem requires greater involvement in revision than the New Critical approach requires. Rather than relinquishing control of the text to the teacher, students must work cooperatively with their teacher-readers in determining what the poem might become, a process that includes the critical consideration of who the poem addresses. For teachers, the task of response requires that they view their students as writers who seek to create not just a text, but a reader as well. Commentary must thus be nonjudgmental and provide the writer with clues as to how the text might better create the envisioned audience. This response, no matter what shape it takes, will be something very different in appearance from comments offered through the New Critical apparatus, as it must reflect the teacher's re-creation of the text. To a certain extent, because of the classroom environment in which this discourse takes place, teachers will retain some authority. But to employ reader-response methods effectively, teachers must willingly relinquish at least some of the authority the traditional classroom environment confers upon them. Interaction and shared authority are at the center of any method of evaluation and reading founded upon reader-response theories.

By perceiving their teachers' readings of their poems as participations in the meaning-making process, students will approach the task of revision differently from the way they do in New Critical settings. While the New Criticism directly addresses matters to be found in the poem in the belief that meaning is expression and expression, technique, reader-response criticism focuses its attention elsewhere. David Bleich notes what seems at first an extreme position, but one my most recent efforts at adapting reader-response methodology reinforce: "The poem itself, as an object of specifically critical judgment, tends to disappear" (quoted in Moran and Penfield 1990, 43). Even in my earliest adaptations of reader-response methods, I found that less attention went to the text than to the evolving relationship between the writer and reader as they determine what the text will be.

Applying Reader-Response Criticism to Three Student Poems: Making Parallel Texts

One major shift in emphasis from New Criticism to reader response is that reading itself and not the text becomes the object of study. In developing a model for using reader-response criticism in commenting on student poems, I wanted first and foremost to reveal to the author how meaning might be reconstructed by a reader. Such commentary would focus on the reader's participation in the making of the text, the reader's associations with subjects and techniques, the reading situation itself, and, as White (1985) notes, "all kinds of other matters outlawed by formal criticism [which] can now be considered as part of the total meaning a reader creates from a text" (92).

Though most of the poets in Turner's *Poets Teaching* rely on text-based commentary, some of them advocate an approach to texts closer, at least in theory if not always in practice, to reader response. Hollis Summers (1980), for one, takes such a view:

> The Reader has not only the right but the responsibility of saying, "This poem works for me," or "This poem does not work for me." The Reader brings what he knows about being in love or out of love, alive or dead, to the words and white spaces on a page that records somebody else's experiences. (87)

Summers notes, "It is the word *teacher* that is bothering me. I am a *reader*, one fallible reader" (87). In doing so, he states much of the predicament addressed in this chapter. What Summers objects to in "the word *teacher*" is the accompanying role as authority over someone else's text. What he accepts of his role in evaluating his students' poems is the task of serving as *a* reader, not *the* reader. He sympathetically adds, "I like to hope that the author has become the reader" (87). That in commenting on student poems Summers ultimately employs something resembling an analytic scale (89) simply reinforces the need for better models of how to see student poems through alternative critical lenses.

Type and Focus of Comments

The three poems below reflect my search for such a model—with all of my failures and false starts. I knew from the beginning that I wanted to improve upon the work I had done with Penney in chapter 3 by approaching poems as unique entities and by respecting young poets as writers who have some notion, albeit in transition, of what they want their poems to accomplish. I realized as well that commentary using reader-response methods would look different on the page than more traditional methods of response. Rather than relying on intertextual comments as the basis for remarks placed in the margins and summary statements, I recognized the need to make a record of my reactions as a reader in a "parallel" text, preferably alongside students' poems.

The parallel text would need to be made *as* I was able to make meaning from each poem and then revised, when necessary, as my sense of the poem's audience was revised, thus enabling me to offer comments that truly re-create the text. I began in the belief that such parallel texts probably would include two kinds of comments: (1) those asking authors questions concerning how they wanted a portion of the text to be read and (2) those analyzing for the student-poets *my* protocol for reading their poems. When I first placed pen to student text, however, I found myself reverting to previously used strategies of reading; only through concentrated effort did I manage to teach myself how to use reader-response methodologies. My responses to the following three student poems show the evolution of my thought concerning ways to adapt reader-response criticism to the evaluation of individual poems.

For each of the three poems on the following pages, I have included the first draft that the authors showed me and, to the right of each poem, my response in the form of a parallel text (see figures 5–7). What these efforts at adapting reader-response criticism to the evaluation of student poems reveal is my attempt to follow four tenets gleaned from available literature:

1. As White (1985) urges, I have attempted as much as possible to ask questions rather than to offer a series of directives about changing the text. Still, I was not always able to limit myself to questioning, and some questions are simply New Critical directives in disguise, advising the authors to make certain specific changes in the technique of their expression.

2. Numerous theorists believe that the author creates a reader as well as a text (see Iser 1974, Ong 1975, and Ede and Lunsford 1988). Accepting this premise means that readers must make every effort to willingly suspend their disbelief while reading, as Coleridge urges, and receive the text as the author intends it to be received. In the same way that an author might adopt a persona for purposes of expression, a reader under these guidelines must accept the persona the author summons. Part of the responsibility of the teacher-as-reader, then, is to advise the author as to how well the particular audience has been invoked and to help the author do a better job of addressing this audience in subsequent drafts.

3. David Bleich suggests that the text as an object of scrutiny disappears under the particular light of reader-response criticism and that the reader's central concern is to reconstitute the text. In my adaptations, certain comments reflect a concern with reading protocols by viewing the poem as a text that requires the reader to recall past experiences with the subject or, if need be, past experiences with poetic technique in order to reach some understanding of the text's meaning.

4. As Lawson and Ryan (1989) note, adaptations of reader-response methods to the evaluation of student writing require that the teacher function as a writerly reader in reconstructing the text. The parallel texts I have provided for my students seem, in this light, the proper form for adapting reader response to the examination of individual student poems.

Looking more closely at my efforts to adapt these strategies to poems by Mickie, Grace, and Jennifer, I find myself relying initially on the New Criticism. This reliance is especially apparent in the parallel text I wrote beside Mickie's poem. In the process of learning how to

The Stop and Go

You filled your car—
a black beachbound Buick LeSabre—
with high-test
and your belly
with MD/20-20:
Mad Dog, Plum Jubilee—
purchased with a crumpled
dollar and borrowed quarter.

You slammed
the last swallow
of grape Kool-Aid-
with-a-kick
and swaggered
between moongreen
ditches like a dark
drunken pin ball.

My father flipped
the OPEN sign to CLOSED—
PLEASE CALL AGAIN!,
exited the shadowy box
of his Stop and Go
shop, and turned
the clattering keys
clicking the door.

Walking along Deppe Drive
in grass tickling
leg beneath jean, father whirled
a fingered key ring
and hummed
a tune of new boots
and a place
called Charlie Horse Saloon.

—title: sounds like a kind of store.

— give me a clear image in strong, detailed language. That the dollar is crumpled helps, but the fact he drinks Mad Dog may suggest by itself all you want.

— another strong stanza, visual. Does "slammed" already suggest "swallow"? The last four lines here are fine. Some might think the pin ball image has become common.

—this seems to be a counterpoint, a parallel action that may be knit back into the poem later. I'll look for it.

— Good. But does "whirled" suggest throwing? Would "whirred" be better here?

Figure 5. First draft of Mickie's poem and my response.

respond to a poem according to the four tenets outlined above, I made several false starts that I will examine as stages in the development of new models for commenting on student poems.

Perhaps these false starts also reflect my difficulty in relinquishing control of my students' texts after years of viewing them from the perspective of exemplary reader. In fact, I felt some uncertainty in adapting reader-response criticism to the examination of the students' texts because, among other things, I found that it requires that I place myself in the uncomfortable and unprecedented position of a reader

He hugged
a brown paper sack
overflowing with snacks:
Doritos, Funyuns, Rold Gold Pretzel-
Sticks, Snickers, and Mars
for two sons waiting
on tri-shaded green
living room shag
to watch
midnight monster movies
with dad.

— Good image. Brings the counterpoint into clearer focus. Promises some connection and perhaps loss.

He closed his light
marble blue eyes
in song as you stealthily
bounced off the curve
near home.
Back hunched, face grounded,
you tweaked
the knob of your Sparkomatic
for late-night soul.
Looking up, you stomped
not in rhythm,
but in panic.

— The two events are so close now. They share a stanza. Nice idea. "stealthily/bounced" is enjambed for effect. "Sparkomatic" would need to be explained to me. Do you need the last two lines here? What would happen if you didn't use them?

My father danced
in starlit chrome and aqua glass
showering your Buick
with chips and dip-
ping his parcelled partner
to the padded floor.

— Beautifully written offering of a tragic scene. Does this suggest a certain beauty in this act?

You sawed the fisted
shifter into reverse
then drove leaving
snacks, shadows, and sons,
continuing your trip,
adjusting the volume,
and tapping
your purple-stained fingers
to a dying
beat.

— The last stanza seems necessary. But the last three lines get pretty direct. Doesn't the driver know what he's done? "Panic" up above would suggest so.

Figure 5 *continued.*

who must negotiate the meaning of texts with the student-authors themselves. After all, I was not always the reader created by a given text. Often, I assumed one reading to be correct, but my student-authors insisted on (or, more often, hoped for) another. Once an exchange took place between us, though, often through an interactive journal (see chapter 7), I could better "see" what they intended. Then I could continue our dialogue in a way that enabled me to participate with them in the meaning-making process. Note that from a New Critical perspective, a reader would clearly not *share* in the re-creation of the text; rather, my experiences highlighted in chapter 3 suggest that the New Critical method would more often entitle the expert reader to *dominate* the novice writer in revising the text.

Additionally, I had to fight two overwhelming feelings: first, my feeling that, since I was not entirely in control of the class (that is, did not dominate the novice writers), I was not doing a good job of teaching, and second, my impression that some of my students, accustomed to more authoritative teaching methods in their other writing classes, thought that I was not doing my job. I had to constantly remind myself that not being entirely in control was exactly the point, that by relinquishing control I might actually be doing a better job of "teaching." In any case, I had to share power in the classroom if I wanted my experiments in using reader-response methodology to be legitimate. Later in the term, perhaps because I gave up some control of the students' texts, I was pleased to see a considerable amount of verbal exchange in their workshop discussions of each other's poems. I was also pleased to note an improved atmosphere for peer commentary, not only over what I had seen before in my teacher-oriented workshops, as I point out more specifically in chapter 7, but also over what my students report to have experienced in workshops in various other writing courses. I attribute these improved interactive workshops to my students' ability to employ the kinds of comments I made on their poems when commenting on each other's poems.

In all, I have noted three types of comments in these early efforts at using reader-response criticism to examine student poems: (1) text-based comments, both directives and questions, that resemble New Critical marginalia; (2) participatory comments, in the form of statements of understanding or questions which construe the author's intention; and (3) protocol identification, focusing on what the reader believes the poem to mean as well as on how the reader constructed this meaning.

Text-based Comments. Text-based comments take two forms. In one, specific advice is offered to direct the author's revision. In the other, questions are asked in an effort to work inductively, so that the author, in answering these questions, will make certain choices necessary, from the reader's viewpoint, to the revision of the poem. Of course, insofar as these reactions are text-based, they are more closely

---

Lucifer on a White Jet

Lucifer wears a pilot's hat flies a white jet to hell
from heaven, wrings his hands misses the mountain
Granite, shale . . . beside her wrenching and stops.
She weaves the moon dark.

Hunters stray white circles for racetracks for red ants
Nothing a diabolical hand hasn't touched
Hell's smoke hisses down
down
      down
          down
to a barren ocean.
Saint, you aren't ours, yet. We will walk together.
You wait, one day you'll belong to us.
In the death jet take hold of the Devil's hand
It will slip and you will fall like the rest.
A fire ant sips immortality.
Lucifer content to fly. He waits to claim those
from the sweet sickening-sweet earth.
You saint, give up. Your pilot is waiting on the White
jet Content to rule from the throne.
Down
     down
         down
to his claws
She deceives while laughter quakes.

— interesting title – what do you want to accomplish? It seems surrealistic to me.

— no punctuation – it makes me read more carefully.

— puts Milton to mind – interesting image.

— "she weaves the moon dark" – nice.

— connections in st. 2, L. 1 are vague to me.

— the downs working down are old, don't work.

— Direct address. "Saint," vs. Lucifer? Seems an unfair mismatch. Who is now speaking? Lucifer? Seems so. Maybe some visual sign/signal (stanza break, italic, etc.) would help.

— repeats "white jet" – why white? Is this an oxymoron (jet = black)? White black – Milton's hell would be "black white," wouldn't it?

Figure 6. First draft of Grace's poem and my response.

bound to the New Criticism than to anything else. No doubt the New Criticism was my starting point in examining these poems, and the process of examining them reflects as well my own gradual understanding of how reader-response criticism might be used in reading and evaluating student poems. Still, one clear result of these efforts is that I came to feel more convinced than ever that it is indeed possible to read student texts differently than I had read them before. Because of the difficulty I felt at first in relinquishing control of the author's process of revision, however, I found it necessary to remind myself from time to time of how I wanted to approach the evaluation of these poems. To facilitate this, I kept the four tenets outlined above on my desk for quick reference.

    The text parallel to Mickie's poem has more text-based comments than Grace's or Jennifer's and merits attention here for that reason. In stanza 1 of Mickie's poem, for instance, my parallel text praises the image but goes on to offer, by directive, advice I might have given Kim in the poem of hers I examine in chapter 3: "That the dollar is crumpled helps, but the fact that he drinks Mad Dog may suggest by itself all you want to say about this person." In response to the second stanza, I use both questioning and directing in a way that now helps me better understand the kinds of questions that should be *avoided* in adapting reader-response criticism to the examination of student poems. I ask, "Does 'slammed' already suggest 'swallow'?," knowing the answer already and using the question to weakly disguise the directive. Then, as if to blame a larger group of readers for this intrusion into Mickie's text, I add, "*Some* might think the pin ball image has become common."

Similarly, remarks alongside Grace's poem make text-based recommendations that are intended, by tone as well as intent, to direct Grace in her efforts to revise her poem. I do offer praise to the text: " 'she weaves the moon' is good." But then later I note, "The downs working down are old, don't work" and "Maybe some visual sign (stanza break, italic type, etc.) would help." Yet these kinds of comments occur less often in my response to Grace's poem and not at all in my response to Jennifer's, suggesting that learning how to adapt reader-response methodologies, like other learning, involves a discernible process.

Nonetheless, I am interested in the fact that, though I consciously attended to the four tenets outlined above, I burdened Mickie's poem with numerous questions which, with their thinly disguised agendas, continued to reinforce the New Critical bias toward the teacher as authority on matters pertaining to the text. As I have said, it is not enough to ask questions. The type of question asked is of utmost importance. Questions based on how the reader has *construed the author's intent* better serve the reader employing reader-response methods than questions advising the author, albeit indirectly, on *how to manipulate the text* in revision. To employ the latter form of questioning is to incorrectly use the parallel text, which provides ample room for the reader to participate in the author's meaning-making activity by asking questions about what the poem might become once revised. To so naturally focus on text manipulation in questioning suggests the difficulty of changing well-rehearsed methods for commenting on student writing. Others attempting to make such adaptations as I offer in the two kinds of remarks discussed below should not become discouraged by the difficult process through which old ideas are overthrown, even by willing and well-armed warriors.

Back to the Ole Drawing Board	— the title is a cliché for starting over.

Back to the Ole Drawing Board

The picture was drawn
simple
black and white.
I thought it needed
something more.
You didn't.

If only
you had let me paint it,
add some shading,
definition.
You were content
to leave it untinged.
Just the outline, you said.
Nothing more.

You controlled the drawing board.
I allowed it
once.
You teased the sketch
with splashes of red, purple,
even green
then left it alone
looking empty, tainted.

Now you're back,
paintbrush in hand,
ready to create a masterpiece.
The outline has been erased.
The easel—thrown away.
You were stuffed
in the back of my portfolio.
I have begun to paint again.

Handwritten response annotations:

— the title is a cliché for starting over.

— picture? drawing? line drawing? which do you mean? I take this as metaphor, right?

— Here's a contrast in views as to what should be added to the skeletal drawing: "You" wants less; the speaker wants more. Is this the central tension of the poem?

— What does it mean to control a drawing board? Can it be controlled? How? If the speaker allows it, did "you" really have control? "You teased" set me up for some upcoming contradiction, right?

— Where did "you" go to make it possible for him/her to be "back"? Okay. The outline & easel are gone. How, if this is metaphor, does "you" get stuffed in a portfolio?. You have a new relationship and have painted this time rather than drawn?

Figure 7. First draft of Jennifer's poem and my response.

Participatory Comments. These comments mirror for the author what the reader construes to be the author's intentions when reconstructing the text's meaning. Often these comments focus on matters of technique. On other occasions they focus on subject. In both cases the reader should try to ask questions that reflect the reader's effort to receive the text as the author intended it. This kind of commentary seems more closely related to reader-response emphases than do the text-based comments above, as here the reader actively re-creates the text and asks the author if this reading, upon reflection, is what he or she hoped would result from the text.

For instance, Grace's title, "Lucifer on a White Jet," provokes the reaction "Interesting title—What do you want this to accomplish? It seems surrealistic to me." Later in the poem, I comment on the direct address to "Saint": "Direct address. 'Saint' vs. Lucifer? Seems an unfair mismatch. Who is now speaking? Lucifer? Seems so." These comments provoke from Grace some further examination of what *she* wants the text to accomplish and do so by offering observations without judgment, simply for the purpose of clarification.

Such clarification is also the goal of my comments on Jennifer's poem, where I believe I do a much better job of reader response. I want Jennifer to know that "picture" in stanza 1 brings to mind several possibilities that she should consider. I indicate my understanding and her possibilities by questioning: "Picture? Drawing? Line drawing? Which do you mean? I take this as metaphor, right?" Alongside the second stanza, I offer a statement against which she can measure her accomplishment: "Here there's a contrast in views as to what should be added to the skeletal drawing. 'You' wants less; the speaker wants more. Is this the central tension of the poem?" Responding to stanza 3, I ask, "What does it mean to *control* a drawing board? How? If the speaker 'allows' it, did 'you' really have control? 'You teased' sets the reader up for some upcoming contradiction, right?" And finally, to the fourth stanza I respond, "Where did 'you' go to make it possible for him to be back? Okay. The outline and easel are gone. How, if this is metaphor, does 'you' get stuffed in a portfolio? You have a new relationship, having *painted* this time rather than *drawn?*"

I find these comments more closely representative of the values and intent of reader-response criticism. Clearly, I have been less a judgmental and authoritarian evaluator than a writerly reader who participates in the making of the poem and who, through questioning, shares observations that make it essential for the author to consider both how the poem has been read as well as how she would like it to be read (perhaps heretofore unknown). From this vantage point, I do not believe that it is possible to appropriate either Grace's or Jennifer's poem. Revision will show that though each paid attention to my questions, they ultimately made their own decisions on how to resolve the various problems.

Protocol Identification. This type of response enables me—the reader—to accomplish two important tasks. First, some comments record what the reader believes the poem means (which is another way of saying that the reader reacts to the audience addressed/invoked by the text). And second, other comments attempt to record how the reader reads the text and thereby makes meaning. If the reader's reactions are not those the author had hoped for, revision should be an effort to better address/create the intended audience.

Several of my reactions to my students' poems record my understanding of what their poems mean. Alongside the second-to-last stanza of Mickie's poem, for instance, I make the notation "Beautifully written offering of a tragic scene. Does this suggest a certain beauty in this act?" In response to Grace's poem, I point out that for me her first stanza "puts Milton to mind—a 20th-century Milton." Later in the poem I note that she "repeats 'white jet.' " Then I ask, "Why white? Is this an oxymoron (jet = black)? White black? Milton's hell would be 'black white,' wouldn't it?" Similarly, many of my reactions to Jennifer's poem, where I simply offer my thought processes as I read down the page, reflect versions of this type of commentary (though by the time I reacted to Jennifer's poem, I had taught myself how to make these remarks in combinations I discuss below).

In the other kind of commentary I offered, I rendered reading protocols that reflected the way I rewrote the text as I read it. These types of reactions are typical of think-aloud protocols (see Swarts, Flower, and Hayes 1984). Responding to Mickie's third stanza, I note, "This seems to me a counterpoint, a parallel action that may be knit back into the poem later. I'll look for it." Later, in response to this same counterpoint, I offer, "Good image. Brings the counterpoint into clearer focus. Promises some connection and perhaps loss." These reactions may either verify the success of Mickie's endeavor or suggest to him a subtle failure that he needs to remedy. From another point of view, these protocols mirror the kind of audience Mickie has created with this draft of his text. If the audience invoked in these reactions is not the audience Mickie intended, he would need to revise accordingly, the specifics of such revision to be determined on his own.

In a similar vein, I note that Grace's poem has few marks of punctuation. Rather than explaining to Grace—as I might have done if I were using New Critical tools to reflect my personal biases—that she should either punctuate or not punctuate (as I recall having told students in the past), I simply note what I see on the page: "No punctuation—it makes me read more carefully." Thus, the task of determining whether and how to revise falls on her shoulders. My comment simply reveals that she has created an audience responsive to her mixture of punctuated and unpunctuated stanzas.

My more recent examination of Jennifer's poem shows some evolution in my ability to use reader-response methodology to evaluate student poems. Most of the comments parallel to her text reveal a mixture of participatory commentary and protocol analysis. In these comments, I offer a reading of the poem focusing on what I believe the poem means and on how I have reached these conclusions. An example already cited above is useful in this context. When I note about her second stanza that "Here there's a contrast in views as to what should be added to the skeletal drawing. 'You' wants less; the speaker wants more," I participate in her poem in a meaning-making way. When I add, "Is this the central tension of the poem?," my analysis reveals a protocol for reading her poem as well.

Effectiveness of Comments

Revisions of these poems reveal something of the nature of each author's response to these comments, responses different from reactions to New Critical commentary primarily in the requirement that the student-authors make the necessary revisions by themselves rather than rely on the teacher-reader's instructions for manipulating the text. What follows are revisions of the three poems:

The Stop and Go

You filled your car—
a black beachbound Buick LeSabre—
with high test
and your belly
with MD/20-20:
Mad Dog, Plum Jubilee—
purchased with a dollar
and borrowed quarter.
You slammed your grape
Kool-Aid-with-a-kick
and swaggered
between moongreen
ditches like a dark
drunken pin ball.

My father flipped
the OPEN sign to CLOSED—
PLEASE CALL AGAIN!,
exited the shadowy box
of his Stop and Go
shop, and turned
the clattering keys
clicking the door.

Walking along Deppee Drive
in grass tickling

leg beneath jean,
father whirred
a fingered key ring
and hummed
a tune of new boots
and a place
called Charlie Horse Saloon.

He hugged
a brown paper sack
overflowing with snacks:
Doritos, Funyuns, Rold Gold Pretzel-
Sticks, Snickers, and Mars
for two sons waiting
on tri-shaded green
living room shag
to watch
midnight monster movies
with dad.

He closed his light
marble blue eyes
in song as you stealthily
bounced off the curve
near home.
Back hunched, face grounded,
you tweaked
the knob of your AM/FM
for late-night soul.
Looking up,
you stomped.

My father danced
in starlit chrome and aqua glass
showering your Buick
with chips and dip-
ping his parcelled partner
to the padded floor.

Scanning the street
with red-rooted eyes,
you sawed the fisted
shifter shakily into reverse
then drive, leaving
snacks, shadows, sons,
and a father for whom
you will forever
mourn.

—Mickie

Lucifer on a White Jet

Lucifer flies a white jet to hell from heaven
She wrings her arms, misses the mountain
Granite   shale   beside her wrenching.
She weaves the moon dark.

Hunters stray   red ants run a race in white
Hell's smoke hisses   a charred ocean.
Saint, you aren't ours, yet. We will walk together.
In the death jet take hold of the Devil's hand
It will slip and you'll fall like the rest.
A fire ant sips immortality.
Lucifer waits to claim those from the sweet
sickening-sweet earth. He deceives
while laughter quakes.

—Grace

Back to the Ol' Drawing Board

The picture was drawn:
simple
black and white
I thought it needed
something more
you didn't.

If only
you had let me paint it,
add some shading
definition
You were content
to leave it untinged
Just the outline, you said,
Nothing more.

You insisted upon
controlling the drawing board
And, once,
you tickled the sketch
with splashes of color
then wandered off as I
giggled with delight

Around the studio,
you peeked over the shoulders
of other artists,
smiling with approval
while our work
was left empty,
tainted

Now you're back,

paintbrush in hand,
ready to create a masterpiece
the sketch you left unfinished
was stuffed
in the back of my portfolio
I have begun
to paint again.

—Jennifer

In general, revisions in response to commentary made from a reader-response perspective are far more extensive and far less predictable than revisions resulting from New Critical concerns. This is because most of the changes made to poems read and evaluated from a New Critical perspective are made in direct response to concerns voiced by the reader-evaluator. Of course, since the New Critical method gives final authority over meaning to the teacher as exemplary reader, we should not be surprised to see students revise as the teacher has suggested they should. Such obedience was not as readily given by Mickie, Grace, and Jennifer. For the most part, only when they felt my parallel text offered something of value did they revise in response to my commentary.

Still, sometimes the changes made by Mickie, Grace, and Jennifer seem to be a reaction to the tone of New Critical authority that inadvertently snuck into my comments. For instance, in response to my comment "Does 'slammed' already suggest 'swallow'?" in the second stanza of Mickie's poem, Mickie revises the original line, "You slammed / the last swallow / of grape Kool-Aid-with-a-kick," to a shorter, more direct version: "You slammed your grape / Kool-Aid-with-a-kick." But where I suggest to Mickie, again using the power of numbers as support, that "Some might think the pin ball image has become common," no change has been made. In a letter to me describing his revision of this poem, Mickie writes, "Pat shared a concern with the common pinball image in the second stanza. However, I kept it because I like the image and it appears fresh to me."

That same letter included information I might have surmised from the poem but did not risk to suggest. "The Stop and Go" is a poem about the death of Mickie's father. Mickie writes, "This poem was an emotional release of a personal tragedy in my life. I used it to share the experience and emotions that I felt in response to the death of my father." Teachers have always been concerned about how to respond to such personal writing. Text-based commentary, of course, tends to diminish the student's experience, as the tools employed in such a reading insist that meaning is expression and technique. But reader-response methods enable the reader to re-create the meaning of the student's poem in a much more participatory and, therefore, sympathetic way.

Mickie's revision is an excellent example of this point. The most noticeable change in the poem, of course, comes in the last stanza. In his first draft, Mickie characterizes the driver who has just killed his father in the language of anger and hurt: "You sawed the fisted / shifter into reverse / then drove leaving / snacks, shadows, and sons, / continuing your trip, / adjusting the volume, / and tapping / your purple-stained fingers / to a dying / beat." So, in an effort to participate with Mickie in making meaning in his poem, I ask in the text parallel to this stanza, "Doesn't the driver know what he's done?" Mickie's revision reflects a substantial change in his perception of the driver: "Scanning the street / with red-rooted eyes, / you sawed the fisted / shifter shakily into reverse / then drive, leaving / snacks, shadows, sons / and a father for whom / you will forever / mourn."

By way of explaining this enormous change in the last stanza of his poem, Mickie writes the following in his letter:

> I had trouble in the first draft's ending because there had never been any real resolution. Life just goes on with little thought on the past. The ending was merely an extended observation based on my emotional bias. It satisfied only my sense of hurt and vengeance. While driving home after receiving Pat's reading, I realized that to remain true to the poem and to myself, I must experience and resolve the poem from the driver's experience: someone who is capable of realizing his error and feeling the torment and regret of his fatal mistake.

This kind of change in Mickie's poem might have come about, in any case, from a more direct text-based evaluation of the poem. But I believe that by my participation in the meaning-making activity—since meaning in this adaptation of reader response is an agreement between reader, writer, and text—I was able to encourage Mickie to reconsider his description of the driver. More importantly, I believe I was able to do so without intruding unnecessarily into Mickie's personal life, making judgments about his painful loss, or reducing his experience to a discussion of technique. With the creation of the text as our goal, we were able to negotiate over a poem, not over Mickie's personal past.

Changes to the poems by Grace and Jennifer were equally substantial, if not as dramatic. Like Mickie, Grace made some of the text-based changes I authoritatively suggested, including deletion of the word "down" as she had placed it working down the page. But Grace does not work out the matter of punctuation noted in my parallel text. And she does not clarify the speaker in line 7 and following.

Nonetheless, Grace's poem is an interesting example of what might happen—and no doubt of what many poets believe often does occur—if the author is not quite sure where she wants her poem to go. Grace has worked toward greater clarity in her revised version, taking quite seriously my question "What do you want this to accomplish?" But in a letter back to me, Grace identifies this as "a strange poem" and confesses that she is "puzzled by it." Lack of a clear purpose or intention in a poem is, of course, something that all poets must deal with, that most accept without question, and that some appreciate about their own creations. To say that poems are often the product of deep and subconscious imaginings is to state the obvious. Such a view of poetry holds for Grace's poem. Still, another benefit of the reader-response method can be seen here. I am able to ask Grace to consider what she hopes to achieve. Though she is not certain what, if anything, this poem might accomplish, her conclusion is one a teacher might appreciate: "I guess I'd like to pursue this one [after the semester ends] because it is so odd to me. I don't hear any echoes of clichés. I like the lines 'She weaves the moon dark' and 'He deceives / while laughter quakes.' " Clearly, Grace has retained ownership of her poem.

Jennifer similarly incorporates into her poem only those elements she finds useful. She is not concerned, for instance, with my reading of the word "picture" in line 1 as being unclear, as she keeps the first two stanzas exactly as they appear in her earlier version. And of my participatory comment and protocol analysis parallel to stanza 2, she writes, "That is exactly what I had intended at that point in the poem, so I didn't change anything there." Stanza 3, however, is heavily revised, since my questions helped her see that she "wasn't as clear there" as she needed to be. In my parallel text, I ask, "What does it mean to *control* a drawing board? Can it be controlled? How? If the speaker *allows* it, did 'you' really have control?" These questions enabled me to participate in the re-creation of the text. Jennifer changes "You controlled the drawing board. / I allowed it / once" to the more definite "You insisted upon / controlling the drawing board." By making this change, she is able to more precisely limit the ways in which this line might be read.

Jennifer also shares my concern with the word "teased" in that same stanza. Offering a protocol analysis, I note, " 'You teased' sets me up for some upcoming contradiction, right?" Jennifer writes, "That contradiction is never really developed." As a result, she revises around the new verb, "tickled," which enables her to make an image of a speaker who "giggled with delight." Finally, Jennifer adds six new lines to the next stanza to respond to my concern that I do not know where the "you" of the poem went. In my parallel text, I ask, "Where did 'you' go to make it possible for him/her to be 'back'?" Her revision clarifies that "Around the studio, / you peeked over the shoulders / of other artists, / smiling with approval / while our work / was left empty."

By analyzing my efforts to employ reader-response criticism in reading and evaluating student poems, I not only taught myself how to read my students' texts differently, but I also began to see the hidden benefits to a teacher of using these methods. For one thing, using reader-response methods allows me to make a much more sympathetic response to students who write from emotional need, as my response to Mickie's poem reveals. And as my response to Grace's poem shows, reader-response methods enable the reader to accept a poem that a writer has not yet clearly envisioned, but at the same time help push that writer toward a greater understanding of the poem.

Reading as a Recursive Activity: Using a Tape Recorder to Comment on a Poem by Matthew

Perhaps the biggest surprise of all in my effort to employ reader-response criticism to comment on student poems was the interference from previously used methods, notably the New Criticism. I realized almost immediately that I would have to teach myself how to be a writerly reader without a model to rely upon. Though such reading is not "natural," I found myself able to quickly improve in my ability to use these methods. But I also discovered that each time I returned to a set of poems, I had to retrain myself to read "differently."

Heartened by my experiences, I set out to use a tape recorder to record a think-aloud protocol of my actual process of determining meaning in a student's poem. Writing down protocols, as I did above, is a self-limiting procedure; it portrays the reading process as a linear and one-dimensional activity. Even when I actively revise my interpretation in the process of understanding a poem, a parallel text does not allow me to accurately indicate what has occurred as I reconstruct the text.

As a result of this recognition of a parallel text's limitations, I set out to determine how a student might respond to a tape recorded version of these comments. Unlike a parallel text, the very nature of oral protocols would enable me to demonstrate to writers that I made meaning of their poems by engaging in a recursive rather than a linear process. I thus chose to provide Matthew, a student in my introductory poetry writing class, with taped commentary on one of his poems. Matthew had already received written comments on another of his poems, comments that relied primarily on the parallel text. As a result, he was able to compare the two methods. Here is Matthew's poem:

Myself, Myself

I watched myself watch myself
Hanging on a wall, splashed
Fallings wept upon the floor,
Bleedings of a seamstress
Seaming the seeming
Lines that are me whole.
Piecefully I gathered myself
To myself,
Etching the moment upon occurrence
That might not, or might, happen again.
Visual cues whispered
In relative blindness, that
    Van Gogh struck me deaf
    Keats' urn bears only his ashes
    Life paints by numbers,
    Knowing I cannot count.
"You call this art?"
Finally incredulous, I asked of myself.
The print, it, I, me, replied,
"It is what you make of it."
Grinning, I ripped myself
In two.

                    —Matthew

I recorded my observations about this poem as I read it and gave the tape to Matthew. I also timed myself to determine if this method of commentary might be efficient. I took only thirteen minutes to record what follows:

Oral Protocol of My Reading of Matthew's "Myself, Myself"

Interesting title. I'm not quite sure what to make of it, but I think that there's an echo here or a reflection. Let me jump into the poem and read a section of it.

"I watched myself watch myself hanging on a wall." That suggests to me a mirror. That you're watching yourself watch yourself and the second self is one that's hanging on a wall the way it would be if the mirror were attached to the wall.

"Splashed fallings wept upon the floor bleedings of a seamstress seaming the seeming lines that are me whole." "Splashed fallings wept upon the floor." We have two water images here—"splashed" and "wept"—but then we find out that these are bleedings which could also splash and weep. Of a seamstress . . . if they're bleedings of a seamstress then chances are that it's meant to be metaphor, so I'm wondering here if by this you mean pieces of cloth . . . pieces of clothing. You watched yourself hanging on the wall in the mirror and in it you see the clothes hanging off of you or the clothes on the floor behind you . . . "bleedings of a seamstress seaming the seeming lines that are me whole." Begins to make me think that that seamstress is a mother, a creator . . . am I right here? It seems like there are a lot of suggestions as to what the seamstress might be. The seamstress is the person who has made whatever it is that you see . . . the "lines that are me whole" have been created by this seamstress.

"Piecefully [I spell it out] I gathered myself to myself." It's almost a statement of getting yourself together or pulling yourself together. That kind of thing. "Piecefully piece by piece" you gathered yourself to yourself and those pieces are the pieces that were sewn together by the seamstress.

"Etching the moment upon occurrence" . . . I'll read it again: "Piecefully I gathered myself to myself, etching the moment upon occurrence." So re-creating, etching the moment upon occurrence. Something has happened; something has occurred and you're trying to capture that and reflect it in the way that you have piece by piece gathered yourself together "upon occurrence that might not or might happen again."

"Piecefully I gather myself to myself etching the moment upon occurrence that might not or might happen again." It's really hard for me to read this independent from the last poem of yours I read, Matthew, where there was that same sense of the cyclical, of things coming back to happen again. I need to re-read. "Piecefully I gathered myself to myself etching the moment upon occurrence that might not or might happen again." I think I need to go a little bit further before I can really understand what happened in that particular four-line set.

"Visual cues whispered in relative blindness." So okay, let's go back. "Piecefully I gather myself to myself etching the moment upon occurrence that might not or might happen again. Visual cues whispered in relative blindness." That whether something will happen over again depends upon what you see in front of you. The thing that you're looking at is yourself in a mirror, that these are the things—"visual cues whispered in relative blindness"—and these are the things that were whispered. There's a comma there: that "Van Gogh struck me deaf, Keats' urn bears only his ashes, life paints by numbers, knowing I cannot count." Interesting. Okay, so what we have here is a kind of confusion, trying to make sense of who you are. Is that what's going on here? Van Gogh who cut off his ear struck you deaf, Keats' beautiful grecian urn is only proof of the fact that he's no longer around, that he's dead, that that urn carries his ashes. And then the irony that life paints by numbers and that if you're looking at the world in order to figure out what's going on, life paints by numbers, but poor you do not know how to count.

Interesting. " 'You call this art?' " Quotation marks around it—someone is saying it to you. "Finally, incredulous I ask of myself" ... so this thing that you see in the mirror may very well be not really a reflection at all. The mirror may really be the mirror of words. So the mirror now may be metaphorical and what's reflected back to you is reflected back through that language ... through your art, that somehow you hope to piece together who you are through your acts of creativity. And then we have to ask, as a lot of people have to ask about confessional work, "You call this art?" "Finally incredulous I ask of myself. The print, it, I, me replied, 'It is what you make of it.' "

Oh oh, that's what I'm doing, isn't it? That's reader response, isn't it?

The print, meaning the words, it, I, me ... the work of art replies, " 'It is what you make of it.' " Saying in effect that art is in the eye of the beholder, that meaning is not in the language on the page. In some sense I think you're saying that meaning is not intention, that meaning is really exactly what I'm trying to do here ... which is ironical ... that meaning is really in my re-creation of what you put on the page and that the language isn't where meaning is found. Meaning is found in the reader that evolves as you put language on the page.

"The print, it, I, me replied, 'It is what you make of it.' Grinning I rip myself in two," again suggesting the concreteness of a page being ripped in half.

I feel pretty good about that interpretation. I think that I'm going to go back through and read the poem and see if this whole idea of you trying to piece your life together through your art makes sense.

"Myself, Myself." Interesting, now that title might mean to me myself the writer, myself the words on the page. Are they the same thing? Do you find out something about yourself by writing that you can't know in any other way, thereby creating other kinds of art ... meanings and self-understandings that you just can't get to except through art.

"I watch myself watch myself hanging on the wall." It sounds like proofreading to me. "Splashed fallings wept upon the floor bleedings of a seamstress seaming the seeming lines that are me whole." So I think that one side of you or one side of the artist, or one side of the "I" character is also the seamstress.

"Piecefully I gather myself to myself etching the moment on occurrence that might not or might happen again." Etching the moment upon occurrence seems now to me—the term etching, the action of etching—seems to me to be making a record of certain experience because that experience might not happen again. Rossetti calls it "a moment's monument."

"Visual cues whispered in relative blindness"—okay, those cues are signals—as to who you are—"whispered" and these are the things that told you—that Van Gogh struck you deaf, that Keats' urn bears only his ashes as in his death. "Life paints by numbers knowing I cannot count"—I think that's—am I getting it here?—that this is . . . that even though you're making art, that it's not easy to know who you are and that sometimes the reflection of you in the words on the page is not exactly what you had hoped it would be? Or is not exactly so discernible that you really understand who you are? In part because that occurrence . . . it's an occurrence that you record on the page that might not or might happen again. If it doesn't happen again, then you can have absolutely no clue as to who you are based upon that experience. In a new experience you may in fact be a different person responding in a different way.

" 'Call this art?' Finally, incredulous I ask of myself. The print, it, I, me replied, 'It is what you make of it.' Grinning, I rip myself in two"—Man, all right, I think I have that, Matthew.

I hope that this is useful. Once again, if I didn't get from it what you had hoped, then I think it would be incumbent upon you to make those changes that would enable me to be the reader that you want me to be.

There are obvious benefits to employing this procedure. For one, and perhaps most important, Matthew can hear for himself my effort to be the reader his text creates. We might be able to argue from one standpoint that the fact that I can be that reader says something not only about my success as a reader, but also about Matthew's success as a writer. Enough of the signals were there so that a careful reading would render what, in the end, is the meaning Matthew claims to have intended. No doubt it is possible for both weak reading and weak writing to occur in a text, making the kind of transaction that Matthew and I had virtually impossible. But, of course, the tape would record those failures and then serve as a mechanism for continued discussion of the text.

Matthew is able to hear how I read his poem, where I place stresses and break units, and from that reading determine something about the form of his poem—at least the form as I construe it as one reader. He is also privy to the private operations of my memory as it is stimulated by his poem, enabling him to "locate" me as a reader. This information will help Matthew determine not only *which* portions of his poem gave me the greatest difficulty, but also *why* I had trouble there. These two factors—what proved difficult and why—should serve writers well as they set out to revise. A writer can thus note that reading is a recursive activity, one in which, as should be obvious in my reaction to Matthew's poem, a reader tests a hypothesis against the text, and if that hypothesis needs to be revised, tests another.

What I liked best about employing this method of commentary is that it enabled me to provide the author with a large amount of information. Some might argue that students can respond better to less information or to some edited version of the information provided here. But from a reader-response standpoint, those who believe so still adhere, on some level, to the traditional view that a teacher's job is to point out specific matters in need of remedy and that the student's job is to fix up a piece of writing as the teacher suggests. The tape recording I offered Matthew enabled him to see for himself how one reader brings experience to bear upon the text, how meaning evolves for that reader through a process of hypothesis sampling, and how the writer might rework the text to better direct and thereby create the reader envisioned.

I asked Matthew to write an evaluation of this method of commenting on his poems since he had poems evaluated both in a parallel text and on a tape recording. This is what he wrote:

Reply to Taped Responses to My Poem

As you stated in class, writing is reading. In having you tape your response to my poem, I was able to clearly view the process of reading.

It [the tape recording] was much more in depth and helpful than a response written upon a page. I felt like I was having more of a discussion with you. I was able to better understand how and why you achieved your interpretation of my poems. From this understanding, I could better decide who was in the right, the reader or me, as far as clarity of intention in my poem's content. From this point, it allowed me a clearer view of how and what could be improved to bring about a better melding of author's intent and reader's interpretation. These changes would hopefully lend themselves to improving the quality of my poem.

I'm glad you let me participate in this. I loved it. I kept finding myself trying to reply to the tape and getting somewhat frustrated when I couldn't reply. I suggest you do this some more. I think it would help other students immensely....

As this note indicates, Matthew has learned a great deal about how "Myself, Myself" has been read by one reader. More important, though, is that Matthew has learned a great deal about the interaction that takes place in the making of meaning between the reader, writer, and text. This knowledge will enable him to participate fruitfully in the workshop situation.

5 Intentional and Unintentional Exclusions: Some Applications of Deconstruction

Like influenza in winter, deconstruction is in the air. Some of us will catch it, others will panic and take shots against it, a few of us will ignore it and assimilate its attendant discomforts along with our other minor and major irritants. A few of us will go stoically on and wonder what the fuss is all about—it's always been here, even if we've called it by other names. The question that a few of us are starting to ask is, "Can we use it?"

David Kaufer and Gary Waller,
"To Write Is to Read Is to Write, Right?"

Part of the problem of evaluating student writing comes out of our deep understanding that we need to consider the process of writing as well as the product before us and that much of what the student is trying to say did not get very clearly into the words on the page.

Edward White, *Teaching and Assessing Writing*

Both New Criticism and reader-response criticism can be—and have been to varying degrees—adapted for use in examining student texts. But adaptations of deconstruction for this purpose might be greeted by some teachers as inappropriate. Jane Tompkins (1990) is unequivocal on this point in her essay "A Short Course in Post-Structuralism": "You can't apply post-structuralism to literary texts" (36). And near the end of her remarkably succinct discussion of deconstruction, Sharon Crowley (1989) concludes, "I am not sure that

Portions of this chapter first appeared in "Some Applications of Literary Critical Theory to the Reading and Evaluation of Student Poetry Writing," in *Poets' Perspectives: Reading, Writing, and Teaching Poetry,* ed. Charles R. Duke and Sally A. Jacobsen (Portsmouth, NH: Boynton/Cook, 1992), 154–74. Reprinted by permission of the publisher.

a deconstructive pedagogy can be realized—the term is in itself an oxymoron" (45).

Still, there are those, Crowley among them, who believe that it is at least possible to *design* a pedagogy based on deconstruction (see also Atkins and Johnson 1985 and Donahue and Quandahl 1989). According to Crowley, that pedagogy would first have to reject the teacher as the authority for disseminating and judging "received" knowledge, a far more extreme position than the shared authority required in the adaptations of reader response described in chapter 4. Crowley explains, "The knowledge which is preferred and privileged at any given moment is so, simply because influential members of the concerned community have subscribed to it" (46). Second, a teacher would have to "teach" writing by focusing on how the writing process differs for each writing task: "The writing process differs to some extent with every situation or task; which also implies that no universally useful model or tactics for generating writing will ever be found" (Crowley 1989, 46). Thus, rather than offering prescriptive guidelines for the making of various kinds of texts, as done in most of the applications of the New Criticism in chapter 3, a deconstructive approach to teaching writing would pay attention to "the constraints of the rhetorical situation in which [writers] find themselves" (Crowley 1989, 46), including the "real" situation of writing in the classroom. And third, if writing is a process of entertaining differences, a course in writing would have to confront its own assumptions about reading and writing. As Crowley notes, "a syllabus for a writing class would always be in revision," since students would be actively involved in rewriting the teacher's syllabus (46).

Crowley concludes with what seems both a caution and a challenge:

> Adopt[ing] deconstructive attitudes toward writing and its teaching will not be an easy matter for either students or teachers, all of whom are accustomed to working within the constraints placed on them by institutions and a culture that subscribes to the metaphysics of presence. (47–48)

If we hear the voice of caution in this passage, perhaps it is because of deconstruction's global implications: its reconsideration of existing reading methods and, of course, its threat to the very existence of certain literary works long privileged and valued by the dominant culture. Yet we might also read these words as a challenge. As with other theories, our job is to determine which of the tenets of deconstruction are most pertinent to our task in the classroom, develop models for using them, and then study their use in the ongoing effort to better meet both our students' needs and our own. Kaufer and Waller (1985) state the predicament excellently:

> It's easy enough for department heads or full professors, bought out of their teaching by prestigious grants, to speculate on self-indulgent play, dehierarchizing hierarchies, finding the tracks along which meaning may (or may not) be possible; but what of those of us who must teach the 8:30 A.M. freshman composition or literature class? What relevance do discussions of *differance*, decentered selves, and grammatology have to the educational acts we (or our teaching assistants) perpetrate in Strategies for Writing or Reading Literature? (66)

Any effort to answer Kaufer and Waller's questions as they pertain specifically to courses in the writing of poetry must begin with the most apparent element of theory stressed by Crowley in the passages above: a deconstructive pedagogy—if such an approach to teaching, reading, and evaluating writing is possible at all—will be founded chiefly on the issue of difference, on analyzing the incongruities in a text, on applying pressure to a poem's seams and thereby uncovering what has been intentionally or unintentionally excluded. Deconstruction thus allows us to give up our search for a poem's privileged meaning and our investment in the authority of the text. More specifically, deconstructive revision will not result in the traditional succession of drafts wherein each is "better" than the last. Since deconstruction is a way of reading rather than a way of evaluating writing, it does not set a standard by which a reader or writer can determine if a piece of writing is finished. A deconstructive revision thus aims not for improvement, but for difference; the idea of "better" implies the notion of privilege, a new hierarchy, an ideal against which the text must continue to work.

What deconstruction enables a reader to acknowledge that the other methods analyzed in this book do not are the complex disagreements warring within any text. Deconstruction thus serves as a useful mechanism for analyzing student poems in a poetry writing class because it does not accept at face value a text's apparent meaning. Rather, deconstruction enables us to analyze a poem differently, beginning with the close reading that New Critics advocate, but continuing on to an examination of what the student has left unsaid but nonetheless suggested in the poem. Gerald Graff (1990) writes, "In order to say something about any subject we presumably repress some of our thoughts and feelings about it, but what we are repressing is betrayed by our words in a way that will be readable by analysis" (171).

In the same way that canonical works are exemplary expressions of traditionally privileged cultural values, most teachers will agree that successful student texts are those which express certain valued elements of subject and technique (see Cooper and Odell 1977; Lawson, Ryan, and Winterowd 1989; and Faigley 1989). Clearly, the meaning of canonical literary works, simply by their representation of traditional values, arises from something other (and more) than an interpretation of linguistic units. Similarly, teachers have long known that student texts are not exclusively about what the student has put on the page. In the same way that applying the notion of "greatness" to literary works requires readers to confront each work's tentative culturally granted status as a literary work, so too do teachers need to confront the subjects and techniques of student works as but tentative in terms of an ongoing process of writing. The existence of both literary and student works as texts depends as much upon the repression or exclusion of certain elements as upon the inclusion of certain other, usually culturally validated, elements. As White (1985) puts it, "If we are limited to what the student puts on the paper, we tend to be literalists, putting aside our intuitions of what the student *meant* to say or our predictions of what the student *could* say if he or she followed the best insights now buried in the present text" (93).

Deconstruction enables us to explore with our students the conflicting forces of signification that constitute the work itself. According to Kaufer and Waller (1985), "A fundamental tenet underlying work in deconstruction is that every interpretation must make systematic omission of incompatible, though no less probable, interpretations" (69). Any effort to adapt deconstruction to the evaluation of student poems must therefore reflect an effort to read differently, so that the conflicts submerged beneath the literal level—that is, those conflicts not readily available to us through our "usual" ways of reading—can be uncovered and brought to the surface. Only after they are brought out can the writer view those conflicts, see if dragging them to the surface will clarify intended meanings, and if so, bring them into the language of the text. For a student, this means revising with attention to the conflicts originally left outside the boundaries of the text, either intentionally or unintentionally. For the teacher, it means attending to how the text works out what Barbara Johnson (1985) calls "its complex disagreements with itself" (141).

Finding Gaps, Silences, and Contradictions in the Text: What Teachers Should Know

In her own interesting adaptation of poststructuralism to the examination of student texts, "What Students Don't Say: An Approach to the Student Text," Margaret L. Shaw (1991) makes an important, commonsense observation about the theoretical basis for the strategies she employs. After attributing the original theoretical foundations for her strategies to the French Marxist Louis Althusser and his student Pierre Machery, she acknowledges the presence of a larger group of theorists linked by "their methodological interest in gaps, silences, and contradictions—the discontinuities of texts" (46). As the title above suggests, my orientation to the strategies discussed in this chapter is no different. The strategies themselves are adaptations of deconstruction as it is currently discussed by composition theorists. But, to cite Shaw again, "what I will take from them [these theorists] is actually something they share with a number of other thinkers from Freud to Jacques Derrida" (46).

The question is, What of this can be readily appropriated by classroom teachers? First, teachers employing New Critical methods know quite well that student-writers make certain choices about what they will include (and, therefore, what they will not) in the texts they write. Because these choices often close off the development of conflicts submerged in the text, teachers often find it necessary to encourage their students to introduce into the text material originally excluded, whether intentionally or unintentionally. Of course, to say, as Kaufer and Waller (1985) suggest critics of deconstruction might, that deconstruction is "merely a trendy New Criticism—a formalist sheep in a snappy new wolf-suit" (68) is to oversimplify. Rather, deconstruction offers us a way to read deeper, to read more closely than even the New Critics urged, by focusing the reader's attention on what the student has failed to say. Among other things, deconstruction gives license for readers to do what many teachers have been doing all along when they have asked students to write more about this or that undeveloped portion of the text.

Second, deconstruction enables teachers to see how the meaning of a student's text arises in the writing process from the ongoing relationship between what is said and what is not. Naturally, teachers must start with what is on the page by making a close reading of the sort that will render the privileged meaning of the text. But they must not stop there. They must then look for the subtle conflicts suggested but left undeveloped in various drafts of a text. In those conflicts they will often find a subject, some details, or a critical tension that the author might decide to bring into the text itself. Of course, all of this makes the issue of revision from a deconstructive standpoint a difficult one. Since the process of a deconstructive reading involves an ongoing effort to turn the text against itself, it is difficult to say when, exactly, a text is "finished." Deconstruction offers a reading, not an evaluation, and does not depend on a set of standards for excellence to measure improvement. My examination of the use of deconstruction with my student Deb later in this chapter shows exactly how this process might continue indefinitely into the future. From this perspective on reading and writing, it may be that ultimately a text is given up only in exhaustion (or at the end of the term).

Third, and consistent with Crowley's description of a deconstructive pedagogy, the determination of whether to bring the excluded element into the text must be made by the student-writer. The teacher's job is to offer a reading that brings to light elements that may have been excluded in the students' efforts to make, as they have long been taught, a seamless text, a text in which contradictions are resolved. Consequently, once a teacher unearths these contradictions, the findings must be brought to the writer's attention in language that avoids a tone of authority and expectation. Rather, teachers must nudge the author—through a letter or note perhaps, but definitely through a text detached from the student's poem—to look more closely at the text, to see it differently, to deconstruct it. In short, one of the teacher's goals should be to enable students to perform their own deconstructive readings.

Applying Deconstruction to Three Student Poems: A Point of Departure

There are those who would insist upon the danger of applying deconstruction to the evaluation of student writing. Who can argue with Shaw (1991) when she writes, "The questions we come up with when we respond to student papers will always be determined by what the paper suggests, not by a theory which is 'applied' in any reductive way" (48)?

Keeping Shaw's admonition in mind, I have tried to avoid using deconstruction as a method of evaluation, except insofar as evaluation implies reading. A standard or set of criteria for use in grading a poem will not likely result from a deconstructive reading anyway. The commentary that does result from such a reading, however, will differ radically from the types of comments we might make using the New Criticism or reader-response criticism. In this difference lies deconstruction's value—not in the application (and oversimplification) of theory, but in the benefits of reading drafts of student poems in yet another way. In combination with other methods of responding to student writing, deconstruction offers a point of view different in kind and focus. Yet here I find Shaw's advice especially valuable: deconstructive readings should not be offered programmatically. Directives helpful in reading one text (or one draft, for that matter) may prove counterproductive in reading another.

Still, we must consider how deconstruction might aid us in reading and offering in-process responses to student poems. Steven Lynn (1990) offers three steps for reading a text using deconstruction. First, Lynn advocates that readers note, presumably through their usual methods of reading, "which member of an opposition in a text appears to be privileged or dominant" (106). In other words, through a process which requires that students make certain exclusions in order to have a text at all, a student produces the work in question. Clearly, this work favors one subject, one set of circumstances, over another. Task one is to determine what those circumstances are. Then a teacher making a deconstructive reading "shows how this hierarchy can be reversed within the text" (Lynn 1990, 106). Though Lynn is not specific on this point, such reversals no doubt can be made on a holistic level, thereby affecting the subject of the entire piece, or on an atomistic level, concerning smaller units within the document. Finally, a deconstructive reading places both the privileged reading and its reversal in question, "making the text ultimately ambiguous" (Lynn 1990, 106).

Lynn's analysis offers, at the very least, a starting point in our efforts to adapt deconstruction to the reading of student poems. We may need to go a bit further, however, to meet Shaw's (1991) lofty goal: "To produce these strategies, we need to rely essentially on one move: turning the text against itself and letting *it* provide a model for interrogating itself," rather than relying on the "codification and application of a set of reading procedures" (47). Still, by observing my own attempt to deconstruct the poems of three of my students, I hope to model the use of deconstruction in reading student writing and then to measure the pedagogical effectiveness of that adaptation.

Type and Focus of Comments

For each of the three poems that follow, I have included the first draft
that the authors showed me and, after each poem, my response in a
letter that deconstructs the poem:

The Swim

His eyes aren't mine.
When the blue widens
I stand at the stern watching
the river erupt into the ocean.
His hand on the silver wheel,
holds the course.
Not mine either.
White peaks of far off waves
lumber toward the hull
like fields of carnations
rolling in the wind.
Wavering,
I look at him sitting
more a stranger than a father,
with his green trunks and black hair
waving in the sea spray
like Neptune
commanding this trip,
trying to push us together
like magnets polarized
with the same force,
repelling each other.
Gulls and pelicans spiral
and dive,
ripping fish into suffocating air
and swallowing them.
He licks his dry lips,
nothing like mine, and smiles,
unwelcomed. It falls
with the force
of the salt water that burns
in my nose.
As I dive and surface,
our eyes meet. Bobbing,
the boat waits.
He stretches his hand out,
fingers rubbing the water
to pull me back,
but I'm too far gone.
Untrusting,
I cough and turn,

keeping the sun from blinding
with its white needles, pricking.
My eyes refocus on the water
moving, moving, moving
away from the boat,
away from him.

—Jeff

Dear Jeff,

In my efforts to use deconstruction in my interpretation of your poem, I've done two things. First, I offer a traditional "close" reading (of the sort we've all been taught to give) to determine which conflict is privileged as central to your poem (from that traditional kind of reading). The second reading flips the poem over to see what has been excluded (reading from this perspective, I am also interested in what you have chosen *not* to include).

This is a poem of separation and initiation into manhood. The privileged conflict from close reading is, of course, between "I" (the son) and "he" (the father). The swim far out at sea is symbolic. The father is increasingly unfamiliar, as suggested in descriptions of his eyes, hand, lips, smile, green trunks and black hair, desire to command, effort to push, etc.

The flip side is the conflict between this known which is repelling and the unknown ("away from the boat, away from him") which is attracting. What is that world (the world that attracts you) like? Does it hold promise of something valuable? Are you only repelled? If you are attracted, to what are you attracted?

In revision, you might consider this flip side as holding elements you might want to include in your poem. Or, you may be content to allow meaning to arise from the decision to continue this exclusion: the element of being repelled may be motive enough to move away!

Dragged Down

A great black sheet covers me
as the sunless morning comes.
My nails are chewed and useless,
my lips get in the way of my teeth
as I try to get out.
The clock demands attention
its daily penance
(I don't believe anymore)

The sheet absorbs my dream-sweat
and uses the leech-filled river I swam in against me.
I sigh and roll over,
escaping
and see my keys on the table

out of reach
as I notice for the first time
that all the fluid has leaked out
of my compass-ball on a chain.

—Lee

Dear Lee,

This is a good start. Let me offer two readings, one of what I see included in the poem and the other of what contributes to this poem (perhaps unknowingly, perhaps wisely, since it's your decision) by being excluded.

"Dragged Down" seems to focus on the moment of near-waking from deep dream ("the leech-filled river I swam in") when we're tempted to fall back asleep. It questions the importance of routine ("The clock demands . . . [I don't believe anymore]"). What's more, various things militate against getting out of bed: "black sheet," "sunless morning," "keys . . . out of reach," etc.

Excluded are possibilities of letting this setting function symbolically. Though I sense some effort to do that in the last two lines, I'm really not sure what you mean there (i.e., I'm excluded from that part of the poem. Do you want to let me in so I can see the symbolism? You don't have to!). Some conflicts not developed: if your dream-state was "leech-filled," why do you want to return to it? Why is the penance in stanza 2 your clock's and not your own (for missing a class? a job?)? How would your nails help you "get out" in stanza 1 if they weren't "chewed and useless"? Hope this style of interpreting helps.

feeding, the love

Before birds could eat, like birds do,
in their own particular way,
I would pull back the carapace for them
with my stubby fingers.

Later, I matured.
Looking down at the melting snow
—sun dancing off the sweat of my evolution—
I dashed mollusks against the rocks.
Sometimes I missed.

Now, I'm supine—peep! peep! peep!
in bed. Pull away the feathers
—clock numbers reflecting in your eyes the sweat on your
    breasts—
peep! peep! peep!
Lower yourself

Outside, the scream of a mouse, owl's talons.

—Andy

Dear Andy,

    In deconstructing your poem, I've had to do two things. First, I've had to "read" your poem as best I can using the traditional means of "close" reading my education gave me. This reading requires that I determine what the poem is about. What I am more sensitive to *now* is that the poem can be read for what it says (or includes) as well as what it doesn't say (or what it excludes). The included conflict in the poem is what I call the privileged conflict since the traditional and accepted method of reading is geared toward helping me find that conflict. Hence, it is privileged. But a poem also can be read for what the author excluded. Deconstruction, then, is an effort to read differently by flipping the poem over and, thereby, examining what has been excluded.

    Here's the privileged conflict, at least as I read this difficult draft of your poem: man now as opposed to historical man. This is a poem about evolution (in fifteen lines). Each stanza offers a "stage" typified by an activity: "I would pull back the carapace for them," then "I dashed mollusks against the rocks," then "clock numbers reflecting in your eyes."

    The excluded conflict, albeit suggested, concerns the gradual change from man-aggressive to man-passive. In what ways do they differ? What actions were required of early man that have been replaced by the machines and technologies of modern man? Marshall McLuhan called this *kind* or *element* of evolution "psychological amputation." For instance, the wheel replaced the legs, etc.

    In revision, you might want to include some of these excluded elements. Or you may allow them to continue to contribute to your poem by excluding them.

In learning how to use deconstruction to comment on my students' poems, I attempted to follow four guidelines suggested to me by what I have read on the subject:

1. One reason for exploring deconstruction after discussing New Criticism and reader-response criticism is because it seems the necessary next phase in its view of authority in reading and writing. As Crowley (1989) has noted, a deconstructive pedagogy "would reject the traditional model of authority that obtains in most American classrooms, where the teacher is both receptacle and translator of received knowledge" (45–46). While the New Criticism requires the teacher to be the authority for received knowledge and reader-response criticism provides a method by which teacher and student share that authority, adaptations leading to a deconstructive pedagogy must provide a method by which teachers can fully empower students to over-

throw the authority granted to teachers by tradition and privilege.

Because I sought a way to place responsibility for revisions to their poems on the students, I tried to *read* my students' poems from a deconstructive vantage point rather than *evaluate* their poems in any way. To accomplish this difficult task, I limited my commentary by writing my remarks in a letter and, thereby, using a "detached text." What's more, in each letter I attempted to teach students how I read by offering an explanation in the first paragraph of what I intended to do in my reading and a reminder in the last paragraph of what options they had for revision.

2. One goal stands out in my mind as critical to the successful use of deconstruction in reading student poems: teaching students how to read deconstructively. To instruct my students in giving deconstructive readings, I have modeled what Kaufer and Waller (1985) describe as "an act of examining possibilities that have been systematically repressed or undefined—and thus not explored" (71). For students to benefit from such a reading of their poems—that is, for students to determine if and how they might revise their poems—clearly they must understand how I have read them. Once they see for themselves the way deconstruction enables them to put pressure on the seams of their poems, they will be able to apply such pressure in workshop on poems written by their peers, as I will discuss in chapter 7.

3. Though I attempted to explain to students in some consistent and understandable way what I did in reading their poems, I did pay close attention to Shaw (1991), who reminds us that the goal is not to apply or adapt theory, but to read a student poem in a particular way. Shaw's advice on this point is valuable: "To provide these strategies, we need to rely essentially on one move: turning the text against itself and letting *it* provide a model for interrogating itself" (47). To do this, I offered two readings of each poem, one interpreting the poem in terms of what it includes and the other interpreting the poem in terms of what it excludes but refers to. More on how I explained this process to my students can be found in chapter 7.

4. A text in the process of being composed would need to be read differently than one finished or nearly finished. Clearly, the

enormous gap, where a gap exists, between the New Criticism and deconstruction is on this very point. A New Critical reading is apt to focus chiefly on those norms specifically pertinent to the making of poems, creating a hierarchy of such elements reflecting the kind of emphases found in "Bizzaro's Biases" at the end of chapter 2. A deconstructive reading, on the other hand, would not consider such a hierarchy to be something determined outside the text being examined or derived from reading numerous texts of its kind. Knoper (1989) clarifies this point: "This is not to say that writing influenced by deconstruction would refuse such markers and devices, but rather that they would be treated always as parts of the general textual economy—not outside of it, not transcendent, not as external controls that would arrest 'the concatenation of writing' " (134). To this end, I avoided the tendency to say that "This is more poetic than that" or "Why not rely on an image here to convey that point?" I focused chiefly on what the students' poems said, rather than on how they said it.

Of course, the question remains: What sort of comments did following these guidelines produce? In looking more closely at my response to poems by Jeff, Lee, and Andy, I note an effort to give my students three kinds of information: explanatory information, interpretative information, and deconstructive information.

Explanatory Information. I offer two kinds of explanations in my comments on these poems. First, in the introduction, I explain my use of deconstruction in language and depth geared to the specific student. Then, in the conclusion, I remind students of their responsibility in revision.

I find my introductory explanations useful both to my students and to myself as I learn how to make such readings. For my students' sake, I attempt to restate and clarify the vantage point from which I am reading their poems. By relying on the personal nature of a letter, I attempt to individualize instruction and explain my goals in adapting deconstruction in a way that satisfies the needs of each student. As a result, the amount of explanation I offer varies, with more going to those students who seem to need something in addition to class discussion and the handout that I give students on how I will read their poems. For instance, to Lee I say, "Let me offer two readings, one of what I see included in the poem and the other of what contributes to this poem . . . by being excluded." Yet to Jeff, using language from my discussion of theory in class, I say that I will offer "a traditional 'close' reading" and then a reading that "flips the poem over to see what has been excluded." Jeff appeared to have a solid grasp of my procedure in class, and I thus felt that I needed to offer less new information to him than to Lee.

But because the label *deconstruction* has come to include a great many things in classes around English departments, some students need and, in fact, request more information. My letter to Andy is a case in point. In another of Andy's classes, deconstruction was introduced in a way that confused him. He asked, as a result, that I explain my adaptation of it to him so that he might better understand how I read his poem. My explanation to Andy is thus much more detailed and personal than my explanation to Lee or Jeff. In writing to Andy, I wanted to make sure he understood my perspective, the perspective of someone attempting to take rather complex theory and find out if, in fact, it might be usefully employed in examining student writing. I point out my own growth, thereby lessening his perception of me as the authority in such a reading: "First, I've had to 'read' your poem as best I can using the traditional means of 'close' reading my education gave me. . . . What I am more sensitive to *now* is that the poem can be read for what it says (or includes) as well as what it doesn't say (or what it excludes)." In this explanation, I attempt to "locate" myself for Andy, hoping that such an approach to reading his poem will empower him to revise for himself, without my appropriation of his text.

Such explanations of my intent in applying deconstruction to student poems help me "locate" myself for my own purposes as well. As with reader-response criticism, deconstruction involves certain problems in reading that require that I reteach myself how to read in this way each time I approach a text. What's more, I needed to state the approach because it reminds me that I offer only the reading I am able to make, not some definitive or authoritative reading. As with certain of my experiences with reader-response methods, I had some difficulty finding a voice that did not resonate authority. I also experienced some of the frustration Crowley (1989) correctly predicts for us when she remarks that "to adopt deconstructive attitudes toward writing and its teaching will not be an easy matter for either students or teachers" (47). No doubt my frustration arose from the constraints placed on me, as Crowley puts it, "by institutions and a culture that subscribes to the metaphysics of presence" (47).

In all, I experienced many of the same feelings in my effort to employ deconstruction as I did when I experimented with reader-response methods, among them the feeling that I was not doing my job—a job that required authoritative responses to student writing—and that my students, schooled in more traditional workshops, expected more direction from me than my methods allowed. I also felt that some students misread my intentions in deconstructing their poems and revised to satisfy what they perceived to be my demands as an authoritative reader. In fact, the three young poets whose work is discussed here represent a full range of possible reactions to the shifting view of authority required in a deconstructive pedagogy.

But there is something more to be said about using deconstruction to comment on student writing. Though the theory brings into question the tradition of authority as it influences not only what is read, but how it is read, the classroom situation lends itself to continued reliance on the teacher's reading as a point of departure for the revisions students might make to their texts. My own students' reactions were varied, perhaps because the course involved a mixture of approaches, not just deconstruction. Some willingly assumed an authoritative role over their texts, while others refused to accept that responsibility (or simply did not know how), and still others wavered between these extremes. Anticipating these reactions, and in an effort to combat this unwanted intrusion of traditional authority, I decided to conclude each letter with a reminder to the students of their role in responding to my comments. For instance, I remind Andy, "In revision, you might want to include some of these excluded elements. Or you may allow them to continue to contribute to your poem's meaning by excluding them."

But again, there is a range of comments here. I fail to further explain to Lee what his role in revision is, the result of which is that he responds to my comments as though they are the voice of authority. But I believe I do a much better job of explaining what I want Jeff to do. To Jeff, I write, "In revision, you might consider this flip side as holding elements you might want to include in your poem. Or, you may be content to allow meaning to arise from the decision to continue this exclusion: the element of being repelled may be motive enough to move away!" What I like about this comment on Jeff's poem (and why I'm disappointed not to have made it at all to Lee and to have made it only briefly in my response to Andy) is that it reinforces the text rather than programmatically restating the theory. In my reminder to Jeff of his responsibility in revising his poem, I note that the motive of repulsion may be enough to help a reader understand why the narrator moves away from his father and his father's boat. In effect, without saying so directly, Jeff has claimed that whatever he must face out there as he swims away is better than the concessions he would have to make if he stayed aboard the boat. In making the concluding comment as I did, I continued to let the poem work against itself rather than making it fit alongside the theory.

Interpretive Information. When I interpret a poem using deconstruction, I first establish the existing hierarchy. In establishing this hierarchy, I claim to be deriving a "privileged" meaning from the text, a product of ways for reading poems received as a life-long student of the New Criticism. But White (1985) notes two kinds of readings, one in which "we are limited to what the student puts on the paper" and one which involves "our intuitions of what the student *meant* to say or our prediction of what the student *could* say if he or she followed the best insights now buried in the present text" (93).

To be able to write anything at all, students determine what to include and, as a result, what not to include. In determining as a reader what the author has included, I must focus entirely on the language on the page, applying traditional reading methods. For instance, as it appears to me in my application of this kind of reading, Jeff writes about the conflict between his narrator's father and his narrator in a "poem of separation and initiation into manhood." As I see it, the conflict appears most clearly in the son's swim away from the boat, away from his father. Applying similar reading strategies, I see that Lee's poem "seems to focus on the moment of near-waking from deep dream . . . when we're tempted to fall back asleep." And Andy's poem seems to be "a poem about evolution." Since my goal is not an exhaustive interpretation of the poem, I feel comfortable making general statements of what I perceive to be my students' intentions.

The benefits of even this much of the deconstructive reading I have set out to make are in some ways greater than those I reap in my adaptation of reader response. Each method enables me to offer a reading of the poem against which students can measure their intentions. But as a part of the deconstructive reading, I am also able to provide my students with a reading that will make it possible for me to offer deconstructive information about their texts. I can thus offer both my intuitions about "what the student *meant* to say" and my best prediction "of what the student *could* say," to use White's language. To remain connected to the theory and at the same time honor the author's own sense of what the poem should accomplish, I tried to offer this interpretative and deconstructive information as merely the product of *my* reading, the reading of one possible reader. Clearly, if the discoveries made are those of but one reader, they are not necessarily things that students must change during revision.

Deconstructive Information. This information is the most difficult to provide, since it requires that the reader find gaps or holes in the included meaning and apply pressure there by pointing them out to the author. What's more, this is a far less stable method of commenting than reader response, as it does not follow guidelines or assume that any two readers might reach the same decisions. The benefit of this approach is that it offers a reading different in kind from any other possible reading. The drawback is that by turning the text against itself, a reader cannot generalize from it, establish a code for reading, set up verifiable guidelines, or determine a stable and reproducible meaning. In fact, a deconstructive reading would militate against the identification of any methods or procedures at all, except perhaps a highly individualized adaptation of the "close" reading performed in an effort to obtain interpretative information.

I cannot stress enough that, no matter how it is framed, how it is presented, students receive only one reading, the teacher's. But unlike New Critical estimations, a deconstructive response encourages students to use this reading only as far as it is helpful and as long as they concur with it. Since this adaptation is intended to provide a reading rather than to generate a set of criteria for evaluation, students retain authority over their texts. Nonetheless, the kind of information rendered provides an unusual opportunity for students to re-examine their own poems. In fact, by playing each text against itself in deconstructing the three student poems given in this chapter, three very different kinds of comments are made, each applying a kind of pressure at certain places in the students' poems without the reader ever making a mark on the page.

For instance, Jeff is invited to think further about the privileged conflict in his poem, but now from a very different perspective. I write to Jeff, "The flip side is the conflict between this known which is repelling and the unknown ('away from the boat, away from him') which is attracting." This perspective on Jeff's poem is not apt to be given using any of the other methods discussed in this book. I ask Jeff, in effect, is there anything out there that attracts your central character as he moves away from his father, or is that character motivated entirely by repulsion? More specifically, I ask him to consider these four questions: "What is that world (the world that attracts you) like? Does it hold promise of something valuable? Are you only repelled? If you are attracted, to what are you attracted?" My last paragraph to Jeff reinforces the idea that Jeff alone has the right to decide if he should offer further description of what he is moving toward. I could see ample reason for Jeff to decide that to define the future would in many ways limit the effectiveness of his character's movement away from his father, a movement from which other considerations might detract. Jeff's revision, discussed below, suggests his ability to hold firmly to his view of his poem and what it should accomplish while at the same time consider the comments I have made.

While I feel somewhat successful in my deconstructive reading of Jeff's poem, I am not as pleased with my response to Lee's poem. What I have found to be true about other methods of evaluation applies as well to my use of deconstruction: some texts seem to demand certain kinds of readings, readings we do not always have models for. To offer such readings when appropriate, teachers need to develop greater flexibility in the way they respond to student writing as well as a wider repertoire of evaluation methods to draw upon. Then teachers could respond to each student text differently, depending, of course, upon the kind of text being read, the author's experience as a writer and reader, and the stage in the writing process at which the response is made.

My response to Lee's poem suggests that different methods might be used to respond to writers at different stages of development and to poems at different stages of "completion." Though I felt that Lee excluded me from parts of the poem by remaining fairly vague, I wanted to be consistent in my approach to his poem. I note, on the one hand, that "I'm excluded from that part of the poem. Do you want to let me in so I can see the symbolism?" But I also add, "You don't have to!" I found it terrifically difficult not to enter Lee's poem and take it over; secretly, I wanted to instruct him so that I could better understand (or provide him with) his intention. Instead, I focused on conflicts that I noted in the poem, but that were generally undeveloped: "If your dream-state was 'leech-filled,' why do you want to return to it? Why is the penance in stanza 2 your clock's and not your own (for missing a class? a job?)? How would your nails help you 'get out' in stanza 1 if they weren't 'chewed and useless'?"

Part of my difficulty in deconstructing Lee's poem rests in Lee's apparent uncertainty about what he wanted the poem to do. Lee's revision will show that, more than either of the other students whose poems are studied here, he made changes in direct response to my questions, resulting I believe either because he needed more direct guidance in revising his poem than the others did or because I neglected to remind him that the decision concerning what to revise and what not to revise was his. In either case, the problem might have been remedied by a decision to use some other method of reading, one more appropriate than deconstruction proves to be for Lee at this stage of his poem.

I am happier with my response to Andy's poem than with my reaction to Lee's, primarily because in an effort to touch upon undeveloped elements in "feeding, the love," my commentary helped Andy better envision where to productively close certain gaps in his poem. I inform Andy that I believe his poem concerns "man now as opposed to historical man." But I also note that this draft of his poem is "difficult." I want to put pressure at the seams between the stanzas. I note, "The excluded conflict, albeit suggested, concerns the gradual change from man-aggressive to man-passive." To place some emphasis on the gaps that make his poem so difficult, I ask, "In what ways do they (man-aggressive and man-passive) differ? What actions were required of early man that have been replaced by the machines and technologies of modern man?" To indicate a potential direction, should he decide to revise in this manner, I cite Marshall McLuhan, who "called this *kind* or *element* of evolution 'psychological amputation.' For instance, the wheel replaced legs, etc." As in my response to Jeff's poem, I add the reminder that Andy "might want to include some of these excluded elements." But I also return to him final authority when I add, "Or you may allow them to continue to contribute to your poem's meaning by excluding them."

Effectiveness of Comments

The young poets' responses to this method of reading their poems can be seen in the revisions that follow:

The Swim

His eyes aren't mine.
When blue widens
I stand astern watching
river erupt into ocean.
His hands on the wheel
hold the course.
Not mine either.
White peaks of far off waves
lumber toward the hull
like fields of carnations
rolling in wind
wavering.

I look at him sitting
more stranger than father
green trunks and black hair
waving in sea spray
like Neptune
commanding this trip,
pushing us together
like magnets polarized
with the same force
repelling each other.
Gulls and pelicans spiral
and dive,
ripping into air
suffocating fish
then swallowing them.
He licks his dry lips,
nothing like mine, and smiles
unwelcome. It stings
like salt water that burns
into my nose
as I dive and surface.

Our eyes meet. Bobbing,
the boat stops and waits.
He stretches his hand out,
fingers rub water
to pull me back.
Hunched and groping,
his confused eyes are mine.
They should be mine,
but to say so
would mean forgiveness
for abandonment
and not caring
what makes
my heart
race.

I'm too far gone.
Untrusting,
I cough and turn to shore,
keeping sun from blinding
with its white needles.
My eyes refocus on water
moving, moving, moving
away from the boat,
away from his hands,
grasping at water
like mine.

—Jeff

Portrait: Dragged Down

> The first day of the rest of your life is the hardest
> one of all.

And a great black sheet covers me
as the next sunless morning comes.
My nails, ragged from clawing at the emptiness
in my chest,
are now useless tools to get out.
Pinned down by darkness,
I try to bite and chew through.

The clock awakes
demanding its daily penance
(I am no longer of the faithful,
yet I still serve the addiction
of habit.).
It screams through the murky room
demanding a touch,
but I don't feel like feeling yet.
Blows will serve.

My sheet absorbs my dream-sweat
and uses the leech-filled rivers I swam in
against me.
I sigh with the breath of a weary soul
with nowhere to go
If I could only get up
light could push away the darkness for a while.

Then I see my keys on the table
out of reach
as I notice for the first time
that all the fluid has leaked out
of my compass ball
on a chain.

—Lee

feeding, the love

Before birds could eat like birds do
I would pull back the carapace for them
with my stubby fat fingers, the rising sun
reflecting in their watching learning eyes
Beaks, bills, red with hunger—peep! peep! peep!

later, looking down on the melting snow
—sun now dancing off the sweat of my evolution—
I dashed mollusks against the rocks below.
if I missed, it was okay

supine—peep! peep! peep!—in bed.
my hunger—clock numbers burn red in your eyes,

the sweat on your breasts
peep! peep!
lower yourself
outside, the brief squeak of a mouse, the click of owl's
    talons

                                       —Andy

These revisions show the wide range of possible decisions that writers might make. Jeff clearly chooses not to emphasize the attraction to his character of what lies ahead as a basis for leaving his father's boat. In fact, he seems inclined to further strengthen the narrator's repulsion from the father. At the other extreme, Lee made changes in direct response to the questions I asked him, perhaps out of a need for more direction and a more authoritative methodology on his reader's part or even as a reaction to not being reminded that my deconstruction of his poem was not intended to evaluate or grade. Andy seemed to consciously close the seams I had opened for him in my commentary, reinforcing the sense of three stages of evolution.

More specifically, in addition to numerous low-level editing changes in which articles were dropped and individual lines tightened, Jeff added ten lines: "Hunched and groping, / his confused eyes are mine. / They should be mine, / but to say so / would mean forgiveness / for abandonment / and not caring / what makes / my heart / race." These lines introduce one new element into the poem: the momentary confusion the narrator and his father experience. Otherwise, the lines seem a direct effort to clarify why the boy is moving away—rapidly. Even the diminishing length of the lines and the quickening pace of the poem seem to suggest his own racing heart. In the last stanza, Jeff adds other information in response to my request that he indicate what attracts him. Rather than leaving the reader with the feeling that the boy might be moving farther out to sea and new difficulties, Jeff indicates something less threatening: "I cough and turn to shore." And, in the new last two lines, Jeff indicates that it is now the water, and not his father, that he most resembles, that he is drawn subtly to the attractiveness of his new life. In short, Jeff is responsive to my deconstructive reading of his poem, but subtly so, making the poem into a clearer expression of what *he* wants to express.

I am pleased that though I influenced the direction of Jeff's revision, I did not appropriate his poem to do so. I cannot say this about Lee's poem. It is noteworthy that Lee made more changes than either Jeff or Andy. In fact, he revises some portion of his poem in response to each of my questions. I ask, "If your dream-state was 'leech-filled,' why do you want to return to it?" In response, Lee adds four lines to stanza 3: "I sigh with the breath of a weary soul / with nowhere to go / If I could only get up / light could push away the darkness for a while." These lines seem to be a versified answer to my question. My second question is "Why is the penance in stanza 2 your clock's and not your own (for missing a class? a job?)?" As a way of reacting to this question, Lee revises stanza 2 extensively, adding four lines in an effort that I surmise attempts to attend to the concern of the person grading his poem. Finally, my third question is "How would your nails help you 'get out' in stanza 1 if they weren't 'chewed and useless'?" To this concern, Lee responds by revising stanza 1 and again adding four new lines, including one that clarifies what he has used his nails on: "ragged from clawing at the emptiness / in my chest." Lee's reaction to my questions leads me to believe that he succumbed to my role as the authoritarian figure in the classroom, the reader whose reading is the one he must adopt. In any case, Lee definitely reacted differently to my comments than Jeff did; Lee's revision brings to mind the revisions John made in response to my New Critical commentary in chapter 3. Naturally, I was disappointed with Lee's reaction, but hardly upset with Lee. Rather, I believe I conveyed something to Lee about my role as reader that made him confuse that role with the role of evaluator and grader. The result is a poem that reflects, as nearly as it could, what Lee believed I wanted him to do with his poem. Again, we have a case of text appropriation. Lee's reaction to my commentary reinforced my growing realization that, as a teacher of poetry writing, I must have a wide repertoire of reading strategies and determine which to use based upon the student, the text, and where I find myself intervening in the student's writing process.

Andy too was very responsive to my deconstruction of his poem. As I look at my comments on both Lee's and Andy's poems, I can see that I attended to the seams or gaps in both of their texts. Yet while Lee seems to me to have hypercorrected (bringing to mind Penney's poem in chapter 3), Andy took from my comments what he could use and adjusted his poem accordingly. Basically, Andy made one change: he added three lines at the end of stanza 1 so that he could achieve a circular effect in the final stanza by echoing those lines. I felt that Andy incorporated my comments into his poem without being overwhelmed by them.

Still, I am not completely satisfied with my role in Lee's poem. One conclusion I have reached about my dealings with this young poet is that I did not do an adequate job of teaching him how to read deconstructively. A second conclusion I cannot avoid is that with Lee, perhaps because of aspects of his personality I could not possibly know (or because of aspects of my own personality), I projected myself as reader, evaluator, and eventual grader, and that projection influenced the choices he made as he revised his poem. To cite Penney once again from chapter 3, "I did allow you to take [my poem] over at first, perhaps because I thought that that was what I was supposed to do." A major task ahead if we hope to make deconstruction useful in reading student writing is the development of ways to convince students that they, in fact, are the owners of what they have written. I am increasingly certain that we cannot help them take identities as writers unless we first show them how by empowering them as readers.

Sharing the Authority: A Letter from Deb

In response to the shortcomings in my use of deconstruction with Lee's poem, I wanted to see what would happen if I used the letter format to further reinforce the shifting relationship of authority between reader and writer, teacher and student. As a result, I asked students to evaluate the effectiveness of my deconstructive reading in return letters. Unlike the return letters in chapter 4, in which students commented on the changes they made to their poems, these letters were intended to reinforce for students the idea that *they* are the owners of their writing. I then studied Deb's reaction to my deconstruction of her text as she wrote about it in her letter to me.

A student in my contemporary poetry course, Deb was a candidate for an M.A. with a creative writing emphasis. She had previously taken several other poetry writing courses, including an advanced class for graduate students, had read the works of a great many contemporary writers, studied the aesthetics of contemporary poetry, and even knew something about deconstruction. In fact, she seemed receptive to any effort on my part to comment on her poems in some novel way. What follows is Deb's poem and my response to it:

My Father's Solitude

Driving into the yard these last nights,
I have heard my father in the workshop,
drilling and sawing and staining
picture frames.
Like cobwebs they hang in every corner
dark, dusty, and deliberate.

Tonight, I wait in the drive,
motor running and car radio off.

I remind myself that
today I have been a good wife.
Have ironed my husband's white shirts and
put the denims out to dry,
have eaten lunch and
(as he told me)
not thought about the size of my thighs,
or picture frames.

On the day of my mother's burying
my father gave me his solitude.
I did not ask for it.
He gave it in his faltering gaze,
his unsteady hand and slow pace.
Then we not speaking
rode back to the family loud house.

Tonight, I wait in the gravel drive
for the lights to go out,
my father to emerge in coveralls and
make his way to the house.
I pull out into the quiet.

Dear Deb,
Let me respond to "My Father's Solitude" by offering a reading of your poem intended to let you know what *I* see happening in it and what I do not see happening that might. What I'd like you to do is revise your poem, if you'd like, and/or write a brief note back to me responding to my comments. Please read "you" in my comments below as a way of addressing the "I" in the poem. It's just easier this way.

This poem seems to take place at your father's house on "these last nights." I see several relationships that you have developed in this poem. The immediate one, and the one that I sense inspired you to write, is between you and your father. He is distant. You know his presence only because you can hear him "in the workshop" doing what, I suppose, are typical male things in the world of your poem: "drilling and sawing and staining," creating picture frames that he hangs "in every corner," suggesting to you the image of "cobwebs."

The next stanza locates us in "Tonight," and a second, more complex (because it gives rise to the first) relationship is developed. Now you are determining if you are a "good wife" by measuring your behavior against some standard. For if you are a good wife (though we're not sure yet what that *really* means, are we?), you can justify your relation with your father (that is, you can remain somewhat distant, observing from outside his workshop) because you have a new relationship with a second man (as this other man's wife) that you are trying to be good at—whatever "good" means in this context. You do list specific things that a "good" wife must do: iron shirts for your husband, dry clothes, eat lunch, and not think about bodily imperfections ("as he told" you) or picture frames. But I think, in truth, you are calling these criteria into question (more on this in the next section).

In stanza 3, you give shape to "solitude" as though it is something that can be given to someone else, like a handkerchief. On the day of your mother's burial, this is what your father gives you—his tangible solitude for you to do something with—though you do not apparently want it. Then you describe *how* he gives it: in "his faltering gaze," "unsteady hand," and "slow pace." After that, two quiet people (you and your father) return to the "family loud house," establishing a kind of difference in your responsibility to your father and the responsibility to him of others in your family.

Going back to "Tonight," you continue to wait for your father to leave before you leave. By making this stanza parallel with your second stanza, you seem to suggest that, in the end, nothing really has changed between you and your father. Rather than having his solitude in your hands, you continue to watch him from a distance. This seems a kind of resolution to the problem of who takes care of the old people when they are no longer independent. But the fact of your watching suggests as well that once he is no longer capable of taking care of himself, you will be there for him, like it or not.

This poem is written in an open form. There are, of course, repetitions of sounds, especially the *-ing*. You have relied heavily on imagery to depict various people in their various roles. Your line breaks are at the end of units of logic, usually after a strong word (rarely after a conjunction and never after a preposition).

On the flip side, I don't see much made of the other side of certain conflicts in the poem. Perhaps by my pointing them out you will care to do something with them (or care not to). Certainly, you may not have intended to do anything with the other concerns that I bring through the window below.

In stanza 1, an interesting juxtaposition is created between the masculine and aggressive (at least, hardly fragile) activity of "drilling and sawing and staining," on the one hand, and hanging these frames "Like cobwebs," on the other. Ironically, these masculine productions hang "Like cobwebs," suggesting a kind of delicateness that seems almost contradictory. What's more, the cobwebs you describe are more like picture frames than cobwebs—"dark, dusty, and deliberate."

Another unexplored relationship (or one only superficially explored in this poem) seems to be between you and your mother. Have you inherited a sense of the wife's role that you cannot abide by? This is suggested in your poem, but developed only in your rebuttal to guilt about your father being alone: that you "have been a good wife" today. Do you feel pressure to become for your father (especially given what you write in stanza 3) *his* "good wife" when he gives you his solitude? Before her death, had your mother carried this great burden of your father's solitude? In her absence, does this responsibility come to the daughter descendent?

Another relationship barely touched here seems to be between you and the rest of your family. Again, this is suggested without quite being developed. You are given your father's solitude. They are not. You are "not speaking," but the house you return to, where your family is (are they there or not?), is "the family loud house."

Finally, another interesting series of juxtapositions exists in your treatment of time. There are these demarcations indicating time: "these last nights," "Tonight," "On the day of my mother's burying." Missing here is a clear sense of what the relation is between these demarcations.

Let me add that the open form, while less restrictive in some ways, excludes from the poem the restriction suggested by a closed form with a definite meter and rhyme scheme.

I hope this gives you a way of looking at your poem. Please show me any revision you make and kindly write me a note indicating whether my commentary was helpful to you in revision.

This commentary is intentionally nonjudgmental. In making these remarks to Deb, I assumed that she knew what she wanted her poem to accomplish, an assumption that perhaps I could not make about Lee. My role is to reflect back to her what she has done (at least, in terms of my reading) and what she has not done but might do in revision.

My intention, however, was to use the letter format as a way of shifting responsibility and authority back to the author. The instructions were simple enough: "Write me a note indicating whether my commentary was helpful to you in revision." I believe that if I had more clearly made this kind of recommendation to Lee, not only would he have seen that the decisions on how to revise his poem were his alone, but he might have better envisioned what he wanted his poem to accomplish. By revising her poem and then explaining which of my suggestions were helpful and which not, Deb regained ownership of her poem.

Here is Deb's revision:

My Father's Solitude

Driving into the yard these last nights,
I have heard my father in the workshop,

drilling and sawing and staining
picture frames. Like cobwebs
they hang in every corner of the barn,
dark, dusty, and deliberate.

Tonight, I wait in the gravel drive
motor running and car radio off.
Reaching into the glove-compartment, I light
cigarettes from a crumply pack and
remind myself (as my mother did) that
today I have been a good wife,
have ironed my husband's white shirts and
put the denims out to dry,
have eaten lunch and
as he told me
not thought about the size of my thighs,
or the wooden picture frames
around every photo.

On the day of my mother's burying
my father gave me his solitude.
I did not ask for it.
He gave it in his faltering gaze,
his unsteady hand and slow pace.
Then we not speaking
rode back to the family loud house
where casseroles covered the kitchen counter
where we nodded our goodbyes.

Tonight I wait in the gravel drive
for the lights to go out,
for my father to emerge in coveralls and
make his way to the house.
Then I pull out into the quiet.

The biggest change here comes in the second stanza, where Deb adds
some context concerning what she was doing in the gravel drive—
"Reaching into the glove compartment, I light / cigarettes from a
crumply pack"—and then responds to my queries about her undeveloped relationship with her mother. I had asked, "Have you inherited
a sense of the wife's role that you cannot abide by?" And later, "Do you
feel pressure to become for your father (especially given what you
write in stanza 3) *his* 'good wife' when he gives you his solitude?" Deb
clarifies this in revision: "I . . . remind myself *(as my mother did)* that /
today I have been a good wife" (emphasis mine). Deb also adds a
telling detail to her image of "the family loud house": "where casseroles covered the kitchen counter / where we nodded our goodbyes."
This addition creates yet another dimension. The loud house they

enter "not speaking" to each other is no longer loud; they nod their goodbyes to each other, again in new silence.

Significantly, Deb does not make much of the other seams that I attempted to unfold for her examination. She does not, for instance, revise her image of the cobwebs in stanza 1. And little is done in the new draft to bring forward her relationship with the rest of her family from her perspective as daughter descendent.

Deb evaluated my deconstruction of her poem in the letter accompanying her revision, which follows:

> Dear Pat,
>   Thanks for your response to "My Father's Solitude."
>   First, let me say that I found the comments very helpful in that you addressed areas in which I had questions of my own. For example, the development of the relationship with my mother. The changes I have made in that area are small—I'd like to develop that further—but I do see a difference between the drafts.
>   Secondly, I agree with your comments on what you see inside the room that I have constructed. However, in the room outside, I am afraid I don't understand the relationship that you describe between the cobwebs and the masculine activity, or rather, I don't see the relationship as contradictory. Am I clear here? At any rate, I am trying to develop the relationships more clearly—I hope that you agree.
>   Also. Do you find that the language lends anything to the tone? And would you say that the opening is strong? or weak?

Deb's response, purely by chance, shows how a model for using deconstruction to evaluate student poems might evolve with an individual student. First, in writing her letter of response, Deb assumes an authorial role over both the letter and her poem. Second, in the final paragraph of her letter, Deb turns the text of the letter against itself, revealing how a deconstructive pedagogy would have to work: "Do you find that the language lends anything to the tone? And would you say that the opening is strong? or weak?" A deconstructive pedagogy must serve the ongoing effort between student and teacher to shift authority back and forth from one to the other. In other words, by asking Deb to evaluate my commentary on her poem, I have given responsibility for the poem to her. The very procedure that enables this transference to occur is one that insists not only upon turning the text against itself, but also upon turning authority against itself. I use my authority in responding to Deb's poem to undermine the very authority I have been granted through tradition and privilege; Deb uses her authority in the letter to undermine her authority as author. Deb writes the poem; I offer a reading; Deb accepts and rejects portions of my reading; Deb returns an element of authority to me in her final questions.

I believe my interaction with Deb reveals something of the pedagogical implications of deconstruction and, in fact, shows how beneficial it can be as a method of reading and rereading, writing and rewriting. Though Deb and I ended our correspondence here with her return note, we might have continued this interaction indefinitely. She is not yet finished with her poem, and I have not yet offered a reaction to her questions. To continue the interaction, though, I would have to consciously attempt to shift authority for the text back to Deb. This effort could take us far into the future, lasting until one of us simply gets tired of talking about "My Father's Solitude" or, better yet, until Deb finds a publisher for her poem.

Clearly, the format used in this chapter makes it possible for readers to attend to elements of a text either consciously or unconsciously excluded. And the responses of students to the use of a second letter indicate that by relinquishing authority for the text, it is possible to empower students to serve as authorities over the text they want to write, if not always the one they have written. Students also seem to learn something about how to read deconstructively.

6 On Becoming a "Resisting Reader": Some Applications of Feminist Criticism

. . . the first act of the feminist critic must be to become a resisting rather than an assenting reader and, by this refusal to assent, to begin the process of exorcising the male mind that has been implanted in us.

Judith Fetterley, *The Resisting Reader: A Feminist Approach to American Fiction*

. . . reading is a learned *activity which, like many other learned interpretive strategies in our society, is inevitably sex-coded and gender-inflected.*

Annette Kolodny, "Dancing Through the Minefield"

Though it is difficult to work out in positive, independent terms what it might mean to read as a woman, one may confidently propose a purely differential definition: to read as a woman is to avoid reading as a man, to identify the specific defenses and distortions of male readings and provide correctives.

Jonathan Culler, "Reading as a Woman" (from *On Deconstruction*)

By applying deconstruction to the evaluation of student poems, I already had some experience resisting the text. So, encouraged by my efforts with deconstruction, I decided to inquire into the ways feminist theory might be used in the writing classroom. After all, if the goal is to read a student text fairly and differently and, in so doing, to offer in-process evaluation of student writing, teachers must consider their gendered relations to the text.

But because I read for gender as a male, I make such considerations self-consciously. It may well be true, as Stephen Heath (1987) posits, that "men's relation to feminism is an impossible one" (1). Still, men must learn to read a text as "sex-coded and gender-inflected." In fact, the underlying motives for my persistence in learning how to use feminist theory are stated excellently by Heath:

> Men have a necessary relation to feminism—the point after all is that it should change them too, that it involves learning new

ways of being women *and men* against and as an end to the
reality of women's oppression—and that relation is also necessarily one of a certain exclusion—the point after all is that this
is a matter *for women*, that it is their voices and actions that must
determine the change and redefinition. (1)

As a teacher who hopes to read student texts differently and, in so
doing, to enable students to retain authority over their writing, my
inquiry into the practical uses of feminist theory in reading poems in
a poetry writing class seems inevitable.

Simply put, of the approaches used thus far in this book, none
deals with the oppressed voices in a text as thoroughly as feminist
theory does, not even deconstruction. While both deconstruction and
feminist criticism search the gaps and seams, deconstruction is a process of determining the *excluded* element by searching for difference, for
what is not in the text but suggested nonetheless. Though it requires a
similar search through the text, feminist theory looks not for what has
been excluded, but for what has been *silenced*; that is, reading from a
feminist critical perspective requires a sensitivity to elements of gender that may typify the reading habits of some, though not all, readers
of a text. In this way, feminist theory seems to me closer to reader
response than to deconstruction, as it requires a reader who is attuned
or sensitized to the silent and the seemingly invisible. As Bahktin tells
us, poems assert an "authorial individuality" which requires that a
single voice rise above others to be heard. Yet multiple voices nonetheless persist in the text, each in a battle or "dialogue" with the other
voices. All voices but the single "authorial" voice, however, are
drowned out; some readers will not even detect their presence.

Though I have in the past recognized the necessity of reading in
this way, I have not always felt capable of offering such a reading, even
if my students' texts seem to have demanded it (see my responses to
Penney and Kim in chapter 3). And the texts that demand it are not
only those written by female students, as I will demonstrate in this
chapter. As Barbara Waxman (1991) says, the goal of employing feminist theory is much greater than simply appropriating a method for
commenting on student writing:

> If we create in our classrooms what Giroux calls an "emancipa-
> tory authority," one that is committed to social empowerment
> and ethics, then we will see ourselves not just as technocrats
> who distribute knowledge and values, but also as morally con-
> cerned teachers who conceptualize and raise questions about
> our curricula and the methods that enable students to develop
> both humanity and sociopolitical *savoir faire*. Feminist theory

> and feminist literary criticism can help the English teacher to
> serve as an emancipatory authority.... (149)

With this realization in mind, I wanted to orient myself to feminist theory both as a male—marginalized even further by Joseph Allen Boone's (1989) reduction of a certain class of people to the group of "older male critic[s]" who lack "a significant 'pre-feminist' past" (173)—and as a teacher who would like to employ feminist theory in an effort to offer fair and balanced readings of student texts.

A major turning point in my investigation came when, in an effort to expand my reading skills, I took home a batch of fourteen student poems. Having announced to my students that I planned to read their poems through a feminist lens, I was dismayed to find myself capable of reading only three of the fourteen poems from what I then considered a feminist perspective. While those three poems dealt specifically with male-female relationships, the others were less obvious. Worse yet, I feared that as a man I had not only missed the point of feminist theory, but had also incorrectly explained to my students the procedure for rendering feminist readings.

I began, as a result, a careful search through the literature to determine why such readings were so difficult for me. In fact, to approach the task of learning how to read student texts as gendered, I found it necessary to consider not only the theory itself, but also the related issue of my being a male employing these methods. Fortunately, I was heartened both by what I read and by the encouragement of my colleagues to continue my efforts. I simply had to work harder.

As Elaine Showalter (1985) notes of early male feminist efforts, "Until men questioned their own reading practices . . . , male feminism was just a form of critical cross-dressing that made female masquerade a way to take over women's newly acquired power" (197). I did not want to masquerade as a woman in my readings. And I certainly did not want to appropriate a cultural position and use it without accepting the risks and challenges of critiquing my own position as an "older male critic." What's more, a man must take quite seriously Showalter's warning that before he can even aspire to make "a genuine contribution to feminist theory," he must "confront 'what might be implied by reading as a man, and questioning or surrender[ing] . . . paternal privileges' " (197). In short, a man must learn how to become a resisting reader.

Some of what has been written reinforced my belief that I could, in fact, be a more effective reader of my students' poems, but only with considerable effort. I wanted to know why I was deaf to the voices at war in eleven of the fourteen student poems I set out to read from a feminist perspective. And I wanted to understand the implications of asking such questions as a man. During my search for answers, I kept in mind Adrienne Rich's ([1979] 1985) words: "It is not easy to think like a woman in a man's world, in the world of the professions; yet the capacity to do that is a strength which we can try to help our students develop." I am certain that Rich is writing to other women here; nonetheless, as a student, I took these words with me into the efforts I have made to help still other students, still other men, develop as writers.

Reading as a Man: Some Deliberations

Encouraged and guided by two of my colleagues, I have read widely in the areas of feminist theory, male feminism, and gender-specific composition studies. The considerations that have resulted from this reading have helped me become a better, though still tentative, reader of my students' writings.

Bernard Duyfhuizen (1988) provided a point of departure for my personal deliberations. According to Duyfhuizen, "Feminist criticism often asserts that reading is both a learned and a gender-oriented activity that male readers have long controlled by expounding, consciously or unconsciously, a masculine perspective on literary value and interpretive significance" (411). In response, feminist critics call for us to revise those readings that have long privileged certain literary texts and espoused certain cultural values over others. Yet Duyfhuizen continues, "Despite some gains in the last fifteen to twenty years, feminist approaches are still only slowly reaching classrooms" (411). No doubt this statement is especially true of classrooms where writing is taught.

As for myself, by being able to offer only three feminist readings out of fourteen poems, I effectively silenced the voices in the other eleven texts. Those eleven poems contained elements which were inaudible to me, voices I could not hear, voices which, albeit inadvertently, had been silenced by my reading. Using a slightly different but nonetheless sensual metaphor, Toril Moi (1989) writes, "The invisible, as feminist critics know, is the place where the phallic eye finds 'nothing to see' " (188). If we see texts through this eye only, and then teach our students to read in this way, we perpetuate the kinds of readings and decisions concerning the canon that result in cold and dispassionate readings of student texts in class and oppression in the wider culture. This patriarchal way of reading persists in our culture; women are taught to read as men, and men are required to live up to certain expectations. If the identity of our nation and its people is buried in our literature, then the way we read that literature will reflect not only our cultural values, but also our attitudes toward people and the power relationships between them. In the words of Elizabeth Flynn (1989), "In urging that we recognize difference, feminist researchers and theorists are urging us to make visible a previously invisible feminist perspective" (52).

Why have these perspectives been invisible? Flynn, citing research by Crawford and Chaffin, concludes "that males and females differ in their interpretation of texts because they have been socialized in different ways and hence have different schemata or mental representations to draw on" (52). Perhaps these schemata explain why one student whose end-of-term evaluation is cited by Dale Bauer (1990) writes, "I didn't appreciate feminist comments on papers or expressed about a work. . . . Others in the English Department have difficulties *leaving personal opinions out of their comments*" (385, emphasis mine).

But the problems related to seeing what has been culturally invisible are not just problems encountered by male critics like myself. Women too must learn to read against the text if they are to read as feminists. Most feminists would agree that women read against the grain quite naturally but are educated out of it. As Kolodny ([1980] 1991) urges, "Reading is a highly socialized—or learned—activity" (104). To read as feminist critics, then, women must unlearn what they were taught. They must become, to paraphrase Culler (1982), women reading as women. And men must become men reading as women reading as women. Most women have been unconsciously coerced into reading as men. Because of this, Fetterley (1978) argues that they experience "the powerlessness which results from the endless division of self against self, the consequence of the invocation to identify as male while being reminded that to be male—to be universal, to be American—is to be *not female*" (xiii). The process by which women reading American literature are silenced is what Fetterley calls "the *immasculation* of women by men" (xx). Fetterley continues, "As readers and scholars, women are taught to think as men, to identify with a male point of view, and to accept as normal and legitimate a male system of values" (xx). A man critiquing his method of reading must thus find the silences of women in the gaps and contradictions of his methods. The "flip side" of reading as a man is reading as a woman.

Fetterley's solution to the problem of reading as we have all been taught—that is, of reading as men—is for the feminist critic "to become a resisting reader rather than an assenting reader and, by this refusal to assent, to begin the process of exorcising the male mind that has been implanted in us" (xxii). In this way, certain voices long hidden in student texts will become audible. Finding these voices will not be a reflection of the teacher's mastery over the elements of the text, but evidence of a dialogue that ultimately questions that mastery, turning it against itself in a critique of the masculine point of view.

Even the term "resisting" as it applies to a reader suggests a dialogue between the privileged reading of a text and the other voices at war with that reading. But the male "resisting reader" must also unlearn the habits of reading that prevent him from reading as a feminist. The goal is not to read as a woman, but to identify a subject position as a man reading a text by resisting the patriarchal elements that our culture has taught us to value. Yet a difficult question remains, one on which Showalter takes Culler to task for not answering: Do men resist the text in the same way women do?

Male Feminism and Ethos

I am increasingly certain that learning to read as a woman—or, as Culler asserts, "to avoid reading as a man"—is difficult for all readers. But it poses a special problem for men that is worth some brief discussion here. For as Heath (1987) writes, "Feminism speaks to me, not principally nor equally but *too*, to me too" (9). In short, Heath concludes that every man who sees the necessity of a feminist orientation to literature and classroom practices must consider one central question, one uniquely related to his subject position: "*What does feminism mean for me?*" (32).

A good place to begin the attempt to answer this question is with Andrew Ross's (1987) common-sense warning that we avoid generalizing about what feminism means to men. Ross observes that "there is nothing unitary . . . about belonging to the categories of *biological men, men-in-practice,* and *theoretical men* at one and the same time, as many men do. For the same individual can be different kinds of theoretical men and men-in-practice, some progressive for feminism, others not, at different times and in different discursive contexts" (88–89). Still, there are those who object to the treatment of feminism purely as theory or as a methodology divorced from real life, as something that exists squarely and only in the academy. Of course, unlike New Criticism, reader-response criticism, and deconstruction, the overt politics of feminist criticism, as Bauer (1990) has noted, are still highly controversial in the classroom. Nonetheless, according to Irene C. Goldman (1990), if a teacher is going to use feminist theory in the classroom, "part of the teacher's task is to unmask gender-based structures and to support students in the process of change and growth that will inevitably begin with that unmasking" (120).

Over the years, though, theorists have been concerned that the process of unmasking gender-based structures in the classroom is an activity performed more believably by women than by men. Men have responded to this challenge in three ways. They have either avoided feminist theory altogether, oversimplified (and thereby marginalized) it, or worked diligently (in some instances almost exclusively) at establishing ethos and asserting their trustworthiness as feminist critics.

James V. Catano, in "The Rhetoric of Masculinity: Origins, Institutions, and the Myth of the Self-Made Man" (1990), voices a concern shared by many conscientious men, a concern over not only whether they can employ feminist approaches to reading in good conscience, but also over whether they can use feminist theory at all. Catano carefully considers the boundaries of his argument: "I am focusing this particular argument on how the ideology of self-making promotes versions of masculinity, in part because my own training as a man makes me most familiar with this version. I also am wary of a male appropriation of gender issues or the female voice, and for that reason prefer to limit the area of my study to the masculine" (422). Catano then goes on to show how "a masculinist rhetoric" presents dangers for all of us, male and female alike, "when it ignores its gendered characteristics" (422). By skimming the gendered surface, Catano "limits the area of [his] study." But by doing so, he also fails to directly confront the real issue: that versions of masculinity render inevitable certain versions of femininity.

Catano's analysis of masculine rhetoric is no doubt a "safer" position than one that tries to use feminist principles and risks appropriation of the female voice. To his credit, however, Catano acknowledges a way in which writing is gendered while avoiding the sin that I fear committing: oversimplifying the very complex issues involved in employing feminist theory as a man.

A tendency toward oversimplification typifies a second response that men have made to the challenge of using feminist theory in their classes. Not all men have worked around issues of gender as neatly as Catano has. For instance, I think Steven Lynn oversimplifies these issues in "A Passage into Critical Theory" (1990). When Lynn writes, "I have only recently stopped being amazed at how easily and enthusiastically my students take to feminist criticism" (110), I cannot help but wonder why it is so easy for Lynn's students to learn how to use feminist criticism while it has been so painstakingly difficult for me (and many others, both male and female). Perhaps what Lynn has told his students about feminist criticism has undercut many of the difficult issues I have felt compelled to encounter in my own efforts.

Then I read on in Lynn's essay: "To practice feminist criticism one need only read as a woman" (110). No doubt intended ironically, this oversimplification of Culler's statement—"to read as a woman is to avoid reading as a man"—overlooks (as Showalter has said of Culler himself) the necessity that men critique their own habits of reading. Then Lynn adds, "Not all texts, *of course*, lend themselves easily to feminist criticism" (110, emphasis mine), and I understand quite well that Lynn too might have taken my fourteen student poems home and rendered only three feminist readings.

The necessity for yet another response can be seen in an exchange that involves Culler himself. In "Reading as a Woman," part of a chapter in *On Deconstruction* (1982), Culler offers a brief history of feminist criticism in which he locates "moments" central to its development. While his account logically hypothesizes that both male and female readers might construct the gender of their reading positions for themselves, Culler does not cite any examples of men reading. Worse yet, nowhere does he refer to himself as a reader. In short, Culler does not establish the much-needed ethos that I have found essential to offering a reading of student writing based on the centrality of gender.

More recently, however, men who believe that gender issues must be addressed in the classroom have taken the time to critique their own habits as male readers. To be believed, to be seen as trustworthy and credible with students as well as others in the professional community, men have found it necessary to "locate" themselves. Take as an example John Flynn's effort at establishing ethos in his essay "Learning to Read Student Papers from a Feminine Perspective, II" (1989). The most obvious identifier is the "II" at the end of his title, since John's wife, Elizabeth Flynn, entitles an article in the same collection of essays "Learning to Read Student Papers from a Feminine Perspective, I" (1989). Then John locates himself further:

> I would claim that even if we admit gender as a first principle,
> an essential attribute of being, my view of reality, and my per-

> spective as a reader of student texts, needs to be elaborated by counting other qualifiers. So I would describe myself as a male, working-class, Brooklyn Irish Catholic, social-democrat, feminist, environmentalist, conservative, antifascist, disabled Vietnam veteran, peace activist, and recovered cancer patient. (131)

Once so identified, presumably John becomes, if not less threatening, more credible: "If we accept gender as experienced by an upwardly mobile, working-class male during the 1960s as a condition of my reading of student texts, then I wish to claim my pedagogy as feminine and women as my teachers" (132). We might say, of course, to avoid oversimplification, that we all read as members of different communities, that ethnicity, for example, also influences our readings of various texts. My point here, however, is that by so identifying himself, John Flynn moves in the direction other men must follow if they hope to establish a subject position from which they can become resisting readers.

Though Patrick D. Murphy (1991) does not take the extreme measures that John Flynn takes in identifying the position from which he uses feminist criticism, he does advocate doing so. Murphy posits that "we need to find ways to break down the position of authority awarded us as teachers from the outset, not in some pseudoegalitarian way limited to just rearranging seats in a circle while simultaneously keeping the grade firmly in our grasp, but in ways that clarify the importance of each student's developing her or his own self-conscious critical posture" (173). To do so, Murphy advocates establishing ethos: "Let the students in on the 'secrets' of why the teacher is doing what she or he is doing (thereby performing a metacriticism of the pedagogy in process), and engage in self-critique and group evaluation of the pedagogy and the subject matter" (173). Only then, continues Murphy, "can [we] break down the myth of 'competence equals patriarchy'" (173). To more fully describe this myth, Murphy quotes Paula Treichler, who summarizes, "Thus behaviors judged as traditionally male—a lecture format, little student give and take, the transmission of a given body of content, little attention to process—seem also to signal professional competence." Murphy concludes that to be effective teachers, men need to overcome what they have learned through the culture they work and live in and begin to teach differently.

To read differently—that is, to become resisting readers—men must be willing to actively critique the reading habits they have learned as men in the culture. In other words, they must consider what it means to read as a man. Without the care and pain of such a critique, men risk using feminist theory irresponsibly, masquerading as women and appropriating the feminine voice. This concern, so well expressed by Elaine Showalter in her now famous "Critical Cross-Dressing: Male Feminists and the Woman of the Year," was brought into the open by the "Men in Feminism" panel held at the 1984 meeting of the Modern Language Association in Washington, D.C. In short, there is a very real danger of feminism being misused by men. In her article, for instance, Showalter ([1982] 1987) notes that male critics—most notably Wayne Booth, Robert Scholes, Jonathan Culler, and Terry Eagleton—most often speak of "women" or "feminism" to speak about "something else." And though she begins with the observation that "we can hardly fail to welcome male feminist criticism when we have so long lamented the blindness, deafness, and indifference of the male critical establishment towards our work" (117), she then convincingly demonstrates that the move to feminist criticism by male theorists is motivated largely by "recognition that it offers the mixture of theoretical sophistication with the sort of effective political engagement they have been calling for in their own critical spheres" (117). In fact, Showalter concludes that "feminist criticism is currently so appealing to male theorists that some feminists are beginning to regard the development with some suspicion" (118).

Interestingly, many feminists do invite males to make feminist readings. As Annette Kolodny ([1980] 1991) suggests when she argues that reading is a learned activity, men can develop some skill in reading as feminists if they are patient and diligent enough to do so. Clearly, such diligence includes reading far more writing by women and becoming less ignorant of women's values and experiences. What's more, while commenting on Culler's attempt to produce feminist readings, Showalter adds another condition:

> I would argue that what Culler has done here is to read consciously from his own gender experience, with an ironic sense of its own ideological bounds. That is to say that he has not read as a *woman*, but as a man and a feminist. . . . Reading as a feminist, I hasten to add, is not unproblematic; but it has the important aspect of offering male readers a way to produce feminist criticism that avoids female impersonation. *The way into feminist criticism, for the male theorist, must involve a confrontation with what might be implied by reading as a man and with questioning or a surrender of paternal privileges.* (126–27, emphasis mine)

Alice Jardine, in "Men in Feminism: Odor di Uomo or Compagnons de Route?" (1987), and Joseph Allen Boone, in "Of Me(n) and Feminism: Who(se) Is the Sex that Writes?" (1989), offer more considered perspectives on what a man must do to critique his own privileged political position. Jardine identifies four reservations that she has about male critics employing feminism. First, "men are jumping on the feminist theory bandwagon at a time when it is experiencing a certain success in the academy" (57). Second, she is concerned about the potential for "appropriation of a struggle, with men telling us how to be 'more sophisticated' and warning us not to fall into theoretically 'regressive' traps" (57). Third, "we feel threatened by men's rather easy transformation of our private struggles into public exchange" (57). And finally, she claims that feminists are "irritated by the prescription and reduction of complexity that has so far governed so much of men's interventions into feminism" (57).

Nonetheless, Jardine offers seven general suggestions about the kind of work men must do to profitably and conscientiously employ feminist theory:

1. "Stop being sophisticated in theory and politically naive in practice."
2. "Read women's writing—write on it and teach it."
3. "Sponsor women students."
4. "Recognize your debts to feminism in writing."
5. "Stop being so reductive."
6. "Critique your male colleagues on issues of feminism."
7. "Stop being *reactive* to feminism and start being *active* feminists." (60–61)

Though Jardine notes the existence of "male allies," she would require that they carry "the *inscription of struggle*—even of *pain*" (58). Men should not mimic women, offer pathos or guilt, or even admire feminists. Rather, they should do the work required of them as they critique their own cultural habits of reading.

Boone too is concerned that feminism might be used irresponsibly by men. He thus ends his essay with "a few observations" that he believes "other men interested in practicing feminist criticism might like to consider" (175). Of them, let me note three that seem most pertinent to this chapter. First, Boone encourages men "to *identify with* feminism": "If you *are* offering feminist interpretations, then go ahead (to paraphrase Showalter's advice) and read 'as a feminist' and not a 'female impersonator': acknowledge both the centrality of feminism and your gender to your practice" (175). Second, Boone argues for establishing ethos: "Men participating in feminism should make their own oppressive structures (ideological, social, psychological) *present* for critique, rather than hiding them under a veil of abstract musing" (175). And third, a male feminist critic must see the necessity of difference and remain determined to acknowledge it: "The male feminist critic must be willing to forge a definition of himself as a man that makes room for the acknowledgement of a difference and a sexuality that is truly heterogeneous" (175–76).

Perhaps the most encouragement for me came from the compromise Janet Todd (1988) makes in *Feminist Literary History* when discussing feminist criticism:

> Women's voice from experience needs to remain at its base and, until men listen to it as well as imagining costumes and modalities for themselves, there cannot really be male feminism or men in feminism. One can, as Mary Jacobus has noted, be male or female to write feminist criticism, but no one can afford to become involved in its debate and practice "without confronting the implication for their own critical position of that debate, that practice." No one should enter it without knowing that he or she takes up a political position. (134)

While a man obviously can never *be* a woman, theorists recognize that a man might learn to make a feminist reading of a text. By guarding against impersonation—Showalter's notion of "critical cross-dressing"—a man might learn both how to use feminist criticism and, more importantly, understand why he should use it. In fact, a man might see all around him methods of teaching that have a feminist basis, as I describe below. But to do so, he must identify his own subject position and offer a critique of culturally valued reading practices. He must recognize the politics of his own "given" and "privileged" position. And while it is true that feminist criticism is overtly political, it might be argued that the other theories studied in this book are political as well, even if covertly so.

Reading as a Teacher: What Teachers Should Know

Elizabeth Flynn, in her Staffroom Interchange essay in *College Composition and Communication*, "Composing 'Composing as a Woman': A Perspective on Research" (1990), notes that "the field has not engaged feminist research and theory in any sustained and systematic way" (83). In fact, so much resistance to feminist thinking exists that Flynn found it necessary to defend the feminist perspective on research she advanced in "Composing as a Woman" (1988), in which she tried to show "how . . . [feminist] research and theory may be used in examining student writing" and to suggest "directions that a feminist investigation of composition might take" ("Composing" 425 and quoted by Flynn in "Composing 'Composing' " 83–84).

Like Flynn, teachers using feminist criticism in evaluating student writing will come under considerable criticism by those who maintain, as Dale Bauer's student does, that a feminist approach to examining literature is a matter of personal opinion and that the classroom is not a place where such opinions should be expressed. So deeply ingrained is this attitude toward feminist theory that Flynn (1990) must conclude, "Despite its perpetuation of enlightened ways of thinking about writing, the field of composition studies has strangely resisted feminism" (88). Perhaps this resistance is as much a matter of not knowing how to employ feminist theory in the classroom as it is a reaction against feminism as a political force that threatens certain privileged positions in society.

Unlike reader response and deconstruction, feminism as a theory affects more than the way texts are read. Like the New Criticism, feminist theory implies not only a position in relation to classroom authority, but an entire pedagogy as well. Much of what has been espoused in this book is consistent with that pedagogy. Indeed, in recent years, feminist theory has increasingly influenced the way teachers approach the task of teaching students to write.

Even a cursory glance at currently fashionable approaches to teaching reveals that many teachers are already employing "feminist" methods in their classes. First, many teachers have begun to approach reading as an activity that can be learned and shaped both by students' experiences in the world and by the texts they are asked to read. For instance, when students are asked to read more materials written by women, they not only recognize the existence of a body of literature written by women, but also confront the struggles and cultural indignities that women have had to suffer. With the range of women writing poetry in the 1990s, few problems in selecting appropriate reading materials exist. But even the survey courses that prepare students for the kind of reading they will do in creative writing classrooms should challenge traditional methods of selection. Barbara Waxman (1989) suggests four ways to change such courses to help students learn how to read differently: (1) include more works by women; (2) pair prominent and less well known works by both men and women; (3) "double" classics with modern versions; and (4) construct a thematic course outline rather than the traditional chronological one (18–20). What's more, if we are going to read different texts, such texts should be read, as Clara Juncker (1988) suggests, through a "receptive, rather than aggressive, mode of reading," which means that we should "abandon our admittedly strong desire to master a text, to penetrate its most secret parts, to divide and categorize" (433), and, instead, ask questions of the text, its origins, its development, its human concerns.

Second, teachers have decentered classroom authority by relying increasingly on less direct methods of instruction and by helping students learn from each other when reading and commenting on each other's writing. To this end, teachers have also come to employ peer group and collaborative learning techniques, including the workshop as I discuss it in chapter 7. Many feminist teachers believe that any teaching that silences students works against feminist principles. Wendy Goulston (1987) writes, "Indeed, if they are women socialized as I and many of us are, they find the male professor's perspective a threatening one to adopt toward their own work" (25). Goulston thus advocates using peer groups and adopting a new attitude toward student writing: "Interestingly, the new approaches to teaching writing adopt a position and utilize skills that have traditionally been associated with female style. They contrast with the rhetorical professorial academic stance of the past. The new teachers' and fellow students' role in aiding students to write well is not to 'profess' and pass judgment, but to question and to wish to understand" (25). Goulston concludes, "Because it assumes that the writer has something valuable to say, this teaching method provides the respect and nurturing support that women students especially need" (25). Carol Stanger (1987) places the process of teaching from this perspective in focus when she writes, "Teaching becomes a process of creating conditions in which collaborative learning can occur" (39).

Third, teachers have come to view the writing process differently. Assignments are now often viewed as a starting point, a point of departure, that can take the student in any possible direction, perhaps even off the assigned topic altogether. Elizabeth Flynn (1989) writes, "For me, an assignment is a stimulus, a way of getting students started, rather than a straitjacket. If students reinterpret the assignment in creative ways, fine. If they misinterpret an assignment, I'm quite willing to work with what they give me" (50). And Daumer and Runzo (1987) offer a wide range of possible assignments that look to "unearth the voice of women" through "untraditional sources," including devalued forms of writing (e.g., journals, letters, diaries) and "community-based" outlets (e.g., blues, spirituals, work songs) (56). Such assignments productively challenge our usual notion of writing in rhetorical modes or in courses such as poetry writing that have a narrow notion of genre.

Further, Linda Peterson (1991) reports that "the topics that women students choose are almost always 'relational'—i.e., they focus on the relationship of the writer with some other person or group," while "male writers more frequently choose topics that focus on the self, the self alone, the self as distinct from others: e.g., a physical challenge in nature, an episode in building self-confidence, a crisis in vocation" (173–74). Peterson's research has three implications for teachers. First, teachers should not "unwittingly privilege one mode of self-understanding over another" in the assignments they devise. Second, "the readings suggested as models for the assignment should include examples by and about both masculine and feminine subjects" (175). And third, "evaluation of personal essays should not privilege certain gender-specific modes of self-representation, nor penalize others" (175).

Indeed, as a result of the above considerations, evaluation must also be viewed differently. Teachers make greater use of peer evaluation, of course, but they also often find it useful to comment on student writing in-process. Juncker (1988) advises that we "continue to emphasize pre-writing and revision in order to make our students aware of the openendedness of writing, of texts always being written" (432). What's more, our comments must be helpful rather than judgmental. As Olivia Frey (1990) asserts, "The adversary method [of evaluation] is not just bad for women but bad for everyone" (523).

From a feminist perspective, evaluation must involve a dialogue between reader and writer about the text as it develops. Dialogue is critical to this approach to evaluation. But of more importance than the invitation to participate is how the dialogue is handled. Rather than a debate format, where the participants/combatants are able to stake out their positions in advance to make an adversarial reading, a feminist approach manages conversations as a deconstructive approach does, cultivating differences. As with my interactions with Deb, authority for the text shifts from reader to writer and back again. And, as with Deb's poem, there is no clearly established point in time or number of drafts that indicates when the process has concluded.

As I've said, many teachers are already using "feminist" methods in their classes. But unless teachers fully incorporate feminist principles as they touch upon the classroom—that is, in devising writing assignments, employing collaborative learning strategies, relying on peer and in-process evaluation of writing, and admitting into the classroom genres that have not been privileged in the academy—the use of feminist critical tools in reading student poems will lack a foundational basis.

Applying Feminist Criticism to Three Student Poems: A Point of Departure

If one of a course's goals is to call upon feminist criticism for assistance in reading student poems, then the teacher must consider the matter of ethos throughout the semester. This means, of course, opening up oneself, one's political stance, and one's teaching methods for critique. It also means being a conscious reader, one who not only recognizes the impact of various literary-critical theories on the reading of student texts, but one who plans on using those methods as well. When Joseph Harris (1989) writes, "One is always *simultaneously* a part of several discourses, several communities" (19), he is saying that one always has subject positions in relation to everything else and that these positions are apt to change.

Teachers who enter and exit various communities during the semester must identify their subject positions by providing their students with an explanation of each critical community, including its expectations and goals. Nedra Reynolds (1992) clearly states a teacher's responsibility here: "We must be responsible for the ways we construct our own ethos—in textbooks and articles, departmental documents, course syllabi and handouts. . . . We must inscribe our identities . . . by beginning with the self and moving outward to the widest possible spaces where writing and the study of writing matter" (12). The importance of establishing ethos will become more apparent as I examine the three student poems that follow.

Type and Focus of Comments

I have selected these three poems, two of them written by men, because they reflect what I believe to be the full range of student reactions to my use of feminist criticism. What's more, the commentary that I offered in response to each poem was given under somewhat different circumstances. For instance, when I set out to read the poem by David, a student in my introductory poetry writing course, I used the detached letter format demonstrated in chapter 5. Finding the letter well-suited to commentary based on feminist critical methods, I also used that format to comment on poems by Andy and Betty. Andy, however, was a student in my advanced poetry writing course, and

Betty showed me her poem outside the context of a class. As a result, I did not have the opportunity to work with her over the period of time I now believe to be necessary to establish myself as a credible and trustworthy feminist critic. Though the range of student reactions will show that not all of my efforts have met with success, I do think that the reactions are of interest nonetheless, particularly for what they say about the need for men—and women—to establish credibility before employing feminist criticism.

For each of the three poems that follow, I have included the first draft that the authors showed me and, after each poem, my response in a letter that offers a feminist critical reading:

Voodoo

She believes in voodoo.
And I can't say that I'm
immune to it.
Although I try to be a perfect
scientist.

She rattles beats in my ear;
she mixes curses to tangle me
in her game.
But I don't play games,
I don't believe in magic.

Maybe it is a science though
but no one ever considered magic
a science, much less a part of reality.
None of them have been touched
by her.

When sounds are made,
and space is curled,
and all the breath she can muster
into one sentence, breaks into the air,
I believe.

Maybe her science can never be a
secured science.
Maybe her science is real.
A science with no math, a
science with no role for society,
just a place for me.

—David

Dear David,
    Let me respond to your poem by employing feminist criti-
cism. As I've said in class, I will make every effort to hear what
you have written in this poem. But in my adaptation of feminist

criticism, I hope to also pay attention to the silences, the elements of the poem that are suggested or implied but not privileged.

[Musician Carlos] Santana's "Black Magic Woman" comes to mind as I read "Voodoo." The central conflict of your poem is between Science and Non-science, between the perfect scientist and the magician. They symbolize power so strong that "I can't say that I'm / immune to it." Gradually, the speaker of the poem says about voodoo, "Maybe it is a science though," and later yet, "Maybe her science is real." The question is what the voodoo symbolizes, what specific power she has, what lure, what ownership.

The element of your poem silenced, I think, is this. From a certain cultural standpoint, we have always been suspicious of women with special undefinable powers. We've burned them as witches, called them whores, made them wear scarlet letters. You call that power voodoo. But you give its special status a more positive connotation. Do you exclude other interpretations of that power? At first you do not seem to *want* to acknowledge that power at all, but in the end you must. Are there gender issues undealt with here? Are there political motives? Or are they only—as they appear here—psychological?

If you reconsider what you've written and revise this poem to reflect a different vision of the woman you describe, please show it to me. Let me be clear, though, that whether you revise or not is your decision. Let me know in writing how you respond to this reading, okay?

friends talking

"Do you
think

I could
be

an actress?"
asked Celeste.

You can be
anything you

want to be.
And

if you are
a *good* actress

you can,"
replied Gentry,

"be
me."

                    —Andy

Dear Andy,

Thanks for showing me this draft of your poem. I hope to employ feminist criticism here in an effort to help you (and me) see your poem in a slightly different way. What I'll do in what follows is tell you what I think the privileged reading is and then offer a reading that focuses on issues of gender as I read them.

This poem is a dialogue between two people (is one a male?) about what it means to be an actress or, especially, a "good" actress. One person simply says that if the other is a really good actress, she can be him (her?). I think you want to play here with irony and humor. The dialogue is a good way to do that.

Let's look at the poem differently now, for its gendered relations. My first concern is if these are two women talking or one man and one woman. Gentry is, of course, ambiguous. Either way, the perception offered in the poem is hierarchical since it makes distinctions between acting "good" and "bad." In effect, if Celeste is an especially *good* "actress" (rather than the genderless "actor"), she can act in the role of Gentry. If Gentry is a woman, womanhood must be an act, a mask, a set of learned behaviors. If Gentry is a man, the poem portrays manhood as the highest activity a woman can engage in. And if Celeste can "be anything," is this to satisfy herself or her audience, since she is acting anyway? Is it a man's fantasy that a woman "be anything" she wants? Would a woman's fantasy of being anything she wants result in her wanting to be a man? And back to the hierarchy. Gentry thinks the best actor can act in the role of Gentry (an ideal). Is Gentry, then, an actor too? If Gentry is a man, are the best women the ones who can act like men? If Gentry is a woman, should other women try to act as Gentry acts in the role of Gentry?

I hope this reading does more good than harm! Please consider these comments as you revise and let me see your revisions. In addition, please write me a brief note highlighting your reaction to this kind of commentary.

Painted Lady

The stainless quill begins its staccato etchings.
Body tensing, taut, anticipating,
Stiletto steady, buzzing
Punching life into the icon marked upon her flesh.
Inflicting sensations; meeting thresholds of torment . . .

Quickly calmed by the lulls of the artist's hand
As it pirouettes to start its course anew.
Soon the hieroglyphic image emerges
As if it had always been a part
of her incarnate soul.

                                                    —Betty

Dear Betty,

Thanks for letting me see this draft of your poem. In the next paragraphs I hope to offer two kinds of readings. In one, I'll describe what I see in your poem from my usual ways of reading. In the second, I'll offer a reading that focuses on the gender issues I see there.

This is a vivid account of getting a tattoo, I think. In it you pay especially close attention to the feelings associated with having a tattoo etched to skin. There are many visual and tactile images here that portray the sense impressions of the experience. In the end, the tattoo is viewed as something that had always been a part of this person, "of her incarnate soul," and that makes the physical element of receiving the tattoo something that brings to the surface this element of her inner being.

Needless to say, there is a significance in the fact that the person tattooed is a woman. I am led to wonder, first, if I would read this poem differently if the person were a man or if a man would have described this experience differently. In any event, these questions of gender seem inevitable and unavoidable. The poem's title suggests to me cosmetic care, from this vantage point, the care men have always expected from women, the care women take with eyeliner, mascara, lipstick, etc. But this care is much more tactile—and more emphatic. Is the quill an instrument of masculinity, like a pen or pencil in some ways? Is the response by the lady, likewise, erotic: "tensing, taut, anticipating"? Does the quill, transformed into a "stiletto" that is "punching . . . upon her flesh," result in physical sensations that are erotic and painful: "inflicting sensations," "thresholds of torment"? When the calm is achieved beneath "the artist's hand," have you restated the masculine desire that their women undergo cosmetic transformation for the pleasure of men and, in this case, for the woman's sexual pleasure/pain as well?

Please let me know if this reading is useful to you. Naturally, any decision to revise is yours, but whether you revise or not, please write me a brief note.

In learning how to use feminist criticism to comment on my students' poems, I attempted to become a resisting reader. And to resist the text, I attempted to follow four guidelines suggested to me by what I have read on the subject:

1. One reason for exploring feminist criticism after discussing deconstruction is that it seemed to be the next logical step in my evolution as a reader of my students' poems. First, I was interested not in evaluating my students' poems using feminist critical tools, but in offering a kind of reading. Second, to offer this kind of reading, rather than searching the gaps for exclusions, as

I did when I tried to deconstruct my students' poems, I made every effort to pay attention to elements of the text that would have been silenced by my usual methods of reading. Acknowledging that readers sensitized to matters of gender might read the poem differently, I looked for such silences quite (self-) consciously. As Myra Jehlen (1990) notes, "One has to read for gender; unless it figures explicitly in the story or poem, it will seldom read for itself" (273).

2. To "read for gender" and, thereby, resist the text in any believable way, students must see the teacher as a trustworthy and credible critic. Teachers must thus incorporate teaching methods consistent with both their stated expectations for student texts and the way they will read and evaluate those texts. They should also try to be an empathetic reader. To these ends, I tried to describe in the first paragraph of my response what I set out to do and, in the second, offer my usual way of reading the poem prior to reading for its gender relations. What's more, I used the letter format to project a less authoritarian voice, to avoid intruding on the text. As Elizabeth Flynn (1989) notes of her reading student papers from a feminine perspective, "My relationship with my students changed. I was no longer merely an adversary. I was also on their side, a friendly advisor" (51).

3. Reading for "gender relations," while something that must be done consciously, came to involve for me a certain way of thinking about—that is, of resisting—language that I did not or somehow could not use in examining the fourteen poems I took home with me so long ago. Myra Jehlen (1983), paraphrasing Adrienne Rich, offers excellent advice for thinking this way: "Feminist thinking is really rethinking, an examination of the way certain assumptions about women and the female character enter into fundamental assumptions that organize all our thinking. . . . Such radical skepticism is an ideal intellectual stance that can generate genuinely new understandings" (69).

A good place to begin generating new understandings is with word choice. Irene C. Goldman (1990) writes, "One of the first attributes of a text that the deconstructivist critic notices is ambiguous words, and one of the first groups of words that feminists find ambiguous is *man, mankind,* and *he*" (124). Thereafter, it is important to notice "certain *kinds* of absences, gestures of exclusion, false assumptions of inclusiveness" (Goldman 1990, 122; emphasis mine) in the text. A reader must be especially sensitive to "inquire into the power relations" (Ebert 1991, 889) suggested or stated explicitly in a text and judge those relations in terms of "gestures of exclusion" or "false assumptions of inclusiveness."

4. Finally, the question of authority is always present, but nowhere more apparent than in the teacher's efforts to employ feminist criticism in evaluating student poems. I am conscious of the fact that many students see feminist criticism as a matter of opinion. In fact, I want to reinforce here the importance of establishing oneself as trustworthy in the classroom. As with deconstruction, teachers who hope to employ feminist criticism in reading their students' poems must use their authority in the classroom to undermine that very authority. This means that the decision of whether to revise or not revise must rest with the students themselves, that they must be encouraged to be less concerned with pleasing the reader and more concerned with expressing themselves, especially if we hope to combat what Joan Bolker (1979) calls the "Griselda syndrome"—the exchange of self for success in the academic community.

Commenting on the three student poems included above from a feminist perspective required some self-examination on my part. First, my intention in employing feminist criticism was to offer a reading of my students' poems, not an evaluation. What's more, I approached the task of making such a reading openly, recognizing that another reader—male or female—using the same methods might read the same texts quite differently. Since feminist readings are outside most students' experiences, I found it helpful to "locate" myself—that is, to identify a place from which I would approach their texts—as I set out to examine their poems. In the end, I opted for a method of identification a bit different from the methods John Flynn (1989) uses in his essay, though I am certain we both set out to examine ourselves as readers. Since I had been identifying myself for my students from the start of the term by helping them see how I might go about the task of writing and revising my own poems, my students needed little additional information about me. What they needed was information about my approach to reading their poems.

Second, I felt obliged to consider the political ramifications of using feminist criticism to read student poems. Dale Bauer (1990) has already pointed out the kinds of resistance teachers often receive when they use feminist criticism in the classroom with students who believe that feminism is just an opinion. In examining my relationships with my students, I recognized the need to respect their views of feminism (or New Criticism or reader response or deconstruction) by offering not a requirement that they think differently, but the recommendation that it is to their benefit as writers to be able to read from the perspectives of different communities, even communities they might not choose to stay in for long. What's more, my goal was always to return the authority for their poems to the students who wrote them. This meant teaching them enough about the methods I used in reading their poems so that they might, in workshop, use the same methods in examining each other's poems. If students decide not to enter a particular community, they must know that the decision is ultimately theirs to make.

Finally, no matter what decision they ultimately make, I wanted my students to realize that from at least one perspective—that is, in the eyes of one community of readers—all texts, both theirs and the ones assigned from the anthology, are political documents. And for some, politics arise from the gender codes that can be found in the language itself. By helping my students understand this particular orientation to language, I hoped they would see that by using feminist criticism in reading their texts, I was not offering an authoritarian judgment, but showing them how their poems might be read by a reader who has been sensitized to gender. As with deconstruction, I wanted students to realize that they are not required to revise their poems just because I read and comment on them as I do. In fact, if my reading indicates that they have succeeded in developing their poems as they hoped they would, or if they think that by revising in response to the feminist reading I offer their texts will be weakened in some way, then I would prefer that they not revise at all.

Since I used the same kind of detached text—a letter—to convey both my feminist and deconstructive readings to my students, the kinds of information I offer from each perspective are much the same. When using deconstruction, I offer explanatory information, interpretive information, and deconstructive information. When using feminist criticism, gender information simply replaces deconstructive information.

Explanatory Information. As with my deconstructive readings, the explanatory information in feminist readings of my students' poems is given both in the introduction, where I explain my use of feminist criticism in language geared to each student, and in the conclusion, where I remind students of their options in revising.

Major differences between the kind of explanation I give concerning feminist criticism and the kind I give concerning deconstruction arise from two considerations. First, I believe that in using deconstruction, a reader determines what has been consciously or unconsciously *excluded* from the text; in using feminist criticism, the reader searches for what has been *silenced*. And second, I recognize a need, both as a teacher and as a male, to establish myself as trustworthy and knowledgeable prior to offering what some students will see as a mere "opinion" about their poems.

David and Andy were both in classes in which I presented the four guidelines given above (and an explanation of these guidelines) prior to reading their poems. Unlike Betty, David and Andy also knew that I hoped to read their poems from various perspectives, including the four studied in this book. What's more, I believe they were willing to accept my reading of their poems as long as it revealed to them something that was, in fact, silent in *their* readings of their poems. I referred to these elements of the text as "silences" to David and as "issues of gender" to Andy. Of the two descriptions, I prefer the first, since it more effectively allows me to contrast feminist readings with deconstructive readings, where I read for what has been "excluded." In deconstruction, we are concerned with differences that have been consciously or unconsciously left outside the text. From a feminist perspective, the differences we hope to find are already in the text. Our usual methods of reading simply leave us deaf to these voices; they prevent us from seeing the ambiguity and irony of privileged language.

In commenting on Betty's poem, I described my reading as one that "focuses on the gender issues I see there [in her poem]." Since Betty was not in a writing class in which I had the opportunity to critique my own methods of reading and writing (as I do in chapter 2), I actually needed to explain much more to her than I do when I simply contrast a "privileged" reading with a reading concerned with gender. For Betty's sake, if not to deepen the understanding of others whose poems were read in this manner, I might have stressed my interest in reading as a way of listening for certain ambiguities, for certain kinds of absences and exclusions, for positionings of power relations in the text. Though a feminist reading, if it is done well, will create some discomfort in the author, the teacher's job is to ready the student so that such discomfort is minimal. Without that kind of preparation, I might have predicted that Betty would not find anything particularly noteworthy in my reading of her poem and, unlike David and Andy, who revised extensively, would not make substantial changes to her text.

My goal with each of these authors was to return authority for their poem to them in the concluding paragraph of my letter. But only Betty was truly outside my range of influence, since she was not enrolled in my poetry writing class. To David, I remarked directly, "*If you reconsider what you've written and revise this poem to reflect a different vision of the woman you describe, please show it to me.*" By commenting in this fashion, that is, by encouraging David to view my reading as viable, I give David the option of either accepting my reading of his poem as an accurate depiction of the woman he is describing, changing the depiction to something else, or refuting my reading of his poem in a return letter.

With Andy, I am far less certain when I write, "I hope this reading does more good than harm." Though I am happy with my reading of gender issues in Andy's poem, I also like this draft of his poem a great deal. My New Critical biases require that I favor this draft because of its ambiguity, irony, and tension. Specifically, I hesitated in making my feminist reading because from a certain critical standpoint the poem strikes me (as David's does to a lesser degree) as quite good. But, as Andy's return letter will show, the implications for gender in his poem have been hidden from his own reading. I could only hope that later drafts be as polished as this early draft.

Using these same New Critical standards, Betty's poem is the least pleasing to me of the three. Yet feminist criticism allows me to ask questions which, if answered, will help her move beyond the kind of generalizations in language that I would have more directly complained about if I had used the New Criticism to respond to her poem. Instead, I remark, "Please let me know if this reading is useful to you."

Overall, I find that the most effective concluding remarks are those, like the ones I write in my letter to David, that return authority to the author, those that ask the author to seriously consider my reading of gender relations in the poem.

Interpretive Information. As with both reader-response criticism and deconstruction, this portion of my detached text reflects an effort to simply read the poem using my usual New Critical methods of reading. Simply put, I ask myself, "If I read without regard for difference as a gender issue, what is this poem about?"

With David, I try to show likenesses. His poem reminds me of Carlos Santana's "Black Magic Woman," a song that likewise engages in a description of the kind of power David writes about in "Voodoo." In Andy's poem, I comment on the element of dialogue and point out that his use of it enables him to take full advantage of the irony and humor of the situation. Perhaps to establish myself as an empathetic reader, with Betty I try to offer somewhat more interpretation. I note her reliance on "visual and tactile images" and her desire to "portray the sense impressions of the experience." Next I try to bring forward her suggestion that the tattoo is really an outward manifestation of something far deeper, a desire or emotion or some other intangible element.

Except where they were the obvious subject of the poem, I tried to keep the gendered elements silent. In David's poem, I must respond to the fact that as a man he writes about a woman. But I carefully avoid characterizing that woman until the next paragraph; here I try to be completely congenial and nonjudgmental—an empathetic reader. Similarly, I avoid any characterization of the speakers when I discuss Andy's poem. Rather, my goal is to make a simple, even if overly so, restatement of what the poem seems to me to be about. In my response to Betty's poem, I feel as though I am tentative about its meaning. For one thing, I try desperately to be accurate, since my goal with Betty, as a poet not in my class, was to prove that I could be a credible reader. Indeed, perhaps part of my tentativeness with Betty stems from the fact that I know I am about to use feminist criticism as a man reading a poem by a woman.

Gender Information. For my own benefit, I found it necessary to "locate" feminist criticism among the various reading communities I entered while reading my students' poems over the semester. By doing so, I thought I would be better able to know when in the writing process feminist criticism would be most helpful to my students. I could also better determine what format to use in commenting on their poems. But even more, I thought that by doing this, I would be more sensitive to issues related to tone. Since feminist criticism is overtly political, I wanted to offer a dispassionate statement about gender, leading the authors to certain considerations without requiring specific changes in their poems.

Feminist criticism, at least as I have adapted it here to comment in-process on student poems, seems a composite of reader response and deconstruction. Like reader response, feminist criticism requires that readers reconstruct the text in light of their past experiences with both the subject and the kind of text in question. More specifically, feminist criticism enables readers to read the text for certain ambiguities, absences, exclusions, and power relations. Unlike reader response, though, a community of readers can learn to become sensitized to the code that makes such reading possible. My goal in reading through a feminist critical lens was much the same as my goal in reading from a reader-response perspective: to show the author how one reader reconstructs the text. If the author's meaning does not result in the kind of response made by that reader, then the author needs to revise. And as will become clear, such revision might be made on every level of the text, from word to overall design and intent. In short, where gender relations are explicit, feminist criticism will enable the author to see if intention matches accomplishment. Where gender relations are not explicit (and this is where students most often feel teachers are offering opinion), feminist criticism offers one way to read the text, a way different from any other and one far more political.

Feminist criticism does this by offering much the same kind of reading that deconstruction does. In fact, I might just as easily have set out to deconstruct David's poem. In the process of writing my remarks from a feminist perspective, I realized that the differences, the flip side to David's poem in particular, would have required attention to gender no matter which of the two critical lenses I set out to use. Like deconstruction, feminist criticism looks for that element of the text that is not readily accessible through our usual ways of reading. It seeks difference—the gaps, contradictions, and seams in the text that contribute to a reader's reaction. Unlike deconstruction, though, these elements have not been excluded in a decision to limit the topic so something can be written. Rather, these elements have been in the text all along and might be found in anything in the poem—from a word or a phrase or the form to the general content of the work as a whole.

Of the various elements in these poems that feminist criticism sensitized me to, the easiest to respond to were the power relations in each text. David writes about a woman's "special undefinable powers," what he calls voodoo, and presents them as a challenge to "secured science." Andy views gender as an act and sees in this something from which we can hierarchically distinguish the good from the bad. Betty's poem likewise deals with the issue of power and constructs in it a hierarchy that I describe as "a restatement of a masculine desire that their women undergo cosmetic transformation for the pleasure of men and, in this case, for the woman's sexual pleasure/pain as well." In short, each of these poems presents the reader with a hierarchy, and in each hierarchy is the suggestion of power relations that a reader can point out to an author by employing feminist criticism.

If such a hierarchy exists—and usually it does—I read to see if the subjugation of women or the domestication of their roles is apparent in the poem. "Voodoo" is reciprocal in its power relations. Though the woman possesses a power to which the speaker claims, "I can't say I'm / immune," this very power "from a certain cultural standpoint," as I say in my comments to David, is why women have been oppressed in society. David seems to have drawn from a stereotype:

> men = science = cultural "good"
>
> women = voodoo = cultural "bad"

Andy's poem is complicated because one of the speakers engaged in the dialogue, Gentry, seems to have taken a position of authority in the poem. I explain this view in my comments:

> If Celeste is an especially good "actress" . . . , she can act in the role of Gentry. If Gentry is a woman, womanhood must be an act, a mask, a set of learned behaviors. If Gentry is a man, the poem portrays manhood as the highest activity a woman can engage in.

And finally, the hierarchy created by power relations in Betty's poem is perhaps the central issue of the poem. I write:

> The poem's title ["Painted Lady"] suggests to me cosmetic care . . . , the care men have always expected from women, the care women take with eyeliner, mascara, lipstick, etc.

Indeed, the woman is subjugated here. I ask, "Is the quill an instrument of masculinity . . . ? Is the response by the lady, likewise, erotic . . . ?" Is it significant that the lady finds calm, as Betty writes in her poem, "beneath the artist's hand"? The hierarchical structure of each poem enables me to find where dominance exists.

Next I read to determine absences, gestures of exclusion, and false assumptions of inclusiveness. In "Voodoo," the notion of a "secured science," a socially and culturally validated science, clearly excludes and trivializes the alternative perception, the "game" women play. The speaker of the poem, for example, says, "I don't play games," excluding the woman's power and playfulness from the serious world, the world, presumably, of men. Andy's poem is similarly positioned against such playfulness. If a woman acts out a role, is it because men expect her to? If a woman can be anything she wants (since she is acting anyway), would she be a man? Or would she act out her role as a woman because it pleases a man? Betty's poem seems to exclude female sexuality, except as the willing recipient of male indulgences. I write, "The quill is a 'stiletto' that is 'punching . . . upon her flesh.' The resulting physical sensation is erotic and painful: 'inflicting sensations,' 'thresholds of torment.' " If women are "included" in the worlds of these poems, they are falsely included. The traditional masculine subjugation of women in these works actually serves as a method of exclusion. Absent in each poem is the balancing effect of equality and equity.

Much of this gendered information comes through sensitivity to language and the sign's indefinite correlation to the signified. Of course, a woman can have power as great as a man's. But in David's poem, only if that power is magical. Like the speaker of David's poem, men "don't believe in magic." Naturally, we all act. But if we do, as in Andy's poem, traditionally assigned roles in society are just that: roles acted out because of certain cultural expectations. Gentry is an ambiguous name in Andy's poem, but whether the "original" Gentry (who Andy told me about in his return letter) is male or female, the poem portrays gender as an acting out or a playing of roles. And finally, though I was very self-conscious in pointing out to Betty the ambiguity I found in much of her language, I felt her poem was the most ambiguous of all (and, in final examination, the most hurtful to women). In getting a tattoo from a man, the woman in the poem goes to the extreme in receiving cosmetic treatment. In my letter to Betty, I attempt to critique my own position as a reader: "There is a significance in the fact that the person tattooed is a woman. I am led to wonder, first, if I would read this poem differently if the person in the poem were a man, or if a man would have described this experience differently." Either way, this poem portrays the act of receiving a tattoo as a painful procedure undergone chiefly to improve appearance, to express the beauty of the soul in some external and identifiable way.

Finally, in commenting on these poems, I relied heavily on questioning. Since many students are unfamiliar with this approach to reading their texts, not only must we prepare them for what we are about to do, but we must also offer gender information carefully, relinquishing any control we might have over their poems.

Effectiveness of Comments

In keeping with the decision I made when I employed deconstruction—that is, to do whatever I could to return authority for the text to the author—I asked each author here to write a letter responding to my comments. As a result, in addition to each student's revision (where a revision was done), I have also included the return letters and an analysis of the effectiveness of my comments in provoking revision from the students.

Here is David's revision:

Voodoo

She believes in voodoo.
And I can't say that I'm
immune to it.
Although I try to be a perfect
scientist.

She rattles beats in my ear;
She mixes curses to tangle me
in her game.
But I don't play games,
I don't believe in magic.

When sounds are made,
and space is curled,
and all the breath she can muster
into one sentence, breaks into the air,
I believe.

Maybe it is a science though.
Maybe her science can never be a
secured science.
Maybe it is real.
A science with no math, a
science with no role for society,
just a place for me.

But no one ever considered magic
a science, much less a part of reality.
And if they even saw her magic
would they condemn?
Would I condemn if I wasn't receiving?

Magic can come from many places.
Magic might come from me.
I'm sure I can call the spirits and
cast a spell.
Maybe I do, but only to her.

We create a world.
We create our rules.
We create voodoo.

In this revision, David shows a willingness to move around stanzas and lines within stanzas as well as to add new lines to the poem; all of this reveals a desire to make major alterations. In my reading, I reflected back to David that certain elements of the power he describes have not been considered: "From a certain cultural standpoint we [I guess here, as *men*] have always been suspicious of women with certain though undefinable powers." David's revision is an effort to identify this power as different in kind from the power over which, I suggest, "We've burned them as witches, called them whores, made them wear scarlet letters." The power David writes about is not this power, and he adds nearly three stanzas to make that point. This magic, he writes, "might come from me. / I'm sure I can call the spirits and / cast a spell." What's more, it is a power he has over her, just as she has it over him: "Maybe I do, but only to her." And his final stanza suggests that this particular magic is unique to the relationship between this man and this woman: "We create a world. / We create our rules. / We create voodoo."

David's revision is extensive, and one that responds to the kind of commentary that provokes questions of gender. My questions are answered: "Do you exclude other interpretations of that power? . . . Are there gender issues undealt with? Are there political motives? Or are they only—as they appear here—psychological?" But these questions are answered through a revision that undermines their very basis. In revision, David makes clear that the power he writes of is the power of love, something magical that happens between two people.

Here is David's return letter:

Dear Pat,

In seeing [your reading] of my poem, first of all, I understood a little bit more about the theory. But pertaining to my poem, I thought that my poem did not fully portray to you the emotions and feelings that were intended. Then upon rereading the poem myself after reading [your letter], I felt that my expression was not quite what I wanted. I noticed that my poem was not the same poem that was flowing through my head.

Fortunately, what the reading offered . . . was somewhat in line with my original intentions. From that point on, each revision I attempted turned out to be closer and closer to my intention. I do not know that my revision of this poem is not over, though. But I now have locked on to my idea so that it is easier to work with. The words flow more easily. Thanks.

David's reaction to my commentary indicates that, to a certain extent, my reading of his poem was useful as a mirror reflecting one reader's response to the poem. Ironically, my questions required that he return to the poem and reread it carefully to see if, in fact, he had expressed what he had hoped to express, especially since I ended up being unable to become the reader he wanted me to be. In revising his poem, then, David makes large-scale change, even insofar as examining the possibility that this magic might be condemned by the arbiters of reality: "And if they even saw her magic / would they condemn? / Would I condemn if I wasn't receiving?" But David seems to have willingly accepted authority for his poem, and he seems to have in mind a clear intention of something he hopes to accomplish, if not in this draft, then in drafts to come.

Here is Andy's revision:

Pompeii Circus Dance

"We can be
anything we
want to be,"
said G.

"Do you think I,
me,
should try,
or be,
an actress?" asked C.

"A good actress," replied G.,
"can be
anyone she
wants to be."

Answered C.,
"If that's true,
then I could be
[pause, smile] you."

I am impressed that, like David, Andy is willing to make major alterations to his text in an effort to respond to the gender issues I pointed out to him. More specifically, though Andy seems to retain much of the same theme in this draft of his poem as in his earlier draft, he seems to enjoy the ambiguity of the names, reducing both to first initials only. Celeste becomes C. and Gentry becomes G. Ironically, while disguising gender as it would assert itself through first names (especially with the name Celeste), Andy retains the sexist usage "actress" rather than introduce the neutral "actor." Still, the speaker who might be identified as female is Celeste, the one who asks if she "should try, / or be, /

an actress." Andy also reorganizes his poem, taking what had been the middle section and putting it first, as though to suggest that the real issue is the ability to "be anything we / want to be" rather than whether Celeste should "be / an actress." This stresses the notion that the primary function of all people on the planet is to act out a role or, perhaps in this poem, a fantasy. Andy also replaces the "if . . . then . . ." structure of the earlier draft with the declaration "A good actress . . . / can be / anyone she / wants to be." And it is Celeste who seems envious now: "If that's true, / then I could be / [pause, smile] you," a departure from the earlier version, in which Gentry presumptuously says, "And / if you are / a *good* actress / you can . . . / be / me."

In any case, Andy's decision that in this poem only a woman can be what she wants, implied in his continued use of the word "actress," is quite interesting in light of comments in his return letter:

> Pat—
>
> Man, I found those feminist comments most interesting. I have revised the poem. . . . Anyway, here is my reaction to your criticism.
>
> Obviously, I changed the title in a big way. I've never been happy with "friends talking" and this title (hopefully) has a phonetic sound to it that will suggest something to the reader. Anyway. I see what you mean about the hierarchies and the relationship of good/bad acting. The ambiguity of the name "Gentry" is unavoidable, however, because the poem was written for two girls I know. I suppose the easiest way to do it would have been to write a damn poem and dedicate it to them. I had to keep the names somehow, so I used their initials, which I then incorporated into some type of rhyme scheme. The effect I was trying to achieve was to emphasize that, through acting, one's persona becomes another. However, after reading your comments regarding roles, which can be gender roles, I realized that there is already a persona at work in an individual: people act all the time. Therefore, to act as something other than the self is to mask the original persona with another. So the actor, then, is the persona of a persona, on a persona. Much like the poet writing the poem becomes a persona of the poet who, in turn, reveals himself—the persona—in the poem. Your reading of the poem fostered a rewrite which produced a poem that I like far better (actually, there were two versions after your reading, but the first just restated the poem really, in a different order). I think the focus now, by expanding from the "friends" talking, includes people in general. Everyone wears masks and facades, and, too often, life itself is not what it seems. In order to push further the point of acting and personas, I decided to include some stage directions in the end to illustrate that nothing is ever

what it seems. So both characters are actors in a sense, because people are always playing a role. I'm surprised that you could get that stuff out of this little poem. . . .

I hope that I have responded to your comments. I feel like I've more or less defended my poem, which is not what I meant to do. I don't think I've been critiqued from such a position before, and the comments greatly influenced my attempts at revision.

Andy, like David, took my efforts at offering a feminist reading quite seriously. Not only has he come to see the gendered relations in the poem, but he has also questioned his original view of role playing and acting. Of course, his conclusion, that everyone (presumably men as well as women) plays roles and performs on a stage of some sort, is undermined by his continued reliance on "actress." Perhaps a return letter might indirectly offer such a suggestion. I am pleased, however, that "the comments greatly influenced" Andy's attempts at revision. And I feel certain that further revision is apt to occur.

I do not feel as positive about Betty's poem. Unlike David and Andy, Betty, who asked that I critique her poem outside a poetry writing class, seemed to benefit very little from my reading of gender in her poem, suggesting perhaps the obvious: that in situations where authority *really* belongs to the author—that is, outside the classroom situation—a reader has very little influence on revision. Betty, who showed me her poem during the summer institute of the Coastal Plains Writing Project (a site of the National Writing Project), wrote this about how she came to write "Painted Lady":

> As I left Garry's Tattoo Salon that Saturday afternoon, words poured in. Out of my purse, I pulled my trusty "fat 'lil note-book" and (of course my eyes were on the road!) began to write them down: "Painted Lady," tocccata (even though I spelled it wrong), hieroglyphic, stiletto. When I got home, the poem be-gan to emerge—at first writing, it was almost prosaic. . . . It didn't give the feelings that I wanted. Getting a tattoo after having the desire for some 15 to 20 years was for me a religious experience. I let the original "poem" lie dormant till Sunday. Upon awakening, other words spilled forth and I had to put pen to paper again. At my breakfast table, after that first cup of coffee sank in, I began re-writing and it jelled. I was able to re-form that thirty minutes of my life into words that felt right . . . and "Painted Lady" took form.

Interestingly, Betty's process up to the point where I offered my femi-nist reading is fairly standard: having an experience followed by jot-ting down key words that might incite an explosion of language later.

For Betty, poems "emerge." "Painted Lady" has a life that can be prodded by the author or left, as she says, "dormant." When it is active, words spill forth, and the writer is compelled to write: "I had to put pen to paper again." Many of Betty's descriptors for her writing are visceral, bodily sensations and feelings of a *need* to write.

In the context of her overall approach to writing this poem, my reading may have seemed to her an unnatural intrusion on an already finished piece of writing, a piece of writing that she felt certain captured *her* experience of getting a tattoo. Betty's return letter follows:

> In response to Pat's feminist reading of "Painted Lady," I was immediately dumbfounded as my eyes scanned the pencilled page. I agree with part of your interpretation that within its lines are phallic and erotic overtones. However, these did not emerge as conscious elements. I read the poem after having read your comments and I too felt its underlying sensuality.
>
> The poem remains unchanged, not because I did not find the feminist response interesting, but because the poem, to me, conveys the experience and my personal feelings. It is complete to me, in and of itself. It became a living testimony for me and I could not bring myself to "harm" it further.

Though the authority for the text returned to Betty, she was kind enough to help me see in her return letter her reaction to my reading. Admitting that my comments left her "dumbfounded" forced me to determine what I might have said that made her so confused. I do suggest that erotic language dominates the poem, and I urge her to see that as I read it, the poem reflects a relinquishing of power to "the artist's [man's] hand." I fear that I might have touched a sensitive area by pointing out the power relations in the poem. What's more, my confession that I might have read this poem differently if it had been written by a man, though my honest assessment, might have made it more difficult for her to accept this man's reading of a woman's experience. In any event, Betty views the poem as a living and organic thing. Though she says she was interested in my reading, she would prefer to stay nearer to her actual experiences and leave the poem without further revision. For Betty, "it became a living testimony" which she could not bring herself to "harm" any further.

My experience with Betty and one other teacher from that same summer institute of the Writing Project showed me the importance of establishing ethos prior to employing feminist criticism in reading student poems. Though David and Andy were in different classes, I had had a history of give-and-take with both students. As a result, both responded to me as a credible critic. Betty's classroom experience with me had an entirely different focus—teachers teaching teachers. I simply did not have the opportunity to sensitize her to what I hoped to do with her poem. I also wonder if she might have responded to feminist criticism differently if the commentator were a woman. Nonetheless, I feel certain that if I had had the opportunity to establish myself as trustworthy and credible, Betty might have been inclined to make the effort to see her poem as I did.

7 Reading the Course in Poetry Writing: Preparing Students for the Workshop

. . . I'd say that most American students are grossly deficient in their reading background and general knowledge. There are lots of people with lots of natural talent, and very very few with any sort of useful background.

Denise Levertov, *New York Quarterly* Craft Interview

. . . no skillful composition is possible without that prior act of decomposition practiced through reading models of composition by others.

J. Hillis Miller, "Composition and Decomposition: Deconstruction and the Teaching of Writing"

The nonreaders, when forced to write, will repeat tired nonsense without knowing they are repeating the sins of a few hundred years of bad writing.

John D. MacDonald, "Guidelines and Exercises for Teaching Creative Writing"

To say that a course in writing is simultaneously a course in reading is to state the obvious. Besides learning how to "read" their teacher through syllabuses, reading assignments, and writing assignments, students in a workshop must also learn how to read each other's texts and texts of each other's readings. This means that students in a poetry writing course must read not only poems, but relationships as well. As a result, we must be conscious of much more than how students respond to their teachers and peers. Because we have become increasingly certain that the strategies students adopt when entering the social environment determine whether they improve as writers, we must identify for students the roles they might adopt in the classroom.

Robert E. Brooke (1991) notes that "for students to use their classroom experience to move from understanding themselves as students to understanding themselves as writers requires a shift in perceived context, a shift in how they understand the classroom where they are acting" (143). To make such a shift, students must learn to act out nontraditional roles in the classroom rather than simply relying on those they have learned through other school experiences. Brooke continues:

> Such a reconceptualization does not happen by itself, of course. To make such a shift, people require some sort of mark or cue, some sort of indication that the other participants in the situation are also changing their understanding of the activity. (143)

Such cues are vital to changing roles in the classroom. Without them, students will continue to operate in terms of normal classroom expectations. If teachers want students to explore other possible identities, then they must provide students with signals to do so. Without "explicit clues to the contrary," the traditional student-to-teacher relationship of examinee-to-examiner will dominate classroom interaction (Brooke 1991, 144).

How does a teacher signal to students that other roles are possible? Brooke argues that "students need to experience a shift in how teacher and students interact, a change in the nature of student roles, if they are not to become fixed in the roles their past schooling leads them to expect" (144). Thus, the critical issue confronted by Brooke in his study of identity negotiation in writing workshops is how to construct a class that enables students to play nontraditional roles and thereby assume identities as writers. To determine how best to empower students in this negotiation, Brooke carefully studies three kinds of class formats: the sequential writing class, the Piagetian-based class, and the one best suited to identity negotiation, the writing workshop. In the belief that "the roles which operate in . . . classrooms will indeed influence the way students learn" (155), Brooke argues:

> By observing the roles available in our own classrooms, we can describe how our students are learning and the kinds of selves we are helping them to become. Such observation, finally, offers us teachers a choice: what roles will we promote? what sorts of selves will we help our students to develop? The choice is, of course, ours, and aspects of our culture's future depend on the choices we will make. An identity negotiations perspective can make these choices clear; the rest is up to us, our students, and the kinds of writing classes we create. (155)

Any effort to advance a theory for student interaction in the workshop situation must begin with Brooke's challenge: that we look closely at what we have created in our classrooms and determine what roles we are encouraging our students to play, both as writers and readers.

Providing Signals: What Teachers Should Know

Brooke acknowledges the difficulty of identifying from his study alone "what sort of writers' roles we ought to present to students" (154). In doing so, he forces teachers to reconsider for themselves the possible roles they empower their students to negotiate in the classroom. Let me offer three points of reference from which we might identify possible roles. On one extreme are teachers who require strict adherence, even in workshops, to the examinee-examiner role promoted through tradition and privilege. On the other extreme are those who attempt to return power and ownership of a text to its author. Between the two are others who try to model a middle ground where authority is a shared matter, a position that through methods of negotiation and collaboration respects the reader, the writer, and the text.

From this standpoint, the four critical theories adapted for use in this book not only provide students with different readings of their poems, but also serve as points of reference for students as they negotiate their identities as writers and readers. The four theories employed here span the full range of authority relationships between student and teacher, author and reader. What's more, this range of relationships influences possible roles students might adopt, particularly when interacting with each other in the workshop.

Teachers must thus help students understand that these approaches to the text are not simply theories of reading. Rather, students must learn that these theories assume that certain relationships concerning the authority of a text are re-enacted in the drama of the classroom. They also assume that the roles students play as readers and writers likewise reflect the identities they adopt in "reading" the poetry writing class, especially as it enables them to interact with their teacher and with each other during the workshop.

The term *workshop* has several possible meanings. What I refer to as a workshop here is not the entire poetry writing course, much of which takes on dynamics quite different from the actual workshop. Rather, the workshop is the time in the course when students comment on each other's poems, either in small groups or as a class led by the instructor. In either case, the workshop, as I describe it in a handout to my students, "is meant to be a time when we help each other improve our poems. As a result, we must work not only on our poems, but on our skills as commentators on writing." This definition is critical since a significant amount of my time, especially in introductory classes, is spent teaching students how to comment on each other's poems using any of the four theories discussed in chapters 3–6. But I also want them to know—that is, I want to give them signals—that these theories carry with them certain expectations concerning the relationship between the student as writer and reader and the text, all of them calling to the forefront questions of authority in the particular classroom situation called the workshop.

Teachers can signal that these roles exist in three ways: (1) by stating in the syllabus those theoretical assumptions that underlie the course, (2) by employing these various roles themselves in discussing both student and professional writing as literary texts, and (3) by reinforcing emerging identities during the workshop.

Theorizing the Course

Teachers need to address identity negotiation from the outset. In terms of what has been thus far established in this book, a teacher might start the course with more than the usual discussion of course requirements by noting that one of the course's central goals will be consideration of various approaches to reading. Students could thus expect to be asked, in light of these approaches, to consider how they perceive authority in the classroom, both as writers and as readers. Once students are asked to consider the issue of authority as it pertains specifically to the poetry writing course, they can better understand why a teacher might employ various methods for reading and evaluating their poems. They will then be encouraged to employ these same methods of reading when they discuss their peer's work in both large-scale and small-scale workshop sessions. Indeed, these methods give students something to base their remarks on besides opinions.

By so candidly stating the goals of the course and periodically restating them, teachers can make certain their students will better understand why things are being done as they are. What's more, by adapting New Criticism, reader-response criticism, deconstruction, and feminist criticism for purposes of reading in the course, teachers will not only encourage students to read poems from a variety of perspectives, but they will also provide a full range of potential roles for students to negotiate as both writers and readers. Each of these theories, as shown in previous chapters, offers a different view of the student-teacher, examinee-examiner relationship. In fact, the critical element of each is its orientation toward authority, both inside and outside the classroom.

A syllabus for a course such as I have been describing might look like the one in the appendix at the end of this chapter. This syllabus differs from other more traditional syllabuses I have used in the past (that is, before employing literary-critical theory in reading student poems) in several ways, three of them theoretical and three practical. The theoretical aspects must be developed over the semester and reinforced by practice. First, students must be told immediately that the course is experimental and that together they and the teacher are setting out to explore one way in which the course might be taught. Second, in keeping with the sense of experimentation, students must understand the role they play by helping the teacher conscientiously record what happens in the course, examining both the methods employed and the outcome of those methods. Third, students must be told that a large part of what the teacher is attempting to do is provide them with methods for commenting on each other's poems during small- and large-group workshop situations. In short, students must know from the outset that they will be expected to base their judgments about poems on something besides opinions and feelings. To this end, my syllabus stresses two areas: that students will learn both "how to read and evaluate poems" and that they will be taught "how to employ methods of literary criticism."

In practice, such a course necessitates three changes from most traditional efforts at teaching poetry writing. For one, students must be specifically prepared for the possible roles they might play in the workshop. To that end, my own course is divided into two sections. In the first, students read extensively the usual kinds of texts, including essays about other people's theories of composing poems as well as other people's poems. In the second, students receive instruction in literary-critical theory by reading materials describing four methods for commenting on literature, methods reflecting a range of relationships between reader, writer, and text as they influence how authority is viewed in the classroom. As another practical change, my syllabus focuses on an adaptation of reader-response methodology for use in helping students more consciously determine what poetry, in general, and their poems, in particular, attempt to achieve. To negotiate this determination, I recommend employing an interactive journal (see chapter 8). And finally, I believe this method works best if teachers require submission of a portfolio at the end of the semester.

Reading Professional and Student Poems as Literary Texts

One way to demonstrate to students the various roles they might play as readers of poems—those they are writing, those their peers are writing, and those professional pieces they are reading—is to analyze poems through various critical lenses. Chapters 3–6 offer adaptations of critical theories to the reading and evaluation of student poems. These models for evaluation are primarily useful, first, if teachers are willing to read student texts the way they might read literary works, and second, if teachers are willing to adopt various selves in reading these works and thereby model these selves for their students. Students could not receive any clearer signal that the roles implied by each of these methods of reading are roles they might adopt as first readers of their own poems and as workshop evaluators of their peers'. In fact, students, like their teachers, must be willing to give up some of their preconceived notions about what it means to be a student and a reader before they can profitably employ critical theory in reading various student texts. Teachers must thus encourage their students to read differently not only by doing so themselves, but also by explaining how and why they are doing so.

To make this point, teachers might discuss a single poem with their classes at different times during the term, each time using a different critical perspective. Though this can be done with any poem, I enjoy using "Everything: Eloy, Arizona, 1956," by Ai. This poem interests students because of its subject matter. What's more, its subject matter makes it perfectly adaptable to various renderings.

Everything: Eloy, Arizona, 1956*

Tin shack, where my baby sleeps on his back
the way the hound taught him;
highway, black zebra, with one white stripe;
nickel in my pocket for chewing gum;
you think you're all I've got.
But when the 2 ton rolls to a stop
and the driver gets out,
I sit down in the shade and wave each finger,
saving my whole hand till the last.

He's keys, tires, a fire lit in his belly
in the diner up the road.
I'm red toenails, tight blue halter, black slip.
He's mine tonight. I don't know him.
He can only hurt me a piece at a time.

This poem is interesting to approach from a reader-response perspective. Before reading and showing "Everything" to my students, which I usually do during the first full class, I ask them to write

---

down, as a way of preparing for discussion, an answer to the question "What does it mean 'to read'?" After discussing their answers, I present to them the notion that reading has less to do with interpreting linguistic units of varying sizes and more to do with their past experiences with the subject they are reading about and the kind of text they are confronting.

I then ask them what set of expectations they bring with them as they sit down to read a poem; I am interested in discussing with them their "poem reactions" and whether their reactions are different when they read for class as opposed to when they read for their own enjoyment (though many students admit that they do not read for enjoyment). This question enables me to determine where I am beginning with a group of students. Many have read little, if any, contemporary poetry and, as a result, their initial expectations for a poem serve as a description of something very different from the poem I am about to show them.

My first question about the poem itself focuses on the author's name. I ask them, "Has anyone ever heard of Ai?" Even in my advanced classes, few students have heard of her. I tell them that usually the first "cue" or signal we use in predicting what will come next in the text is the author's name. To give them a specific example of this, I ask them to compare their predictions for a text written by Woody Allen to their predictions for one written by William Shakespeare.

Next, by using an overhead projector and a transparency, I show the students the title of the poem, "Everything: Eloy, Arizona, 1956." I then ask, "On the basis of this title, what do you believe the poem will be about?" Though the author's name was their first cue, students are better able to make predictions about the text from the title. But, having read little contemporary poetry, their predictions are tentative and usually inaccurate. What's more, few of my students have been to Arizona, and even fewer can remember from actual experience the events of 1956. Nonetheless, I am able to encourage them to see reading as an activity in which readers posit one hypothesis about what a poem means after another, testing these hypotheses as they move along and revising them as necessary, as a writer might revise a text.

After this, I show the students the poem's first two words, "Tin shack." Then I ask them to close their eyes and, using their imaginations, to construct a tin shack based upon their past experiences. I give them thirty seconds to perform this imagined construction. Then I say, "What does the tin shack look like? Does it have a door? Is the door on the left? the right? in the middle?" Once we have located the door, I ask them to swing it open and step inside. Then I ask them to close their eyes once more and construct the inside of their tin shacks by imagining a detailed picture. After about thirty seconds, I give them the opportunity to describe what they have seen. Sometimes, depending on the amount of time I have for this activity, I ask them to write down what they have seen inside the shacks they have constructed.

I suppose the point is obvious: students come to understand how their assumptions about what Ai intends reflect their individual experiences. When I show them what is inside the tin shack Ai has imagined, they begin to understand the power of detail and the impact of the image. I continue to discuss this poem to its conclusion in this way, showing the students one line at a time and asking repeatedly, "On the basis of this line, what do you think will come next?" Overall, I am able to successfully introduce to students the notion of reading as a process of rewriting, a notion I will return to and reinforce later in providing students with parallel texts in response to their own poems.

Ai's poem is also well-suited to a New Critical interpretation, one that analyzes the poem on the basis of features found in the text itself. Usually I discuss this poem from the New Critical perspective during the third week of class. Before discussing the poem, though, I ask students to answer the following question: "What do you believe to be the basic features of a poem?" We discuss their responses and then read the poem with this list of features in mind.

Usually students begin by attempting to decide what an appropriate subject for poetry might be. Ai's poem, a kind of love poem, is an interesting twist on poetic subject matter for most students. But by beginning with the subject of the poem, uncovering through discussion the poem's central conflict, we begin a discussion of meaning that focuses on where meaning comes from. We make some simple distinctions at first between reader-response methods and New Critical emphases, between how a reader's experiences influence one kind of reading as opposed to another kind of reading that focuses on the features of the text.

I then ask students to find as many of these features in the poem as they can. They point out that the language seems to paint a picture, as they have already seen, especially of the tin shack. They like the description of the highway, what someone will inevitably call a comparison: "highway, black zebra, with one white stripe." They also like the repetition of certain sounds in the poem: "shack" and "back," "white stripe," the "t" sound in "when the 2 ton rolls to a stop," "shade" and "wave," "tires" and "fire" and "diner." And someone inevitably points out the double meaning of "piece" in the poem's last line.

The next week we discuss Ai's poem once more, this time in the belief that often, in writing about a subject in poetry or in any other genre, writers necessarily exclude certain material in order to include the material that they do. I describe this approach using the broad term *deconstruction.* I also use the passage that follows to describe this reading procedure to my students:

> Think, in your analysis of what the author has intentionally or unintentionally excluded from the poem, in terms of this analogy.
>
> As in the construction of a room in a house, a builder places certain things *inside* the room. But by doing so, there must be other things, those outside the room, that have been excluded.
>
> Sometimes drafts of various kinds of writings give us windows to look through so that we can better see those things that have been excluded. Often these exclusions are notions in conflict with those in the poem that the author has either overlooked entirely or consciously decided not to include.
>
> What I want you to think about as you read a poem is what you see outside, through the windows, that might in some way help us better understand what the author set out to do. Consider this question: Would the room be improved by bringing this excluded element into it?

The title of Ai's poem introduces an interesting problem for students learning to read in this way. I like to ask them to write down a response to this question: "If Ai's poem includes 'Everything,' what has it excluded?" This question gives rise to an interesting discussion, usually focusing on what it might mean to have *nothing* in Eloy, Arizona, on the one hand, or what *everything* might include outside Eloy, Arizona, on the other. In the process of discussing these two excluded elements of the poem, students come to see this method of reading as basically nonintrusive, dealing tangentially with what is in the text— and providing yet another way of reading for those who would read strictly from the perspective of their own past reading experiences.

But students would like to say more about "Everything: Eloy, Arizona, 1956." They enjoy discussing the poem from a feminist perspective as well. To that end, I ask, "What is not being said, specifically, about the persona?" And perhaps they would profit from examining the text from a Marxist perspective: "What is the speaker's social status? What might *everything* be to someone with greater wealth?"

While I find it useful to discuss one poem from these various critical vantage points, I also assign my students readings from the required anthology and, placing students in small groups, ask them to read the poems using one of these methods. Once they have worked in small groups, we reconvene and discuss what they have decided about each poem. In this way, they are prepared for the kind of reading I plan on giving their poems due to me that day.

Additionally, and in some ways more importantly, I want to raise the issue of discourse authority. I explain to students that each method of reading I have introduced views the authority for meaning differently. I then ask them to respond in writing to the following as preparation for discussion: "Which of these methods of reading do you prefer? Why? How is meaning determined in the method you use? Describe as fully as you can the kind of person who prefers to determine meaning in this way." Then I place students in homogenous groups—the New Critics with the New Critics, etc.—and ask them to read their answers to each other. Each group chooses one person to record what is said, particularly each group member's description of the kind of person who might employ a given method.

Students make up some interesting characterizations. But the most important outcome of this activity is that it gives me the opportunity to tell my students that each critical theory can be viewed as a personality type, as a viable role that they might adopt as readers and writers in the class. I also want them to know that they can adopt different personalities at different times, that they need not foolishly stay in character. But I remind them that I do want them to act out various roles until they have found the one they are most comfortable with as a reader and writer. What's more, I stress to students that acting out these roles is crucial to serving themselves as first readers and their peers as critics.

Negotiating Identity in the Workshop

In recent years, I have found it useful to make an audio recording of an early workshop session and critique it with my students during the following class period. Through these tapes, various identifiable personalities come forward, and students seem to actively negotiate identities as readers and writers. One such tape recording follows, a discussion of a poem by Kate. My goal in analyzing this workshop session is, first, to suggest that these students, after having been taught several literary-critical methods for reading and evaluating each other's poems as literary texts, are especially well-qualified workshop participants. Second, I want to show that as students interact with each other through these reading methods, they are at the same time negotiating roles in the classroom. Indeed, the tape shows students trying out one personality after another, proving and broadening Brooke's (1991) conclusion that "the ways they [position] themselves in relation to the available roles of student and writer [determine] their learning" (81). The fact that students shifted from one role to another, as I have already pointed out, is agreeable to me. I have come to believe that such shifts in the personalities students adopt as readers and writers are necessary if learning is to take place.

I have intentionally included some discussion that might seem irrelevant. These exchanges between students, sometimes coarse and often more related to the people involved than to the poem, are actually vital indicators that something is happening to the identities of workshop participants. Brooke describes this behavior as "underlife": "patterns of behavior which show that individuals resist aspects of the assigned role, that there is more to them than this" (74). Brooke, drawing on the work of sociologist Erving Goffman, distinguishes "contained underlife," which might be seen as a natural part of classroom interaction since it provides comic relief, and "disruptive underlife," which is an effort to undermine interaction in the classroom altogether and bring about change.

On the next several pages, I have included Kate's poem, a transcript of the workshop discussion of the poem with my comments interspersed, and an examination of the various roles students play, reflecting both their critical approach to Kate's poem as well as the personality that using that approach requires them to negotiate.

[*Kate reads her poem*]

A Lovely Dream

I was a nymph, a dryad,
clad in black tights,
sinew and skin. Legs
flexing with easy power,
I danced on the table
in the kitchen,
up and down the circling
staircase. Pirouettes on one foot,
three, four consecutively,
my hair fanned out around my head
like a Maypole as I spun.
Gravity had pardoned me,
giving me immunity.
Young men in navy blazers
gazed at the gazelle in black tights.

When one drew near
I stopped to talk.
A lizard's tongue darted
out of my mouth, shaking spit.
I saw the backs of blazers
and well-trimmed shaven napes
gather around my undemanding,
easy-going sister. She offered
me no veal from the buffet.
I did not like the way
this dream was going, swam
out of the manor's hall
until I was inches from being home.
I turned over in my blanket.

From just beneath the surface
of sleep, I heard something not from
the banquet room.
It was a shhh shhh sound
like the old Edge Shaving Cream commercial
with the credit card flicking across
the man's cheek
or like feet brushing over
my carpet. My eyes
snapped open. I could feel
the displaced air. Someone was there.
I am lying on my stomach,
my face half way in the pillow,
turned away from the bedroom door.
Shhh shhh. The sound approaches
the bed. Perhaps only a burglar.
He only wants to steal my jewelry.
I don't move, hardly breathe,
pretend to be asleep.
shhh shhh
Closer. Oh God. It's not
just a burglar.
How will I fight?
Go for the eyes,
I remember daddy said once at dinner
between bites of rice-a-roni.
Easy for him. No fear.
Why be afraid if you're not a target?
More hunters turn up for doe season.
I will fight somehow. But first
I wait and listen.

I can hear breathing.
Does he have a gun
or a knife

or just his bare hands?
My unblinking eyes
look on the floor
and see nothing.
Pause. Then a thud in my ears.
Air rushing around my head.
The bed frame rocks.
I leap up, turn around,
my hair flying from my head
like a Maypole. There is nothing.
I run to the switch. Light
erupts in silence. Furniture,
papers, empty space. I check
the livingroom. Two startled cats
squinting and blinking.
No one in the kitchen.
The closet empty.
Behind the shower curtain,
only the dripping faucet.
I go back to bed
after checking the deadbolt.

Dawn eavesdrops through my window.
Under my quilt, head on pillow,
hair spread out like a fan,
I lie quietly,
a ragdoll to be flung into a corner.
The clock blinks 5:59 a.m.
and I am alone.

[*Discussion ensues*]

PB: Thanks for reading your poem, Kate.

Kate: Excuse my dramatic interpretation.

Lee: It's in the poem, Kate.

PB: Comments?

Mary: Did this really happen?

Kate: Yeah. It was a dream within a dream.

Mary: A story within a story.

Lee: Yeah, or "the invisible man."

Kate: I dreamt that I woke up—this is something that really
    happened—I dreamt that I woke up and someone was in
    my room and then I really woke up.

Lee: How do you know?

Kate: Because there was no one there when I woke up.

Lee: So that's why you were annoying in philosophy class?

[*Some laughter*]

PB: Okay, let's focus on the poem. What comments do you have?

Lee: I like the narrative.

Janet: Your dad and rice-a-roni.

PB: You liked the specific reference to commercials?

Lee: There's a lot of humor in it. I mean . . .

Mary: I think she should submit it to a *USA Today*.

[*Commentary: Right from the start certain interactions are made, primarily between Kate and Lee. Kate finds it necessary initially to establish her ownership of the text and the credibility of her narrative. She points out that this is her real experience and that only she knows exactly what happened.*

Lee provides a healthy dose of underlife, perhaps to break the ice since the first element of discussion comes from the author herself, or perhaps because he is uncomfortable with his role as commentator/evaluator of Kate's poem, or even because (as it seems later) he is uncomfortable with the subject of her poem. To assuage these feelings, Lee establishes a prior relationship with Kate by referring to her alleged behavior in philosophy class, making a connection not just outside the poem, but outside the class itself.

The course instructor, PB, attempts to refocus efforts on the poem, not the unrelated discourse. The discussion continues.]

Joe: There's a lot of bite to it. A lot of these things have an impact . . . in their exposing not only the way women have to deal with men, but with the way men view women.

Mary: And in this poem, the threat of being raped . . .

Joe: The threat? The threat? Not only the threat of being raped . . .

Kate: But the way the world glosses it over.

Joe: Yeah. Exactly.

Angel: Aren't men afraid in the night, too, when they're alone sometimes?

Joe: Not of being raped.

Lee: No. Not real men.

[*General laughter and a man yelling "Oh! She's comin' in!"*]

Joe: Actually, rape is not funny. It's not a sexual act. It's an act of violence.

Kate: Right.

Jim: I think you should create more . . . more images of it. You kind of glossed over it too. I thought you really needed some kind of a threat.

Kate: What do you mean? Like actually should have been somebody there?

Jim: No, no. I'm saying, if you're trying to really show that fear, I think you should probably portray it more fully.

Kate: I was thinking the whole poem portrayed that fear.

PB: Talk about that. What prevented you from getting that fear, Jim?

Jim: Um. Perhaps the laughter in the room when Kate read— you know, the Edge commercial and the rice-a-roni. I mean, maybe it was just the word choice there. Maybe it's too wordy. Maybe cut down on the words?

Joe: I thought the details and objectivity distanced the speaker from us and from the event. . . . [*addressing Kate*] It was al- most like you were giving a statement to the police. You know, first this happened, then this, then this . . . in a timid kind of voice, . . . intimidated, or something.

Jim: I think you need some more verbs that are fear-provoking. Well, have that kind of tingling edge to them.

[*Commentary: Students seem more involved now in discussing the poem. Joe plays several roles in this early portion of the workshop. At first he offers a deconstructive analysis of what's not included, exactly, in the poem. Later he refocuses the class after Lee's interruption. Joe seems to have information that he wants to explain to people.*

Jim enters the discussion with text-based commentary, offering observations about word choice and imagery, in the belief that the poem might be more exciting, fear-provoking, if there were better description.

Kate takes an intentionalist perspective in discussing her poem, not yet comfortable with the fact that her poem is under scrutiny. The workshop continues.]

Andy: I thought that it wasn't even real fear. It was that every- thing was said to this person—the man that didn't come home all night long. It's all full of examples of what he missed and what he put her through, and like, there's promised rewards and stuff of what he'll get if he comes home. And then she's comparing herself to a ragdoll thrown into a corner. . . . And then, "every single woman" sort of signifies that because by saying she's single—she's unmarried—he doesn't really have to come over . . .

Joe: But it also implies that every woman, that every *single* one, goes through this fear.

Andy: Well, I didn't look at it that way.

Angel: I didn't necessarily see it that way either.

PB: Go ahead, Angel.

Angel: I don't know that it necessarily dealt with the rape idea. At the beginning, I saw the speaker's resentment toward her sister. That contributed to developing the individuality of the speaker herself as being different from her sister and preferring it that way. But I think she experiences this fear of being alone *because* she's different.

Scott: I don't know. Maybe there's too much focus on the hair, making these two women sound like the same woman.

Angel: Aren't they different?

Scott: I think they're the same person. I mean, I wasn't focusing on Kate's beautiful, bright hair . . .

[*Laughter*]

Joe: If you're trying to get to fear, that could be a nice way to deal with it. Use the hair image, but . . .

Mary: . . . getting [the hair] pulled back . . .

[*Commentary: Andy challenges the thus far agreed-upon interpretation of the poem, that it is a poem about a woman's fear of rape. Andy's point is that this poem is spoken to the absent husband-lover who left this woman alone. Later Andy will return to this interpretation after he has thought it out more thoroughly.*

Joe takes the role of moderator here. Sensing that others agree with the original interpretation, Joe offers some further explanation to Andy, trying indirectly to get Andy to agree that the poem is about fear. But before he can develop his line of reasoning, Andy undermines further discussion by stating quite simply, "I didn't look at it that way," echoing one tenet of reader-response methodology, that we read in terms of our experiences. If Joe's and Andy's experiences are different, then they will read differently. When Angel lends her support to Andy, PB asks for clarification.

Scott's examination takes us back to the text, to the image of hair repeated in both sections of the poem. Before Scott can make serious recommendations to Kate, he kids with her. Several students go on to suggest how the poem might be fixed.]

Scott: [*addressing Kate*] You have a contrast here between a very feminine quality—that's when you're dancing— and that fear that has to accompany that quality [independence] that you so want to possess. The fear has to accompany that. I mean, what do you do when you dance like that with a guy?

[*General "ooh"-ing here*]

Joe: Well, that really isn't the point . . .

Scott: [*addressing Kate*] Well, I know what your theory is about being a woman in reality. To achieve equality you must almost become a man. I think that you're using that . . . that came across really clear, feminine submissiveness is something that you have to be cautious of . . . or this fear is generated by . . .

Janet: . . . by being feminine? being who you are?

PB: Jon.

Jon: [*addressing Kate*] Sticking strictly to the poem, if you're trying to develop fear quickly, the middle stanza on the third page has all the qualities you need, I think: "the thud of my ears, / Air rushing around my head, / The bed frame," etc. And then a little further down the page, "the light erupts." That kind of jogs you right there. The shortness of those little passages. But I don't know . . . when you talk about "Dad eating rice-a-roni" that doesn't strike fear in my heart.

PB: Okay, what does that do for the tone of the poem? Is that what you're responding to, Jon, the tone? Does the rice-a-roni and the reference to the Edge commercial and the credit card, and returning to that three or four times . . . what does that do for you in terms of your feelings as you read the poem?

Jon: Obviously, it isn't ironic, but it brought out almost an amusing, a light sort of quality, and then you realize at the end that it was serious and it didn't have that serious impact that I thought it needed. But that third stanza, that did it . . . by then it was too late for me. I was hooked into the events that unfolded.

[*Commentary: Scott attempts to introduce yet another way of reading Kate's poem, one influenced if not by his sensitivity to feminist issues, then by his awareness from other dealings with Kate of her particular views as a woman. Scott's portion of the discussion is still characterized to a certain extent by participation in "contained underlife."*

Joe attempts once again to explain the earlier view, but Scott interrupts him, since Scott's prior information about Kate's beliefs gives him what he believes to be greater insight into the poem than others without that information might have.

Jon, who has patiently awaited his chance to speak, is called upon and does what he promises by sticking to the text in his response. Jon quotes directly from the text in making his point.

PB again assumes the role of director and clarifier by calling on students and restating what has thus far been said. Discussion ensues.]

Angel: I want to know if the fear is actually what you were trying to get to, because I didn't see the fear as being the point of the poem. And I'm asking you, Kate, was that what you were trying to get across, because everybody's going on about the fear aspect and I saw the poem as focusing on development of the individual herself.

Kate: Yeah. I didn't really have the fear thing in mind for . . .

Mary: I mean, if you aren't really, really afraid you might be trying to make light of it. I mean, she's already woken up, and there was nothing there, so . . .

Lee: No, I disagree . . .

Angel: I want to know why everybody's skipping over the whole first part of the poem. I mean, I really do. There's some . . .

Lee: If you'd shut up and let people talk . . .

[*Some laughter*]

PB: Well, Lee, why don't we let Angel talk first about that part of the poem, and then you?

Angel: I did [talk about the first part of the poem]. I thought I did. Okay, the first part of the poem is about being an individual. . . . She's being who she is: when she opens her mouth, "A lizard's tongue / darted out" and whatever. But the sister is undemanding and the guys go for her. I saw that [the sister] as being an individual but lacking . . . not having that aloneness that being an individual . . . that you have when you're an individual, sometimes. And how that sometimes goes against what you wanted most to achieve, but you've got to be who you are. But then she goes on . . . the sister thing . . . and she didn't like the way things were going in the dream. I wanted to hear more discussion of that first part, but everybody just went completely to the part in the bedroom and overlooked the first section . . .

Lee: Hey, that's the dirty part!

[*Commentary: Certain roles in the workshop are becoming clearer. Earlier, Andy's interpretation divided the class. Since that interpretation, Joe has had trouble being heard. And Kate has chosen to sit silently, letting others interpret her poem.*

Now Angel offers a restatement of her earlier view and addresses Kate again, asking for Kate to make a statement of intention. Mary (sitting beside Kate at the seminar table) answers for Kate.

Lee continues to supply underlife. Interestingly, though Lee's participation has revealed "contained" underlife, his response to Angel that she "shut up and let people talk" is dangerously near "disruptive" underlife. As a result, PB intervenes and Angel voices some dissatisfaction about the direction discussion has taken.]

PB: Yeah, go ahead, Joe.

Joe: I thought it was a part of setting up the exploitation and stereotyping important to the poem. It seems like the whole time the characters are being exploited by the media, and Kate gives us representations of how people should look. [*addressing Kate*] You know, you're a dryad and the guy with the Edge commercial, and that's such a man . . . that's how we want to look. And you're the nymph and you even talk like a nymph. Then we go to your sister and, well, she must not be a lady. She can dance like one, but she's not and . . . it's setting up . . . it seems to me like it's setting the stage for this something that's about to happen.

Lee: Jon, you don't like the shhh, shhh thing, but I thought that was kind of a nice . . .

Jon: Use of onomatopoeia.

Lee: Well, no. I was going to say that that's something that Kate would have written. But let me rephrase that and say it's a nice image of maleness and sort of subtly . . . well, in general, that is strictly associated with males. When you see girls running around with credit cards on their legs and so . . .

Kate: Well, if I rubbed my legs together, I could start a fire.

Lee: Please don't.

Mary: Just try and stop her.

[*Laughter*]

PB: So, is this poem about personalities, about specific female personalities?

Angel: I think that maybe she's dealing more exclusively with herself and her individuality and that sort of thing, and then you skip completely to this dream within a dream and have this other something totally different. The first one's maybe the fear of being who she is and then maybe resentful of her sister and then it goes to just fear in general.

Andy: The sister is representative of her faithfulness to this man that didn't show up. That's what the sister is. She's saying, "Look, man, they're messing with me because I was looking good, and I stuck out my tongue and drove them away because you're the one I want, but you're still not here. . . . "

PB: Andy, so wait. I mean, just to clear things up—you don't see this as a potential rape?

Andy: Not at all. Through this whole fear thing, she's saying "What if something had happened and you weren't here?

I was very scared, I was by myself, I couldn't sleep."
That's what she's saying: "I need a man with me."

Angel: . . . Kate, tell me what you were trying to say. What
was your intention . . . ?

Andy: [*reading as Angel addresses Kate*] . . . "I lie quietly, / a
ragdoll to be flung into a corner." And you're still not
home.

[*Commentary: Joe addresses the text from a sociopolitical perspective,
focusing on the subversion effect of ads on our views of men and
women.*

*Lee makes an effort to redeem himself after his disruptive intrusion
earlier by asking Jon a question related to Joe's observation. Lee takes
the opportunity to make a response more appropriate to the environment. Perhaps in response to this effort (and a signal, perhaps, that Lee
has been given an identity in this workshop), Kate introduces some
humor that others follow up on.*

*Andy and Angel have not yet been convinced that their interpre-
tations of the poem are incorrect and forward those views, now better
developed, once again. So overlapping are their alternative views of the
poem that they seem to work in tandem: Angel explains as Andy reads
from the text.*]

Kate: You know, Andy, it's funny that you see that. When I
first wrote the poem . . . when she woke up, and she thinks
she hears the guy in there, I was going to make a reference
to the fact that her boyfriend wasn't there with her. And at
first, when she heard the noise, she thought it was her boyfriend because he wasn't there with her. And then I
thought, "Wait a minute; I don't want that there." I want
to take away the fact that the guy should be there to make
her safe. I didn't want that in there.

Lee: Strike another blow for feminism.

Mary: Yeah . . . Andy just kind of got it by mistake . . .

[*Laughter*]

Andy: That was reverse sexism!

Mary: That [reverse sexism] was a wonderful part of the
poem, I think. The veal, and the buffet, and the shaven
neck, . . . um, blue blazers. And I love it about . . .

Angel: Yeah, those are great details.

Dennis: I think it dehumanizes men to call them veal.

Mary: [*continuing*] . . . the light erupting, and . . .

PB: People are responding here, Kate, to the first page, the sexist treatment of men that sets up the sexist view of women.

[*Commentary: Kate comes across as intentionalist in her response to Andy's interpretation. She says to Andy, "Funny you should see that . . ." and goes on to explain that though Andy has shown considerable insight, she decided against explicitly leaving a boyfriend or lover in the poem to protect the woman. Nonetheless, one must assume that clues enough were left in the poem for Andy to reach his conclusions about it.*

Kate's statement of intention gave cause to considerable underlife concerning male-female relationships, which had already been given some attention earlier in the workshop. Interestingly, this discussion, which began playfully, developed into a serious concern about sexism in the poem. Mary sees as "wonderful" descriptions that Dennis believes "dehumanize men." This is Dennis's entry into the workshop, and he challenges the direction of discussion. PB again clarifies the issue and tries to get Kate, instead of Mary, to respond to Dennis's concerns.]

Angel: I liked the first page because it was dealing more so . . . it showed more of the person . . . it showed more of the inside of the speaker and part of the scenery than part of the sounds and the lights even though I liked some of the things you described on the later sections.

PB: Okay, Angel. Did you like the imagery?

Angel: . . . the lizard's tongue, the Maypole, the dancing, that helps develop a persona. And that's what I liked about it. And the other parts didn't, I think, blend well.

Mary: There's something threatening in her sexuality.

PB: In the first section of the poem?

Mary: You get the woman as powerful and then you go on to the woman as powerless. And both of them are kind of like the way it has to be: either she's in control because of sex, or else, if it's a physical kind of control, she has none at all. And the thing about her talking—it doesn't matter. What you say, what you think, doesn't matter. You know? It's not going to get you out of here. I really felt that way.

Lee: I also wondered if one of the young men looking at her at the beginning . . . if one of them is what kind of comes after her at the end or if that's somehow . . . you understand what I'm saying . . . if that's somehow related to the second dream?

Kate: Not specifically. . . . That's not the way it was in my mind. They are the big consumers. Yeah, they are the *male role*. But, see, they are dangerous. Maybe I should bring that in. One of them follows me while I stir around the room. That'd be interesting.

Lee: That's just the thing I got, you know, that's kind of . . . that's what it starts out with—the men—and she's kind of dancing around and . . . I don't know, for some reason it reminded me of . . . what was that movie with Jodie Foster in it? I mean where she was dancing. It had nothing to do with what she was trying to do, but it got her in trouble. And that's just what, you know, when the guy shows up in the dream at the end, that's the first thing that was suggested to me . . . that one of those young men had decided to come and say hello.

Mary: That's a lovely euphemism!

[*Commentary: Angel changes the direction of the discussion, away from a male-female dispute and back to the poem. When asked if she likes the imagery, she reinforces her earlier assessment of the poem's first section and points out imagery she prefers over the other parts (those Mary identifies as "wonderful").*

Angel's response brings from Mary a serious feminist interpretation of the poem, spoken with a tone of authority unheard from Mary earlier. Lee, now with similar serious intent, offers another observation about the males in the poem. Kate wants people to see the poem on a larger level, with the men as symbols of the male role.

Lee continues to draw from outside experiences by perceptively comparing the scene in the poem with the scene in a Jodie Foster movie. The conflict between Mary and Lee continues. PB again refocuses discussion in what follows.]

PB: Well, it's an interesting concept that you had, Kate, of letting one of the men follow you from one dream into the next. I think that's interesting. Do you want to work on that?

Kate: But I think that would be too easy. It would give away the fact that the second dream is a dream. I didn't want to give that away until the end. But, the thing about the commercial and how things are mundane or ordinary in a frightening situation is because people will do that . . . people will think of the dumbest things when they're in a dangerous situation. And I just kind of want that to be there.

PB: Well, what it did for me was it relieved a little bit of the pressure. You were building some pressure here and this was like a relief valve. You know, your dad eats rice-a-roni.

Lee: I mean, it's the San Francisco treat.

[*General hysteria*]

[*Commentary: Prior to Lee's interruption, Kate engaged in a very interesting negotiation of her identity as author of the poem. Much of her reaction at this point in the workshop is an effort to assert ownership of her poem. She justifies her use of commercials because this is what, to her way of thinking, really happens when people are in threatening situations.*

When PB suggests that she could work on connecting the two parts of her poem, she claims that such a connection will make the poem "too easy." This is an important moment in the development of her identity as writer. Rather than insisting that such a connection will improve the poem (since it will only improve the poem as the teacher reads it), it is important for a teacher to back off. To that end, PB offers a reading protocol. In effect, he says, this is how I read those commercials. In the end, the goal for the teacher is to support the emerging writer's identity.]

PB: Kate, what do you want us to talk about with regards to the poem that we haven't spoken about?

Mary: I was just gonna say I thought this was good because if these conservative guys in blue blazers that see women as products or objects of beauty and she [the poem's persona] draws them in. They set standards in a capitalist society.

[General grumbling from the men]

Kate: They're the ones that make the rules. Madison Avenue, you know?

Joe: It's not just the men in blue blazers. There are a lot of women out there too.

Kate: All I wanted to know with this poem was that nobody was bored.

PB: Oh look it, Kate, your poems are never boring.

Kate: And if the language sounded bland. I was kind of worried about that. Sometimes I slip into that.

[Commentary: The effort continues in this section of the workshop for people to more firmly establish their identities in relation to the text and to each other. PB continues to reinforce for Kate her ownership of her poem. Lee and Mary continue to confront from different vantage points their orientation to the feminist issues raised by the poem. Kate becomes increasingly vocal.]

Angel: I want to tell you that I wasn't very clear on the second, the dream, ending, especially when she got up and unlocked the deadbolt. The poem wasn't clear there about her realizing it was a dream and that nobody was there. I wasn't really clear on that. I guess now I think that a person had been there and then left. I just wasn't clear on the dream ending.

Kate: I didn't think that. The way it happened was that when I had that dream, I woke up at five o'clock in the morning thinking that someone was in my house. I woke up the second it happened and I was so frightened I couldn't go back to sleep. So I stayed up for an hour. And *I wrote it all down,* and that was the first draft of this poem. Then later on, as I was telling Rick [her boyfriend] about it, he said, "You were dreaming." I said, "Oh my God, there's a ghost in my house." And he goes, "No, you were just dreaming that you woke up and that it happened." And after a while and I was thinking about it and I said, "Yeah, I guess that's what happened."

Angel: See that's why I couldn't tell if . . . see even you didn't know.

Lee: Yeah, if she couldn't tell, you couldn't either.

PB: Kate, anything else?

Kate: Well, I wanted to know if not knowing whether it was a dream or not was good or bad. You know, if it's a mystery at the end.

Angel: I kind of liked not knowing, because I actually thought that maybe somebody was there.

Lee: Yeah.

Angel: That was my interpretation.

Kate: Yeah, because I kinda wanted the feeling that it lingers and kind of follows you everywhere. And you can't get out of that feeling that there's someone there. That works better than just saying "Oh, it's a dream."

[*Commentary: In this portion of the workshop, Angel's role solidifies. She prefers the first section of the poem still, but now voices what in the second section she is confused about, insisting that more clarification needs to be given there. Kate continues to assert ownership of her poem. The fact that very few others are commenting at this point underscores either that they have said all they want to say or that they have begun to view Kate as the authority over her poem.*]

Kate: [*addressing PB*] What do you think?

PB: What do I think?

Kate: Yeah.

PB: I would like to know that it's a dream. I would like that clearer. Because I think that that way you can really work on the connections between the two dreams. That will free you to do that a little bit, and I think that you have a point that you want to make and I think that by clarifying the dream, that'll give you the opportunity to do that as well. Thank you for asking. You're the only person all semester who asked me for my opinion. Besides "Did you like it?"

[*Commentary: This is an interesting exchange between Kate and the teacher. In it, Kate relinquishes control momentarily, and the teacher offers an overall assessment of what he believes needs to be done: that she needs to connect the two dreams and free herself to work on subtly incorporating the message others have referred to throughout the session. And while the teacher's final remark is an example of underlife, it also signals for everyone in the workshop that various roles are possible besides the traditional role of examinee-examiner.*]

Mary: Okay. I have one question. I have a question to the male audience. Was this poem interesting to you or were you like "Oh God, another one of these heartsick babes?"

PB: [*to Kate*] Do you want just a male response?

Kate: Yeah, I want to see if it makes any impact on a guy because of course a woman's going to respond.

PB: Let's talk a little bit more about that. Do you think that a woman is going to respond differently?

Lee: You have to.

Kate: Yeah, I think that a woman's going to identify with that and I just want to know . . . I mean, I don't want the poem to just be for women. I want them . . . I want men to be able to relate to it too.

Lee: If you want men to have some concept of . . .

Kate: Because what is the main reason women live with fear is that men don't have any concept of the way they [women] feel.

Scott: So it's more informative [for men]?

Kate: Well, I think it's for both. I'm not making any decisions.

Lewis: I read the poem two ways. It had the impact, the serious impact, for me to feel what you were trying to come across with. I mean, I don't know. I read that and to me it was more of an ironic reading of the simple fact that here was a woman in the first dream who was very aggressive in her sexuality and in the second dream here was the same woman who was fearing sexuality. You know, the brutal or aggressive sexuality of the man, and . . .

Joe: Rape isn't sexual; it's a crime of violence. There's nothing sexual about it.

Lewis: You have to see what I'm saying . . .

Kate: Yeah, I do. But she's not fearing her *own* sexuality.

Lewis: Okay, but this was male aggression coming out, especially if you're reacting to the male actually coming up to her. As I saw it, but . . .

Hal: It's okay for a woman to be aggressive, but not for a man?

Mary: Well, if you're going to be aggressive and rape somebody . . . come on!

Joe: I don't think we're talking about that.

Lewis: I'm not necessarily saying that rape is sexual. I'm saying that these are the two aggressions coming out, that
here were the two roles and it was the reversal of the
two—here she is in one sense and then turning right
around when something was very likely to occur . . .

Lee: It's not an exact reversal of roles. And also . . . I'm sorry,
but . . .

Lewis: And very often that is, to men, that if a woman is out
sexually, being sexually aggressive, or that she's asking for
it. And this is what I saw happening when I read it. But
that I guess what I'm saying that the sense with the commercials and everything and I don't know if it was the simple laughter coming from over here that broadened it so
much. Because I didn't really laugh the first time I read it,
until, you know, she made a joke and then it seemed hu-
morous to me, but . . .

[*Commentary: The initial effort in this section of the workshop is for
the teacher to return the authority to Kate. Though Mary says she
wants to know how the males in class respond to the poem, the teacher
makes certain that's what Kate wants to find out and then redirects the
conversation toward a discussion of theory: Will males by necessity
read the poem differently than females?*

*Lewis enters the discussion for the first time, offering his analysis
(in response to Kate's request that males discuss their reaction to her
poem). And as though just because he hadn't said anything so far he
must have missed the flow of conversation, Joe and Lee offer the
previously agreed-upon guidelines within which Lewis is to offer his
interpretation of the poem.*]

PB: One response that I have—something I really like—is that
I think that the first dream, the very first dream is one extreme; the rape scene, which is another extreme; and then
there's the wake-up scene, which is neither of the two.
And that works effectively for me because I think that
you're characterizing two things here that are worthy of
characterization.

Dennis: I want to talk about something. I want to give my response and it borders on what you're saying. The lovely
dream in the first part sucked immensely. I was like "Oh
yeah, I wanna read this." And even where we had the lizard's tongue, I saw that as her being in charge, powerful,
and I thought "Oh, that's okay with me, let's keep going
here." Then the next thing I thought is "Ah shit, we got a
rape here. All right, I'll suffer through a rape." But then it

turned into a dream, and I thought "Oh, good." And the cats blinking their eyes, and I thought "That's wonderful!" Yeah, I'm like "Great! I don't want to read another poem where the woman has her body dismembered."

Lewis: I liked this poem because I really kept expecting that this happened to be in the bedroom when she was back and I really expected this person to still be there. Or for her to even wake up—literally wake up—and him be there . . .

Kate: And just stop it there?

Angel: Maybe the fact that they were fearful of . . . or that you thought the persona was gonna get raped is showing them that our everyday fear is that we're going to get raped even though ninety-nine percent of the time, it might not happen. But still, that fear is still there regardless if it happens or not . . .

Kate: Especially when you're walking home at 9:30 at night . . .

Angel: . . . and the fact that she might and it's still showing you the fear is there.

PB: That's why the title is so effective, I think.

Kate: What were you going to say, Lee?

Lee: Well, I was just going to answer your question from way back, and say that it was an interesting poem . . . from a male point of view. Well, from a male point of view, but, I mean, I wasn't sure in reading it whether you were trying to address a male audience specifically and show them what it would be like to have that fear.

Kate: Did you feel like I was attacking you?

Lee: No. I mean I didn't think it was predatory. I felt the tension, obviously, that everything else. . . . You're trying to show the male audience what a rape is like, but that's not what it came across as to me. If that's what you're trying to do. I got the tension and sort of what you were saying—you know, you're relieved when it's a dream and you're kind of like "Wait, is she going to open the closet, and there he is . . . ?" But, you know, if you were trying to portray for a man what a rape would be like, if you [he] were the victim, then I wanted something more.

[*Commentary: The session closes out with a sense of summary. The males continue to assert their "maleness," as Kate urged, by offering their responses to the poem. The tone of Dennis's reaction is authoritative. Lee and Kate disagree about what the poem means but do so in a way that reinforces identities established early in the workshop.*]

Kate: Okay. Let's go on to the next dead mule.

Lee: I'm filibustering because the next one's mine.

PB: Nice job everyone. Lee, would you read your poem for us?

The students explore a variety of roles in this workshop. And the range is far greater than this tape recording indicates, since we never hear from three members of the class who are present. For purposes of analysis, though, let's take each of the theories discussed with this class during the term—New Criticism, reader-response criticism, deconstruction, and feminist criticism—and see how students tend to align themselves in the workshop with one or more.

Kate is from the start the authority on matters pertaining to her poem. From the outset, she functions from an intentionalist perspective, indicating what she intended and showing how her accomplishment matched her intention. Kate seems well aware of the fact that any changes made to her poem will be made because *she* wants to make them, not because anyone else in the room wants her to do so. A wonderful example of this is her verbal exchange with the teacher, who, having correctly read that she was considering changing her poem, recommended that she go ahead and do so. Not only did she prefer not to make those changes once the teacher suggested that she might, but she felt that to do so would make her poem "too easy." Still, in a matter of minutes, she returned authority to her teacher by asking him what he thought of her poem.

Despite her strong sense of ownership over her poem, Kate experimented, as far as she was able, with other possible roles. In fact, she sat silently for the large middle portion of the workshop. But when she did relinquish control, Kate's friend Mary seemed to take up defense of the poem as a kind of surrogate authority—both as Kate's friend and as a woman sympathetic to the subject of the poem.

Mary is clearly the spokesperson in this discussion for the feminist perspective, one clearly necessary if the workshop is to usefully address the special issues raised by Kate's poem. Mary negotiates this identity in a very interesting manner. Before seriously addressing the issues that she must address in this workshop, Mary acts out contained underlife. She describes as "wonderful" descriptions of men as veal, as wearing blue blazers, as having the napes of their necks shaved. Then, when a male member of the class objects, she takes a much more serious role, pointing out intelligently the very issues Kate would want readers to confront.

In addition to orienting herself to the class through a feminist stance, Mary reinforces much that Joe offers from a sociopolitical perspective. Joe seems to have information he wants to share with others. This approach to the workshop seems to suggest that by providing readers in the class with information they did not have before, Joe can change the way they read Kate's poem. Repeatedly, however, certain students less comfortable with the workshop situation (Lee and Andy) interrupt Joe. Nonetheless, when Joe is heard, he makes excellent observations about commercials and how they influence our perceptions of ourselves and others. In addition, Joe seems tuned in to the political ramifications of such influences, offering, as Mary and Kate do, information unstated but clearly suggested in the poem.

Lee presents the most interesting instance here of role negotiation. No one in this workshop is more often out of bounds and off the subject than Lee. Right from the outset of our discussion of Kate's poem, Lee attempts to bring irrelevancies into the room, most notably that he and Kate share a philosophy class. What's more, he is the one who provides comic relief. I believe these elements of underlife need to be accepted and contained in the classroom rather than stifled. Yet on two occasions, this underlife was not contained in the workshop: when Lee told Angel to shut up and when he claimed that Mary's view was "another blow for feminism." Peer reaction to Lee's remarks suggested to me that these ways of relating to peers were not acceptable to the group as a whole. Lee must have felt this as well. After each of these occurrences, he seemed to more seriously attend to the poem, offering an interesting reading and truly engaging with Kate in an exchange of perspectives on the role of men in the poem. Lee's negotiation required him to exhibit that he is, after all, not contained by this workshop or by the identities available to him in the course. This same display of underlife, however, required him to take on an identity of one who, as a reader, shares in the making of the poem. After his two disruptive interventions, the alternative might have been exclusion from discussion altogether.

Andy and Angel play the roles of challengers in the class. Both offer strikingly different views of the poem, alternative interpretations that they want the others to deal with. Andy's view arises from a close reading of the text. When he discusses the poem, he cites specific lines and offers his view of their meaning. Angel insists that more attention needs to be paid to the first section of the poem. Late in the workshop, she seems to voice disappointment that the others have not looked at that section more closely and examined it as she would want them to. Both of these readings reflect New Critical emphases, not just because the comments are text-based, but also because these students expected others to read the same passages they had and reach the same conclusions.

I am also interested in the variety of ways authority is offered in the classroom. Dennis and Lewis offered their observations only after Mary and Kate asked the men to respond to the poem. And when they did respond, they did so from their authority less as readers and writers than as men. That, after all, was what they were asked to do by the other authority in the class, the poem's author.

The workshop provides students with an excellent opportunity to improve as readers and writers, especially if they are given the tools with which to respond to their peers' writing. And as this transcript suggests, students do more than simply voice their views based upon the critical tools they are given. When they adopt a critical perspective for oral exchange in the workshop situation, they are also by necessity negotiating their identities. We need to remember that we read the world by using the same tools of perception, the same lenses, that we use when we read a poem. Once this point is clear, we will be better equipped to develop our curriculum based on adapting critical theory to the evaluation of student poems.

Appendix: Sample Syllabus

Course Purpose

Only recently have theorists considered how a course in poetry writing should be taught. As a result, one of the purposes of this course will be to explore how to create an environment, intellectual as well as emotional and physical, in which the traditional method of instruction—most often called the workshop or studio method—might work best for student-writers.

In this course we will make every effort to enable students to improve their writing skills by helping them become better craftpersons, better critics of each other's works, and better judges of what constitutes poetry—and, if possible, good poetry—in 1992, while at the same time recording and examining methods employed in achieving these lofty goals. In short, the overriding purpose in this course is for us to take an excursion together, with each of us, in the final analysis, determining our own destination.

Course Objectives

During the term, students will be asked to work through a minimum of six poems, two of which (perhaps three, depending on the number of class participants) must undergo workshop scrutiny, done either in direct response to class-based writing activities or outside of class on the writer's own. Two of these poems may be reworkings of earlier efforts, provided they are truly reworkings, as the drafts which must be submitted with final versions in a portfolio at the end of the term will show (see below). Students will also be asked to review a book of poems published within the past ten years. Students must learn how to competently (that is, by basing judgments on something besides opinions and feelings) comment on student and professional writing. Students should also learn:

- how other writers compose poems
- how they themselves compose poems
- what is contemporary in poetry
- what is traditional in poetry
- what the present publishing status is for poets
- how to write and revise craftily
- how to read and evaluate poems
- how to employ methods of literary criticism

Course Procedures

This course will be broken into two parts:

1. Early in the semester, students will be presented four kinds of information as preparation for enlightened discussion during the workshop. First, students will read about the composing process of other writers, especially Richard Hugo, who have written extensively and excellently about writing poems. Second, students will read poems from the text by Smith and Bottoms and discuss the types of poems to be written during the term. Third, students will read materials explaining four critical methods—New Criticism, reader-response criticism, deconstruction, and feminism—as well as demonstrations modeling how these methods of reading may be employed in providing commentary on student poems during the workshop. And fourth, students will be asked to read a wide range of professionally written poems in an effort to view them through each of the critical lenses cited above. This reading has as its goal the preparation of students for active and productive involvement in the workshop that will follow.

2. The second half of the term will be the workshop. A workshop or studio method of instruction involves public scrutiny of works produced by students. In scrutinizing the works systematically, commentators help the author to improve as a writer and themselves to improve as critics. This workshop will differ from other workshops principally in the way students will be prepared for it by means of the kinds of readings done early in the term (see above). What's more, the workshop will be structured so that two kinds of informed comments are made: those that point out a poem's strengths and those that point out how a poem might be improved (as opposed to simply pointing out the poem's shortcomings).

Thursday of each week during weeks 4–7, students must submit two items: a draft of a poem and an answer to the central question in the course, that is,

"What kinds of things would you take into consideration in evaluating a poem?" The instructor will react to both items, making comments on the answer to the question that students should consider in revising their answers. Hopefully, students' answers to the question will evolve over the term to eventually provide the instructor with a list of criteria for use in evaluating the students' portfolios and determining their final grades. The answers to the "course question" should be stapled together, with the most recent answer on top. Some students may be required to turn in the answer after the seventh week if a satisfactory list is not created by then. Our goal is development of a satisfactory checklist, that is, a checklist that reflects an agreement between both the student and the teacher concerning how the student's portfolio drafts will be evaluated and graded.

For additional feedback on your poems, you must make them available for workshop. These poems (tentatively, a minimum of two) must be typed and reproduced clearly, one copy for each class member, including the instructor. Poems to be discussed in class must be available one week in advance. I don't want to mess around with taping someone's poems to my office door!

A typical class will begin with a writing task of some kind, followed by discussion of that task and its relation to the assigned reading. We may work often in both small and large reading/writing groups.

Attendance and Assignment Policy

Students are expected to attend all classes and university-sponsored literary events. If students cannot attend class, they are expected to contact the instructor. Additionally, assignments are due on the set date unless other arrangements are made.

Please do not call me with the most offensive of all questions: "Did we do anything in class?" Instead, make a phone pal today who you can call upon to answer that question.

Workshops will be arranged through a simple sign-up procedure. I will pass around a sheet with the days of workshops designated. We can profitably and sanely discuss perhaps three to four poems in an afternoon. If we find that we can discuss three to four poems and have time left over, other poems can be presented to the class for reactions.

Assignments

1. Portfolio with six poems: All of the drafts of these poems should be turned in at the end of the semester in a folder we will call a portfolio. I will assess each portfolio and comment where necessary using the final checklist in response to the course question (see #4 below) as a basis. Comments on early drafts will come from the instructor in the form of written evaluations using various literary theories, in conference sessions as needed, and in workshop by the entire class. Remember: Four of your poems will be submitted to the instructor with your journal and two will be workshopped by the entire class.

2. Workshop: Failure to workshop two poems will result in a point deduction from your final grade and will no doubt be reflected in the quality of poems submitted in your portfolio.

3. Book review: I will provide you with books to review. These books will be recent publications and, as a result, a strong review might have a chance of finding a publisher.

4. Answer to the course question: If you do not actively and courageously answer the assigned question during weeks 4–7 (or later), you will receive zero points for this portion of the course. However, if you have made an effort at developing a list but are unable to develop a satisfactory one, we will have a conference on that matter alone. If a satisfactory list does not appear forthcoming at that conference, you may opt to have me employ "Bizzaro's Biases" (to be discussed soon) in determining your final portfolio grade.

Percentages of each assignment toward determining a final grade are as follows:

> Portfolio: 50%
>
> Workshop: 15% (on an all-or-nothing basis)
>
> Book review: 30%
>
> Submission of poems on weekly basis: 5% (on an all-or-nothing basis)

Grade scale: Each assignment will be graded based on 100 points. I will then weight the assignments and average them to determine a grade based on 100 points. Then I will apply the following scale:

> 93–100 = A
>
> 84–92.5 = B
>
> 75–83.5 = C

I will use attendance and participation, as I have noted them, to determine grades in the event you are between them. For instance, if you have good attendance and participation, I will increase a high B to an A, a high C to a B, etc.

Texts

Smith and Bottoms, *The Morrow Anthology of Younger American Poets*
Hugo, *The Triggering Town*
handouts

8 Grading Student Poems: Adaptations of the New Criticism and Reader-Response Criticism

. . . teachers need to alter their traditional emphasis on a relationship between student texts and their own Ideal Text in favor of the relationship between what the writer meant to say and what the discourse actually manifests of that intention.

Nancy Sommers, "Responding to Student Writing"

It would be ideal if some instrument could be developed that could measure a writer's capacity for success and then just enough acclaim, money, and praise could be doled out to keep the writer going.

Richard Hugo, *The Triggering Town*

When we grade writing, we imply that students have reached the end of their writing processes. Such a view of the text might hold for papers receiving the highest grades. But if the goal of the writing process is the construction of successful pieces of writing, then we must conclude that papers receiving less than the highest grade are unfinished. As a result, we must reassure students that grades are meant simply to indicate where in the process of

Portions of this chapter first appeared in the following articles and chapters: "Evaluating Student Poetry Writing: A Primary Trait Scoring Model," in *Teaching English in the Two-Year College* 17 (1990): 54–61; "Interaction and Assessment: Some Applications of Reader-Response Criticism to the Evaluation of Student Writing in a Poetry Writing Class," in *The Writing Teacher as Researcher,* ed. Donald A. Daiker and Max Morenberg (Portsmouth, NH: Boynton/Cook, 1990), 256–65; and "Some Applications of Literary Critical Theory to the Reading and Evaluation of Student Poetry Writing," in *Poets' Perspectives: Reading, Writing, and Teaching Poetry,* ed. Charles R. Duke and Sally A. Jacobsen (Portsmouth, NH: Boynton/Cook, 1992), 154–174. Reprinted by permission of the publishers.

writing their texts they have advanced to at that particular point in time called the "deadline."

This view of grading is common in a profession which has not very often gone public on the subject. Though thorough, Wendy Bishop's (1990) summary of research on evaluation, particularly of student poems, reveals just how little has actually been done. And because of the many emotional issues raised by the subject, most of them related to authority in reading the text, we should not be surprised that even less scholarly activity has focused on grading, or that very little of that activity has focused on the grading of student poems, either as individual pieces of writing or as representative "best" pieces in a portfolio.

Developing an All-Purpose Portfolio Guide

Still, the wisest—and most practical—commentator among us on the subject of grading poems is Bishop (1990), who recommends using a combination of portfolio evaluation and response sheets. According to Bishop, this procedure works best if the teacher follows three "practices":

1. Begin a portfolio system by outlining goals for portfolios *as used in that class*, and write a guide that details what is expected from a portfolio in each grading category (A, B, C, etc.).

2. Share this guide (or concepts from the guide) with students during class discussion, in conferences, and in mid-semester evaluation commentary.

3. Use a formalized response sheet . . . for critiquing. By checking off materials received and recording responses *in categories*, teachers are forced to look up from the mass of writing collected and evaluate it as a whole effort. The checklist can include an "improvement" category or a "participation" credit as well as an evaluation of portfolio draft quality. (166)

While Bishop's response sheets seem to shift the emphasis from quality of writing alone to objectifiable matters—such as whether the required assignments have been included in the portfolio—ample space is given over to commentary on the writing itself—"improvement" and "evaluation of portfolio draft quality"—and to classroom-related activities—"participation." When a grade is finally given, it thus seems to measure both the student's willingness to comply with course requirements and the student's success in writing poems. Of course, deriving final grades under this method admittedly relies upon the teacher as sole judge, as the author of the "guide that details what is expected." Indeed, we must remember that teachers develop response sheet checklists to reflect what they value about writing and what they have emphasized during the term.

In developing my own guide for examining poems from the New Critical and reader-response perspectives discussed in this chapter, I wanted to reward the quality of student poems as measured against an agreed-upon list of characteristics. My checklist also reflects my concern that a minimum number of poems be included in the portfolio, that I note which poems are nearest to completion, and that I offer advice on where poems ready for publication might be submitted. Additionally, I think it is important to indicate which poems are furthest from completion and how those poems might be revised once the course has concluded.

The checklist that I developed from these concerns (see figure 8) can be used in adapting either the New Criticism/Primary Trait Scoring model of grading or the reader-response model. I actually use this checklist in both my advanced poetry writing course and my introductory course, though I require fewer poems in the introductory course. I find that by devising a checklist such as this one, I am forced to examine what I value as a teacher of poetry writing and what I have emphasized in my course. As my views on teaching the course change, I will likewise have to change my guidelines.

But there are problems in grading that a response sheet checklist or a set of guidelines does not solve. Judgments concerning grades fuel teachers' emotions. Some teachers believe that the authority in the classroom should belong entirely to the teacher. On the other extreme are those who believe that students should have substantial room to make decisions about their poems, including decisions concerning their grades. By adapting literary-critical theories to the grading of student poetry, we can consider a range of possible answers to the question of authority in the classroom. Individual teachers can then determine which system suits them best.

Among other concerns to consider is the fact that many teachers still favor grading individual pieces of writing when they are due rather than grading the best pieces of writing available in a portfolio, as Bishop recommends, at midterm or at the end of the semester. Since there are advantages to both methods, and since teachers will continue to grade poems by employing one method or the other, this chapter will discuss approaches to both styles of grading.

ENGL 5840: Advanced Poetry Writing
Dr. Patrick Bizzaro
Spring 1991

Evaluation of Portfolio by _____

1. Poems in Relation to Checklist

   A.

   B.

   C.

   D.

   E.

   F.

   G.

   H.

2. Poems Nearest to Completion

3. Where to Submit Poems from #2

4. Poems Furthest from Completion

5. What to Do to Finish Poems Listed in #4

6. Overall Evaluation of Portfolio, Considering 1–5

7. Grade:

Figure 8. Sample response sheet checklist.

In many ways, the models that follow represent the first attempts to publicly adapt theory to the grading of student poems. I am thus inclined to be cautious, reminding myself that the focus of all evaluation, including evaluations that render grades, must be on how the text might continue to be revised. The least we can hope for from our grading procedures is that students will understand how their grades have been determined and why they have received the grades they have. The most we can hope for is that our students will respond to our commentary at the end of the semester as Grace did in chapter 4, that is, by stating their desire to continue to work on their poems even after the semester is over.

Objectifying the Grading of Student Poems

Any method used in grading student poems must meet several objectives. First, it should acknowledge that each individual poem has its own integrity. If we think seriously about what we ask students to do when we call on them to write poems—and here I mean beginning poets of all ages—we must inevitably see that we are asking students to generate texts that represent their current understanding of what constitutes poetry. That understanding may include a wide range of things and certainly will change with new experiences in reading and writing.

Second, any method for grading poetry writing that hopes to guide students in the writing of a less random variety of texts (that is, that influences their understanding of what constitutes poetry) requires considerable interaction during the term between writer and instructor. Interactive techniques for in-process evaluation, such as workshops, conferences, and interactive journals, are often called into service to meet this need. Nonetheless, though each technique offers unique opportunities for influencing student writing, each must be handled carefully, as my experience in interacting with Penney shows (see chapter 3). The goal is not so much to establish hard and fast boundaries as it is to permit what Petrosky (1989) calls "the play of multiple voices and selves" (218). When using workshops, conferences, and interactive journals, instructors should thus approach each poem as a unique entity, with a life, a set of characteristics, and a direction not only different from all other kinds of texts, but from all other poems as well.

Overall, any system used to grade student poems should possess six qualities:

1. It should offer students options as to how they want the final grade for their poems to be determined. Consequently, a teacher should be able to employ more than one method of reading, evaluating, and grading student poems and should be able to explain these options to students.

2. It should reflect semester-long emphases. To this end, teachers should employ the critical methodologies that they have emphasized in examining both student and professional poems during the term, methodologies such as New Criticism, reader-response criticism, deconstruction, and feminist criticism.

3. It should provide criteria agreed upon by both the student and the teacher. This can be accomplished in several ways, all of which require in-process evaluation of writing which enables students to revise before submitting their poems as part of a portfolio.

4. It should apply these criteria either to individual poems or to groups of poems. In consultation with the teacher, students can strive to develop criteria unique to each separate poem or inclusive enough to apply generally to a set of poems written with a unifying goal.

5. It should reward careful revision. Regardless of the system the student chooses and the criteria the teacher and student agree upon, revision must be the goal of all evaluation. This is particularly true of evaluations that accompany grades, especially if we hope to encourage students to continue to write after the course concludes.

6. It should reveal evaluation to be an ongoing activity. Teachers must see poems periodically during the term, not just when they are turned in for grading, so that students will see both evaluation and grading as natural parts of class activities.

Of the four critical methodologies discussed in this book, only New Criticism and reader-response criticism are adaptable as methods for determining grades. Though deconstruction and feminist criticism provide teachers with ways of reading poems, these methods of reading work against the authoritarian notion of grading (though some kind of self-evaluation, as discussed by Bishop [1990, 168–70], might be possible). What follows, then, are efforts I have made at applying New Criticism and reader-response criticism to the grading of student poems.

Method One: Adapting New Criticism and Primary Trait Scoring to the Grading of Student Poems

By treating each text as a unique entity and focusing "attention on just those features of a piece which are relevant to the kind of discourse it is" (Cooper 1977, 11), teachers can make an important connection between the New Criticism and Primary Trait Scoring. In fact, when combined with interactive teaching strategies, this way of evaluating student poems can serve as one of the optional grading methods that students might choose for their poems, provided, of course, that its New Critical emphases are explained and employed during the term. Through a conference with the student, this method establishes agreed-upon criteria that the teacher can then apply either to an individual poem or to poems in a portfolio. Students will thus clearly see how they have been evaluated and why they have received the grade they have. What's more, they will be able to revise, if they so choose, since the method identifies what they have and have not accomplished in a piece of writing.

Grading an Individual Poem Using the
New Criticism/Primary Trait Scoring Method

I studied some uses of this method in my evaluation and grading of a poem by Alvin, a beginning poet in my introductory poetry writing class. The first draft of the poem that Alvin permitted me to see and discuss with him during a conference in my office follows:

Morro Bay

A moon that's endured events before my birth
Casts its timeless beams across my horizon.
Muted sheer beams of mimicked solar fire.
The ocean is my horizon with no words
To lull my thoughts to peace from a distant shore.
Without looking—I know the waves have erased
My footprints as surely as my past troubles.
Remembering the sunlight of today
With its silently roaring shimmering warmth;
The running hand-in-hand with my special someone
Through the reaching fingers of the briny waves—
I kneel down to write a word in the wet sand
As the high rocky walls echo my quiet laugh.
The wind sighs discontent as the waves again
Remove all blemishes from these sands of time.
Soon I've reached a ridge of earth that I know
Is the rendezvous for things that might be,
Morro Rock stands guard thirty yards from shore.

In the day's healing rays, sun-lovers bask
On its benign covertly laughing face—
At night, the Rock's a sleeping behemoth
Tolerating the ocean's vain struggle,
Never ceasing to replace land with water,
My thoughts fly out to the vast audience
Formed by the sparkling stars and stately moon.
And taking my place—I begin waiting.

In conference, Alvin and I agreed that this was a good first draft. The poem confronts with some sophistication a very serious subject that gives rise to the central tension in the poem: a time in the poet's life when he experienced a relationship both tentative and short-lived. To express the strong emotion of this experience, Alvin's poem relies on imagery, indirection, even strong rhythmical lines. All of this adds up to a good discovery draft.

Alvin and I then devised a list of primary traits to guide us in revision and to enable me to grade his poem. I wrote down in the form of contractual agreement the following observations about those guidelines which Alvin and I had agreed upon:

1. It is difficult to write a general poem about the ocean and shore and their relationship to the self. The poem needs to focus on a specific experience which suggests personal distress and recovery.

2. Since the poem is very general, Alvin has fallen back on perceptions that are usual rather than unique. A good example of this tendency is "my past troubles" in line 7. We agreed that in revision Alvin should work on making images that show past troubles rather than tell about them.

3. Similarly, Alvin must avoid clichés of the sort found in greeting cards, such as "my special someone" in line 10.

4. Alvin repeated certain concepts after they had already been suggested. For instance, "timeless" (line 2) repeats "before my birth" (line 1), and "sighs discontent" (line 14) seems redundant.

5. Overmodification, such as "silently roaring shimmering warmth" in line 9, needs to be simplified.

6. Weak modifiers, such as "briny waves" in line 11, need to be strengthened.

Through this conference interaction, Alvin and I were able to treat his poem both as a self-contained entity and as a text that could be revised to more satisfactorily contain the characteristics that we agreed constitute a poem in general and his poem in particular. Specifically,

Alvin agreed to regularize the rhythms of lines, write stanzas to reinforce regularity, use conversational syntax and language, avoid clichés, rework overmodified lines, avoid repetition, and focus on a specific experience at the shore. By the close of our conference, Alvin knew that his grade would eventually be determined by how nearly his revision reflected these suggestions, and I knew exactly what criteria to apply in evaluating and grading that particular piece of writing.

These primary traits reflect Alvin's growing understanding of what constitutes a poem and meet the criteria that I have set for a system suited to grading student poetry. What's more, during their individual conference sessions, I was able to discuss with Alvin and his peers those characteristics of writing typical of their specific poems, thereby preparing them for workshop sessions later in the term.

The revised poem reflects Alvin's effort to responsibly attend to the guidelines generated in conference with me:

Morro Bay

The moon looms as deeply scarred as my heart
Casting timeless beams across my horizon,
Muted sheer rays of mimicked solar fire.
The shoo-wish, shoo-wish of the ocean's waves
Carefully licking at my toes.

Two forms climb Morro Rock—
I kneel down to write a word in the wet sand.
The sighing wind whipping her name from my lips—
I can't even hold her when I'm alone.
Thirty yards from shore stands the benign behemoth.

Although today began like all the rest
We never knew that a shouted "Hello"
Could cause her soul to butterfly away—
A fall so quick the laughter trailed behind.

Tonight the stony dinosaur sleeps deep
Tolerating the ocean's vain efforts,
Never ceasing to replace land with water,
And knowing nothing of my own struggle
To find a way to share laughter again.

In agreeing to use Primary Trait Scoring, I agreed to measure how much Alvin did to improve the poem in accord with the guidelines decided upon in conference by the two of us. Clearly, Alvin is not finished with this poem; while the new version reflects some improvement in specificity and image-making, it has the kinds of new flaws that suggest more work is needed.

In any case, I did not have to approach the task of evaluating Alvin's poem blindly. Nor did I have to evaluate Alvin's poem against some ideal poem—intuitive or otherwise. And by using Primary Trait Scoring, I was able to avoid the tendency to grade Alvin's poem against poems written by other students in the class. I simply returned to the list of primary traits that Alvin and I had agreed upon in conference and determined as best I could how fully Alvin had met the objectives set forth for revising "Morro Bay."

Alvin's poem received a grade of A-. Two points are important to an understanding of how I came to this grade. First, an A- on this poem may be something different from an A- on another of Alvin's poems, or from an A- on a poem written by someone else in the class. Since my goal was to coach Alvin toward the best poem possible as suggested by his early draft, I had to realize that the poem he ultimately produced would necessarily be limited by what he had to work with. In other words, Alvin could only operate within the framework of his first draft. Second, my judgment in giving Alvin a grade within the context of his early draft, all other matters aside, needed to reflect the list of primary traits that he and I had agreed upon. Only then could I feel certain that Alvin had moved his poem as best he could toward a goal that he and I had both agreed was worthy of his efforts. Alvin's grade had to reflect how closely his revised version realized the poem he and I had envisioned and objectified by creating a list of primary traits.

By adapting Primary Trait Scoring to the in-process evaluation and grading of Alvin's poem, I was able to approach the poem as a unique entity, envisioning as I did what that poem might become and sharing in conference with Alvin how the envisioned poem might be written. The final grade is an attempt on my part to reward careful revision and at the same time provide Alvin with both reasons for the grade he received and, if he should be so inclined later, a plan for revising the poem after the course has concluded.

In my dealings with Alvin, I found myself conscious of things I might have done to assuage Penney in my evaluation of her work (see chapter 3). Though I met with both of them in conference, I simply *presented* Penney with a list of criteria by which I would measure her poem. In my interaction with Alvin, however, we reached a compromise which allowed him to feel as though he had some control over the future of his poem. Rather than doing a lot of guesswork, as Penney no doubt did, Alvin had a very clear sense of how to revise. And while Penney must have felt that the grade on her poem would be determined by my personal whim, Alvin knew exactly what would be measured in his revision and had a part in developing that list. He must also have felt some security in knowing that his other efforts would be similarly measured by criteria that respected each work as a unique entity.

Grading a Portfolio Using the New
Criticism/Primary Trait Scoring Method

As I have already said, students are given the opportunity to decide how they want their portfolio to be graded. In addition to employing the primary trait method described above in my work with Alvin, students are free to send the kind of note Grace sent to me:

> Pat,
> I agree with your list of "Bizzaro's Biases" and would like you to evaluate my portfolio according to your criteria. . . . I suppose I want you to use New Critical theory to examine the effect of the text of my poem, reader-response theory for the emotional reactions (if my poems create any reactions), and deconstruction to see how deeply I can go into the poems to find out what I'm not saying and maybe should have said. It could be that later I will find the true poems by using deconstruction.

Grace had a clear notion of how the theories emphasized in my course might be applied in reading and evaluating her poems, but opted for "Bizzaro's Biases" (see chapter 2) as much out of concurrence as out of a sense of difficulty in reaching some conclusions on her own about her poems. Using "Bizzaro's Biases," then, I wrote up a response sheet checklist evaluating and grading Grace's portfolio (see figure 9).

Perhaps the clearest distinction that I can make between my response sheet and the others I have seen (see Bishop 1990) is my stress on the poems themselves in light of previously established criteria. I believe it is important to stress that students have several options for how they want their poems and portfolios to be graded. What's more, I want to provide students with the kind of evaluative material that will enable them to revise their poems later, submit poems to a literary journal, and, most importantly, understand both how they were graded and why they received the grade they did. Finally, in keeping with the belief that final grades should be a logical stopping place in the course sequence, my comments on Grace's portfolio follow earlier evaluations made on these same poems through some interactive teaching method, either journal response, conference, or workshop.

ENGL 5840: Advanced Poetry Writing
Dr. Patrick Bizzaro
Spring 1991

Evaluation of Portfolio by Grace

1. Poems in Relation to Checklist

   A. "I Fade": I'm having some trouble finding the most recent draft. Your letter is helpful for me to read and, I suspect, for you to write. This is an excellent poem, as workshop reaction testifies. Handwritten draft is ready to be sent out!

   B. "Sunset / an unwound clock": This is a strong image with a hint of narrative toward the end. The second line throws me a bit. But the end is very strong. Would you consider a line of its own for "eat it?" Watch verbs.

   C. "Lucifer on a White Jet": This is much clearer and more accessible than your earlier version. Is Satan "she" or "he"? There's more narrative here, making the poem much easier to follow. Good work.

   D. "Winter Yards": This poem has changed a lot from the earlier draft. It's very different, less compressed, expanded almost to involve some creation of setting and character. I'd urge you to return to the verbs in revision.

   E. "I was walking . . .": is still an early draft. But it has many fine qualities to it, including clear and concise language. Some great line endings: "I keep trying to hold on to all that I have / left"—nice enjambment. Try to compress, look at verbs.

   F. "Going Back to Where I Said Goodbye": This is a very moving poem. The opening stanza seems to promise sentimentality, but the next two stanzas offer quite a different (and disturbing) image of reality. Nice ending!

   G. "Wild Irish Ties": Very powerful and moving poem. The images are sharp and clear, easy to follow. Please don't draw the comparison to Plath's "Daddy" in the direct address of your last stanza.

   H. "Carteret": This might be the best in this batch. Very strong from start to finish. You might rethink line breaks in the last stanza.

2. Poems Nearest to Completion
   A, C, F, G, H

3. Where to Submit Poems from #2
   try *St. Andrews Review* (see me for address)

4. Poems Furthest from Completion
   D, E

5. What to Do to Finish Poems Listed in #4
   rework the subject-verb combinations

6. Overall Evaluation of Portfolio, Considering 1–5
   very nicely done; a lot of hard work and spent emotions

7. Grade: A

Figure 9. Response sheet checklist evaluating Grace's portfolio.

The same should hold true for grades determined through other critical methodologies, as in my adaptation of reader-response criticism.

Method Two: Adapting Reader-Response Criticism to the Grading of Student Poems

An adaptation of reader-response criticism to the grading of student poems confronts us with a challenge different in kind from the challenge presented by New Criticism and Primary Trait Scoring. For while the New Critical method requires readers and evaluators to focus chiefly on the text, reader-response methods require them to focus on the reading process itself. This is because reader-response theorists believe that a writer creates not only a text, but a reader as well, who, in turn, re-creates the text. From the reader-response perspective, then, the grading procedure must enable students to identify the kind of reader they hope to create. After getting students to describe their texts in this way, a teacher must influence that description until both the student and teacher agree on how to best create the desired text and reader. Once this agreement is reached, teachers must willingly become the reader that the text summons (as described in chapter 4). And to determine a final grade, the teacher must ultimately employ the description of the text devised in collaboration with the student.

One means to a collaborative description of a text, and thereby to what a text should accomplish, is through interactive journals in which students submit weekly answers to the question "What kinds of things would you take into consideration in evaluating a poem?" In response, teachers can make suggestions about things to look for in the next week's reading assignments and attempt to influence students' revision of their answers. The product of these negotiations—negotiations not over the text of the poems, but over what the reader should construe the text to be—should be a list of features for use in evaluating either individual poems or groups of poems as submitted in a portfolio at the end of the semester. And because these interactions reflect the students' growing awareness of what their poems should achieve, each student's list should be somewhat different from the rest.

Grading through Collaboration: A Preliminary Study

I set out to determine the accuracy of my belief that interactions through a journal result in different lists for each student and thereby reflect students' unique awareness of what their poems should achieve.

To do so, I studied the journals and poems of two beginning poets, Lisa and Chris, and used the information I gleaned as a foundation for my use of reader-response methodology in grading student poems.

Lisa was a junior art major taking poetry writing as an elective. Her first answer to the course question—"What kinds of things would you take into consideration in evaluating a poem?"—was as follows:

> I would consider a good poem one that expresses one's feelings. If I can read what someone has written and understand what they are trying to say, then they have done a good job in writing. I think a good poem should include abstract ideas that provide an image. Almost like a short story and a painting all rolled up into one.

I responded favorably to Lisa's description of a poem as "a short story and a painting all rolled up into one." Considering her major in art, I was not surprised to note her interest in the making of images. Still, I wanted her to explore the notion of what might result in a good poem; it was not enough, to my way of thinking, to say a poem is good simply because one can "understand what they [the writers] are trying to say." My response to her, written in the margins of her notebook, was thus an attempt to get her to think more specifically about language in poetry: "This week look at the way language is used—what kinds of words are most often employed in poems? What language makes poems like paintings?" My goal was to have her look at the poems assigned for class reading in a different, more discriminating way.

Over four more exchanges, this interaction resulted in a slight shift in Lisa's view of what a poem should be. A list of criteria nearer to my view—that is, a compromise reflecting four weeks of negotiation—took shape, reflecting an interaction that respected the writer, the reader, and the text:

> Things I would take into consideration in evaluating a poem: imagery, imagination, the way the author expresses him/herself, if s/he's able to put a picture in my mind, free verse, an interesting arrangement of words and sentences, if the writer tries something new.

The biggest difference between this statement and Lisa's earlier statement is her focus on the kind of language that seems to be employed in the making of the poems we discussed in class. Lisa's view retains her natural preference as an art major for the visual scene. But by stressing "imagery" and "a picture," she has settled on the use of language best suited to making vivid, visual poems.

This view of poetry was one I could easily accept and use in grading Lisa's poem, "My Favorite Spot":

My Favorite Spot

grass,
lots of it.
green space smothered with dandelions—
baseball field to right,
steeple to left,
bells chiming with the wind.
behind, the gravel road I travel.
in the middle, on a hill
me.

As a result of the procedure followed thus far, I was able to evaluate this poem in terms of what Lisa and I had already agreed should be accomplished in writing a poem. "My Favorite Spot" is marked by imagery that is clear and visual. Of course, while imaginative, the poem is restricted in some ways by being, it seems, a remembered scene, one that may simply be truly and accurately represented in the poem. Nonetheless, I felt that Lisa did an excellent job of creating an attractive picture and that she used the word "me" at the end to excellent effect. I enjoyed the way she arranged the poem on the page as well. Since Lisa achieved all that she set out to achieve, as indicated by her interactive journal, she received an A for her poem.

Chris, a junior chemistry major, also took the poetry writing course to fulfill elective credit requirements. He answered the course question as follows:

> To me, poetry provides a catharsis for those feelings that are inside of me and which I have difficulty expressing verbally. I would take the emotional meaning (my own interpretation) into consideration when evaluating a poem. How does it make me feel? What does it do for me? What problem or happiness is this poem solving? I also dislike poems that have a rigid rhyme.

Chris is more closely involved with his own reaction to a poem than Lisa was: How does the poem make him feel? What does it do for him? In a sense, Chris sees the activity of reading reflected in the activity of writing; both are problem-solving efforts. In part, his reaction to a poem captures him first as writer, then as reader. I wanted to help Chris focus on "those feelings that are inside" and which are difficult to express, since surely poetry contributes to the expression of emotions usually restrained in common discourse. I wrote, "Good start,

Chris. Notice in this week's readings that writers often communicate inexpressible emotions by relying heavily on comparisons. A poet might recognize that the word 'love,' by itself, suggests a great many things to a reader. But if that emotion is compared to something tangible and specific, the writer can do a better job of limiting the reader's interpretations of what is meant."

Four weeks later, Chris wrote the following response to the course question:

> The poem would have to have meaning for me. I guess that is just another way of saying the author presents a problem and solves it. The poem would have to have visual imagery so that I can picture the scene vividly—either in my brain or in my heart (as is the case with extended metaphors). I tend to like free verse and poems with plenty of metaphors, even surrealistic poetry. A poem that is stiff, pure rhyme with no imagery, is dull to me.

The biggest change here is Chris's acknowledgment that comparisons can be used to help the reader understand the writer's emotions. He may want to "picture the scene vividly," but what he also wants is metaphor.

The following, untitled poem adequately reflects this perspective on poetry:

> I am taking part in a great experiment
> in which the only exit will be final.
> The experimental procedure will be
>   thrown by the wayside, in an attempt
> to achieve the moon.
> Indeed, the outcome will be fantastic
>   and the effects irreversible,
> for time is a power greater than any man
>   and the travel across space will
> be for all to watch, to ponder.
> Those with me will never return,
> as well,
> but they know the cost, and the future is
>   on our backs to ride to the end
> only to get off and ride someone
> else's later.
>   We can't wait. We pass greatness so
> others can reach new heights
>   higher than time and ideas
> of the mind.
>   We have achieved much more than greatness.
> We have drawn a CORRECT conclusion.

This poem seems to satisfy much that Chris and I agreed upon in our interactions over the course question. The poem, a versified analysis of the scientific method, certainly would have meaning for Chris and other scientists. He presents a problem, both in form and content, and solves it. He also indirectly expresses his exasperation over the details of the scientific method and its inherent limitations. His interest in surrealistic writing is evident throughout the poem. All in all, given the standard generated through our interactions, I judge this to be a fine poem, very different from Lisa's poem, but successful nonetheless, an A.

By generating a set of criteria, reader response as it is adapted here satisfies the central concerns of most teachers who study and evaluate student poetry writing: first, that the method of evaluation acknowledge the integrity of each individual poem, and second, that it provide the opportunity for continued interaction between writer, reader, and text. This study enabled me to see that students do, in fact, bring their personal experiences to bear upon their writing and reading. For instance, Lisa, an art major, made extensive use of imagery both in answering the course question and in writing her poem. Chris, a chemistry major, explored the potential of metaphor and simile to explain unexplainable matters and, in the end, wrote best about the scientific method.

I reached several other conclusions that I eventually hope to test further. For now, though, I present them merely as hypotheses for others to subject to experimental scrutiny. First, I believe that when we teach students to write poetry, we teach them to generate texts that represent their understanding of what constitutes poetry. This certainly seemed to hold true for Lisa and Chris. Second, this understanding of what constitutes poetry includes a wide range of things. While Lisa describes poetry as image-based writing and writes a poem that depends largely on her use of imagery, Chris thinks of poetry as an expression of emotions conveyed best through comparison. The resulting poems are very different; both, nonetheless, are poems. To evaluate them—as different as they are—by using the same list of criteria would violate their integrity as poems.

I also believe that a student's understanding of what constitutes poetry will change over the term, though it may never parallel the teacher's understanding (nor does it have to). In fact, influencing students' views of poetry is part of my responsibility as a reader who is an active agent in making meaning in their poems. They also succeed in influencing me.

No doubt a wide range of texts called poems is submitted to an instructor for evaluation over a term. That this range of texts is possible simply verifies what we find in examining volumes of poetry published by reputable presses. Still, in evaluating poems by adapting reader-response criticism, we must open communication with our students, freely negotiate, and eventually compromise so that they may write poems that are both theirs and invoke an audience capable of reading what they have written.

Grading an Individual Poem Using Reader-Response Criticism

To further explore the possibility of using reader response in grading student poems, I studied my interactions over time with Terri, a student in my undergraduate introductory poetry writing class. In spite of the fact that she was in an introductory course, Terri was actually an experienced student-writer, having written poetry without instruction for some time and having nearly completed requirements for her master's degree in English literature. In this particular adaptation of reader response, I asked Terri and her classmates to respond one time each week in their journals both to the poems assigned and to the same question Lisa and Chris responded to: "What kinds of things would you take into consideration in evaluating a poem?"

What follows are three of my interactions with Terri, showing more precisely the evolution of her thought on poetry, and one of her poems, graded in accord with the criteria she and I agreed upon as characteristic of the poems she hoped to write. Note that these interactions differ markedly from those I had with Alvin using Primary Trait Scoring, particularly in the process of negotiation and in our joint ownership of the final list.

> **January 11**
>
> *Terri's Entry:* If a poem touches me in any way, such as if it brings a similar event in my life to mind, then I find it valuable. If I can identify with the author or situation in any way, then I usually find the poem important in some way. The only time I do not find a poem worthwhile is if it does not make any sense to me. After reading a poem, I want to feel impressed or touched in some way. I do not want to be left sitting there, thinking to myself, "What in the hell did that mean?"
>
> *My Response:* How does a poet manipulate language in the making of imagery? Are some kinds of images more confusing to you than others?

February 15

Terri's Entry: My ideas have developed somewhat in the area of my biases in evaluating poetry. I now put more importance on using colorful verbs and very descriptive adjectives. I have become more concerned with avoiding the use of any "to be" verb forms or the word "so." Enjambment is vital because I like the breathy quality it evokes when reading an enjambed line aloud. A good example of this is May Swenson's "The Watch." Once again, I'm affected the most by poems that evoke a passionate response, whether that emotion is happiness, sadness, anger, loneliness. Poetry for me should be introspective and have *feeling*. Poetry like Merwin's "A Door" does not interest me because I can't seem to find any meaning in it.

My Response: Let me ask a few questions. First, what, exactly, makes a verb colorful? Second, in terms of enjambment, how about the *surprise* it makes possible? And third, was your reaction to Merwin the same even after our discussion in class? Why not explore for yourself the difference in language between a poem like Swenson's and one like Merwin's? Excellent exploration this time, Terri.

February 21

Terri's Entry: Response to your questions and comments from last week's answer to "What do I look for in evaluating a poem?"

You asked, "What, exactly, makes a verb colorful?" Colorful verbs, to me, are lively, passionate, and feeling words. Verbs that dance on your tongue. Verbs that stand out on a page. Sometimes the duller verbs can't be avoided, however.

I never thought about enjambment causing surprise in a poem, but now I see what you mean.

Even after our discussion of Merwin's "A Door," I still couldn't find any meaning that I could identify with. It didn't create any mood or feeling for me.

One aspect that I've failed to mention in my area of biases: Structure is vital to me. I like poems that aren't traditionally structured—for example, any one of e.e. cumming's poems, William Carlos Williams' "This Is Just to Say," May Swenson's "Women Should be Pedestals," or Nikki Giovanni's "Dreams." I like the cummings and Swenson poems because of their structure and lower-case usage. Thematic structure in "This Is Just to Say" is especially interesting but hard to do myself.

My Response: Thanks for responding to my earlier questions. As far as colorful verbs, you describe the way they sound and look; how about the *way* they mean? As for the poems you list, do they reflect in their structure a natural order of understanding—that is, that something occurs to you, as reader, piece by piece—in the way the author presents the image? Certainly, Williams could have presented the picture in a different word order. Also, don't give up yet on Merwin or on surrealism.

Clearly, Terri's journal reflects her growth as a writer able to converse with me about her personal preferences in poetry. Her first journal entry (January 11)—written the first day of class and submitted without an accompanying draft of a poem—was brief but to the point, reflecting what she had brought with her into the class in the form of past reading and writing experiences. Admittedly, Terri prefers poems that she is able to understand—poems that "make sense" to her—because they concern experiences similar to those she has had. This observation on her part gave rise to my concern over what exactly happens in language that makes sense to Terri as opposed to language that does not.

In her entry of February 15, Terri is far more specific, if not about what makes sense to her, then surely about what does not: "poetry like Merwin's 'A Door.' " I can see as well that she has benefited from class discussions concerning verbs, enjambment, and feeling in poetry. But I question her in my response because I want her to take her personal preferences one step further, making them more useful in helping me understand what she values in *her* poems.

Terri submitted the following draft of a poem with her February 15 journal entry. I was not surprised to receive in that poem a draft which so nearly fulfills Terri's expectations of what a poem should accomplish. As in my grading of Alvin's poem, I was able to approach Terri's poem with some notion, albeit one derived from negotiations taking place *outside* the text, of how to evaluate it.

> I remember
> never being able
> to understand
> your words
> for they were
> old and indistinguishable
> already.
> By the time I was able to be interested
> in you and your past
> You were 74 and I felt silly asking you to repeat
> yourself over and over.
> I still sleep under the expertly sewn quilts you made for me.
> They warm me as your love once did.
> The big black Bible,
> which I remember always lying upon your coffee table,
> now lies upon mine.

My father, your youngest son,
reminds me of you as he grows older
and his voice grows gruff
and his eyes grow weak.
You are one of the cornerstones in my childhood
and I only hope that I can become
half the woman you were.

As I told Terri, this draft accomplishes much of what she and I would want her poem to accomplish. First, it is a direct treatment of a subject for which she feels passionately. What's more, her imagery is clear and understandable, high priorities for Terri. Yet since this is but a draft, and since I was supposed to respond to it in terms of our mutually determined criteria—that is, since I was supposed to read her poem as she would want me to—I recommended that she look more closely at her verbs; by consolidating her language, she might remedy some of the choppiness of the poem's rhythm. Additionally, though the enjambment is often effective (it is clear that she has given some thought to line breaks), she might want to consider restructuring her piece once the language is tightened.

Because this was a draft, I withheld a grade until Terri resubmitted the poem in her portfolio at the end of the semester, hoping that she would continue to revise the poem in accord with the features she and I had identified in the in-process evaluation of her draft. And because I did not evaluate Terri's draft against *my* ideal poem, but against the one described jointly by the two of us, I would hope that my comments accurately reflected to Terri how she might better address readers who perceive poetry as she does.

In her final journal entry of February 21, Terri takes us both a step further, incorporating her personal biases and mine (since she conscientiously responds to my questioning and class discussions) in the development of a growing sense of what I should evaluate in examining one of her poems. I should keep in mind that a poem Terri would like to have written must possess a surface simplicity. What's more, I should pay close attention to the strength of her verbs in creating an overall mood or feeling. Indeed, her poem should convey some passionate feelings, which I construed to mean something she feels strongly about. Finally, my responses should help her in structuring her poems, including the use of enjambment for effect.

When Terri submitted the final version of her poem in her portfolio, I continued to read from what I construed to be the perspective of the reader she hoped to create. I thus used our mutually agreed-upon list of criteria as the basis for a grade, since those criteria reflected semester-long negotiations between us concerning the development of her text.

Grandmother

I remember
never being able
to understand
your words
for they were
old and indistinguishable
already.
By the time I was able
to be interested
in you and your past
you were 74 and I
felt silly asking you to repeat
yourself over and over,

I still sleep
under your quilts,
warm as your love,
and the big black bible
from your coffee table
lies upon mine.
In my father, your youngest son,
I see you as he ages
his gruff voice,
weak eyes.
You are all around me.
I hope I can become
half the woman you were.

This poem received an A. Terri did an outstanding job of writing the poem she and I agreed she should write. It reflects the passion, imagery, enjambment, and surface simplicity that she and I agree her poems should possess. And I am convinced that she can talk with me knowledgeably about her poem as well, since she contributed significantly to its description.

The chief benefit of using reader-response techniques in this manner is that they enable the teacher to read and evaluate student poems while keeping the student involved in negotiations over what the student's poem should accomplish. Such a negotiation occurs not over word choice, imagery, and word order in the text, but in the student's journal. Here meaningful interaction can occur between the teacher, the student, and what David Bleich calls the disappearing text, the re-creation of which is ultimately the cause and focus of any interaction. Another effect of such an effort is that the text is not appropriated by the teacher; in fact, I made no intertextual comments on Terri's poem. The kinds of comments I made, however, reflect a belief that the reader's task is to reconstruct the text, which necessarily involves responding to the document in terms of past experiences with both the subject and with the kind of text it is.

I consistently attempted to address Terri's poem with the kind of reading usually reserved for established literary texts. But as long as one of its purposes is to satisfy course requirements, the student poem will be treated as that peculiar breed of writing that gets evaluated by a teacher, in spite of its identity as a literary text. Nonetheless, by collaborating in the determination of what the poem should be, Terri effectively participated in a methodology that lessens the teacher's authority over a student's text. What Onore (1989) says of the composition classroom aptly describes a rationale for this and other experiments in evaluating student poems from the reader-response perspective:

> If the composition classroom is to be a context for exploration and risk-taking, for finding and solving problems—in short, for learning—then power must be shared. Such changes, of course, imply that teachers and students alike might be able to swim against the whole tide of their personal and cultural histories—a monumental task, to be sure. Nonetheless, challenging the tradition of teacher- and textbook-dominated learning is necessary, since otherwise teaching and learning may be doomed, Sisyphus-like, to repeat endlessly the same endlessly unproductive efforts. (232)

Both Terri's journal description of what her poems should accomplish and her poem itself suggested to me that students may compose poems and perhaps other texts that reflect their current understanding of what that text is. Thus, by using reader-response methods, teachers, students, and texts interact in a way that results in not only a text, but also in a description of who the intended reader might be, as how the text must be read will determine. Interestingly, the evolution of Terri's journal reflects what I consider tremendous growth in her recognition of what poetry, in general, and her poem, in particular, might accomplish. In that sense, the journal proved to be a useful place for learning. What's more, in reading other students' journals and poems as I have Terri's, I found it possible to grade entire portfolios at the semester's end using the same checklist format as I used with the New Criticism/Primary Trait Scoring method.

Grading a Portfolio Using Reader-Response Criticism

To employ a response sheet checklist based on reader-response journal collaborations of the sort used with Lisa, Chris, and Terri, I gave my students two options. First, if they submitted a series of closely related poems in their portfolios that might be graded by my reference to a single list developed collaboratively, they could submit just that list as a basis for grading their poems. But if they set out in each poem to do something markedly different, something that could not be described in a single inclusive list, they would need to take the second option. In this alternative way for having their grades determined, they would need to develop with me a different set of criteria for each poem.

The Single-List Method. Jeff G. developed a list of criteria for evaluating his poems that I was able to apply to each poem in his portfolio. Here are the four interactions that took place in his journal as these criteria evolved. After each journal entry, I offer the observations I made in my effort to negotiate with Jeff over the criteria I would ultimately employ in examining and grading his poems. Here is Jeff's first entry:

> First of all, the subject must have a "world." From the poem it should be evident that it is occurring somewhere that can be imagined. That also means there should be an order to events. Clichés should not be used, nor should million-dollar words such as "love" or "anger." Imagery should be specific enough to show these things. Imagery, for that matter, should be very specific and address the senses.
>
> As for wording, word choices should serve both active voice and emotive responsibilities. Choices of verbs should show the emotion of the moment. Similarly, there should be an awareness of the action of mono- and multisyllabic words for both emotive and rhythmic purposes.
>
> For rhythm, rhyme, and musicality purposes, there should be a use of assonance, consonance, alliteration, etc. Enjambment, or line breaks in general, should be functional to the piece. So should the punctuation.
>
> In other areas, there should be a general tightness of the piece. Every word should be a functioning unit getting double usage wherever possible. Redundancy should be eliminated as should padding. Do not count on the drama of an event to dramatize a poem. Also, do not think a triggering subject has to be kept in a piece. Know when to take out lines that aren't working.

Jeff is a writing major and knows at the start what he wants his poems to accomplish. In the margins of his journal, I respond to his notion that there should be an order to events with the question "Does it have to be linear?" Jeff has taken courses in fiction writing and that influence is apparent in his desire to write narrative poetry. In response to his notion that verbs should show the emotion of the moment, I write, "And verbs should connect in some unusual way with their subjects." Beside his third paragraph, which comments on rhythm and rhyme, I ask, "Should sound somehow reinforce the subject?" I also reinforce certain of his notions with "good" in the margin and respond to his comment that a poet should know when to take out lines that aren't working with "Exactly—sometimes the hardest thing to do is give up a 'precious' image that, in the end, just doesn't work." My summary comment is intended to reinforce much of what Jeff has written in this first journal entry:

> Jeff,
> This is a well-considered piece. I think you and I agree on many points. I've asked related questions in the margins. The goal is for us to have some sense of what a Jeff G. poem should accomplish against which I can set poems from your portfolio. This is a great start.

Jeff's second journal entry follows:

> A poem must have a world with an orderly, but not necessarily linear, way of presenting things. Clichés and large, undefinable words such as "love" should be described using imagery. Images should be very specific.
> Words should be active and should add to the emotion of the poem. The sounds of words, therefore, should be equal to the wanted effect (for example, multisyllabic words slow reading and seem more intelligent).
> Awareness of consonance, assonance, enjambment, etc. should all add to the subject of a piece.
> There should be a tightness of the piece to avoid redundancy and padding.
> There should be an awareness of the feelings of an event.
> Lastly, I believe in finding the power in simple words, not thesaurus words.

In this entry, Jeff has economized his criteria, focusing on the ones that he and I both think would best characterize his poems. I am happy with this list, and with Jeff's effort, and write the simple summary comment that follows:

> Jeff,
> Why not, in your next effort, make a final list of these characteristics that I can use with your portfolio. Good work!

Jeff's third entry is this final list of criteria:

What a Jeff G. Poem Should Do

1. A poem should have a world with an orderly, but not necessarily linear way of presenting information.
2. Clichés and larger undefinable words such as "love" should be described using imagery.
3. Images should be detailed and specific, trying to find original parallels.
4. Words, especially verbs, should be used to reinforce the emotion of the poem.
5. The sounds of words and the beats of the lines should also reinforce the emotion of the poem (use of mono- and polysyllabic words).
6. Redundancy and padding should be avoided.
7. Line breaks should be used to emphasize end words and allow multiple interpretations of individual line endings.
8. Through the various devices mentioned, there should be an awareness of the emotion of the event.
9. The words of the poem should attempt to find the power of simple wording rather than "thesaurus" wording.
10. Images should appeal to the senses.

Jeff has an excellent list here that aptly describes how he wants his poems to be read. By so delineating what a poem should accomplish, he has more than adequately determined the reader he hopes to create through his poems. Jeff's grade will be based on how well his poems create this reader. My job will be both to willingly become that reader and to determine how effectively the reader is created by examining Jeff's texts in light of the criteria he enumerates in his last journal entry. My reaction to each poem in his portfolio will thus be made on an "all-purpose" checklist.

The Multiple-List Method. Dennis devised a series of checklists, one for each poem he submitted in his portfolio. These criteria enabled me to grade each poem on its own terms, terms I collaborated on with Dennis in his journal to create. He also provided me with an explanation of what he felt would be a fair method for grading his poems:

A standard I feel would be most educationally valuable and functional for me would be one which recognizes that I was experimenting with different poetic techniques in each of these eight poems; therefore, while my poems should show progress from the first attempt to the almost finished product, and my level of maturity requires that my subjects be more than "puppy dogs' tails," and my level of education requires that my beginning efforts be more than amateurish and my finished products be accomplished, still, my neophyte use of poetic techniques should be judged mainly for showing variety and exploration from the most basic to the accomplished but not advanced. Individual standards will need to be made to fit individual poems.

In the space that follows are three examples of how the sets of criteria that Dennis gave me differ from poem to poem:

"Flotation Marriage" Checklist

____effective visual image

____attractive word choice

____adult message

____decent title

____visual appropriateness

____non-confusing structure

____appropriate voice

"Poetry Reading" Checklist

____effective visual image

____attractive word choice

____adult message

____decent title

____visual appropriateness

____non-confusing structure

____appropriate voice

____clear allusions

"Could We Talk?" Checklist

____effective audible sound

____attractive word choice

____adult message

____decent title

____visual appropriateness

____non-confusing structure

____appropriate voice

____sense of frustration

There are, of course, certain similarities in the criteria for each of these poems. But by placing stress on elements unique to each poem, Dennis and I were able to focus on the critical way each poem might be read differently from the next. And because Dennis took the care to suggest that the reader his poems create would note these differences, I paid special attention to them and indicated in each case whether he succeeded in creating the text and reader that his criteria said he would.

9 The Teacher's Many Selves: Negotiating the Course in Poetry Writing

Teaching is exciting and interesting, and it is an honorable profession. But I don't think it nourishes a writer. Many of the people you are talking to are too much like yourself; it's too much like a conversation going on inside your own head.

Galway Kinnell, *New York Quarterly* Craft Interview

The most effective teachers of writing are traditionally those who are the most human and the most demanding of their students. Whatever their curriculum, they establish themselves or other defined audiences as live and sympathetic readers willing to participate in the quest for meaning that is writing.

Edward White, *Teaching and Assessing Writing*

Like their students—indeed, perhaps because of them—teachers too negotiate identities during the writing course. In fact, the best teachers of writing are not necessarily the best writers or the best readers, as we have long and perhaps erroneously assumed. Rather, the most successful teachers are apt to be those who are best able to adapt to the texts their students write and accept the roles their students negotiate. They are those who play various roles in the classroom, who can adopt numerous personas, and who willingly experiment with authority, both in commenting on student texts and in classroom interaction.

As shown in chapters 3–6, comments on student texts can cover a range of distances, from the long-range perspective of teacher authority in text-based commentary to the up-close-and-personal perspective of shared authority in reader-response methods. Classroom interaction can reflect the changing relationship that these theories advance between teacher and student, enabling teachers to negotiate for themselves and model for their students the various identities that their theories promote.

But if they hope to help their students negotiate various identities as readers and writers, writing teachers must first know themselves as readers and writers. For the methods that teachers employ in reading drafts of their own poems often influence the way they read their students' poems. Course design and course readings tend to reinforce these methods of reading. Teachers must thus be willing to throw aside their personal biases as readers and writers when it seems wise to do so; they must be willing to read their students' work flexibly, through alternative critical lenses. And to do this, they must develop both a sense of when to intervene in their students' writing processes and insight into how particular student texts should be read. This book offers some guidelines in making such determinations.

First, if teachers of poetry writing evaluate their students' poems by adopting methods such as those advocated by poets in Turner's *Poets Teaching,* or if they use methods advocated by Cooper and Odell in *Evaluating Writing,* they are most likely responding to their students' texts from a position that relies in one way or another on the New Criticism. In fact, the New Criticism has so permeated our methods for approaching student texts that we hardly ever take time to notice its influence. Quite simply, most of our current models for responding to writing are text-based, and though we know that we should be reading and evaluating writing differently, there are very few models for doing so. What's more, whether we use text-based methods consciously or unconsciously, the very existence of the New Criticism in our methods for reading student texts and in the suggestions we make when we advise students on how to improve their writing suggests that the authority for meaning is in the text itself and that improved writing will be the product of text manipulation. This approach to reading is evident in the way we interact with students as well. Because the norms or features used in text-based evaluation can be found in other texts, the person who has read most extensively—almost without exception the teacher—is the "best" reader and therefore the true authority in the classroom. The student's job, then, is to revise the text as the teacher has suggested. If the text that results sounds as though it might have been written by the teacher, or, in any case, by a student who has made an effort to write the text the teacher envisions, we should not be surprised. This method of student-teacher interaction offers students a very limited number of possible classroom roles.

Second, those of us who would like to offer our students more control, both in making their poems and, since it would seem necessary to do so, in their educations, need to make a concerted effort. I cannot emphasize enough the importance of examining our own writing and reading processes. We cannot offer alternative approaches to the evaluation and reading of student texts—or, for that matter, to the roles students might play in the workshop—until we make this examination. Often teachers read and evaluate drafts of their students' poems the way they read and evaluate drafts of their own writing. But such readings may not always be appropriate for addressing student texts; they will, in any case, no doubt result in a teacher's appropriation of a student's poem. By studying their own reading and writing habits, though, teachers will be better able to employ alternative methods when a student or a student's poem requires them to do so.

Third, using literary-critical theories in reading student writing, both at different stages in the writing process and at different stages in a writer's growth toward maturity and independence, enables students to play various roles in their relationships with their teachers, their texts, and their peers' texts. Many professional poets (that is, those published widely) acknowledge the difficulty that they and their colleagues have had in breaking free of their mentors. One solution to this kind of apprenticeship would be for teachers to signal to their students that other relationships besides the traditional one of examiner to examinee can be developed in the classroom. Each of the critical theories examined here—New Criticism, reader-response criticism, deconstruction, and feminist criticism—provides teachers with the opportunity to signal to their students that alternative relationships are possible. Since each of these methods views authority differently, teachers who read and evaluate student poems by adapting these theories are simultaneously inviting students to interact with them differently. These interactions range from the traditional role of teacher-as-authority in the use of New Criticism, to the shared authority of reader-response criticism, to the exclusive authority that students have over their texts in deconstruction and feminist criticism.

Finally, both the comments teachers make in response to their students' poems and classroom discussion of various critical theories and the views of authority that they imply can make students aware of the possibility of changing roles in the classroom. The form comments take differs from method to method. The most intrusive form for commenting is the New Critical model, which involves the teacher in writing on, over, and around the student's text. The reader-response method, since it involves shared authority over the text, requires the use of something similar to the "parallel text" discussed in chapter 4, a text alongside but never on the student's text. Finally, the model best suited to a deconstructive or feminist reading is actually a "detached text," one that is on a page visibly separate from the student's text. This sort of detached text might be a letter, as shown in chapters 5 and 6.

But it might also take other shapes; whatever seems most effective in a particular interaction. In any case, the chief signal that a detached text sends is that since the teacher has made no marks on the student's poem, final determination of what needs to be changed is up to the student.

Class discussion of these various critical perspectives enables teachers to "locate" themselves for their students and help their students see the various selves that a teacher-as-reader might play. After all, if teachers are unable to play these roles, students will not be able to play them either. In fact, unless the teacher models these selves, students may not even know that such roles exist. Modeling is not enough, though. Students must be given the opportunity to play these roles as well, perhaps through the kind of activities suggested in chapter 7. Only then will they be able to enter a workshop discussion of each other's poems capable of commenting from a variety of vantage points and, thereby, able to negotiate identities for themselves among their peers.

Reconsidering the Text of the Course: Which Role and When

The central issue in adapting literary-critical theory to the reading and evaluation of student poems is not only the development of models for *how* to employ it. For each student's poem, a teacher must also know *which* role to play as reader and *when* alternative roles might be more usefully employed. Certain reconsiderations seem warranted.

Reconsidering Course Design

On the one hand, teachers model literary-critical methods for their students so that the students can employ these methods themselves in commenting on each other's poems. On the other, teachers want to provide students with various kinds of readings so that they can experience for themselves the various relationships possible in the writing class. To achieve both of these ends, however, teachers must provide their students with readings of their works that come from a number of vantage points. Yet how can we incorporate this into the course design?

Any method for incorporating adaptations of theory into the course should reflect the teacher's values and emphases. I employ New Criticism, reader-response criticism, deconstruction, and feminist criticism when necessary. Other teachers might decide to offer different kinds of readings. In any case, the theories should be employed so that students can learn how to use them in commenting on each other's poems and, in the process, negotiate the identity that reading requires of them.

In introductory courses, it is useful to begin with the kind of reading students are most comfortable and familiar with—most often from a New Critical perspective—and then move into those that might be more challenging for them—probably adaptations of reader response, deconstruction, and feminist criticism. Regardless of the sequence teachers decide upon, they must keep their students informed about what kinds of readings to expect and continually locate these readings in classroom activities.

On the other hand, teachers might decide to work in the opposite direction by commenting on student poems early in the term using methods most apt to help in subject development—probably reader-response criticism, deconstruction, and feminist criticism—and reserve until the end of the term those methods that pay special attention to the features of the text—New Criticism. Of course, this approach would similarly require teachers to identify for their students what they are doing and why. We must not forget that one of our goals is to help students learn how to employ these methods for themselves and thereby negotiate the identities that the methods require.

Reconsidering a Teacher's Flexibility

We should not become inflexible about flexibility. Teachers need to be able to model several roles in evaluating student poems, and to do this, they need to be able to call upon a repertoire of evaluation methods. But my experiences have shown that I must be willing to adjust to my students rather than programmatically employ a reading method that might, in the end, do some harm. Clearly, some poems demand certain types of readings. When we run into such poems, like Penney's in chapter 3 or David's in chapter 5, we should offer the kinds of readings that seem appropriate.

Take my response to Penney's poem. In my efforts to study ways of adapting literary-critical methods to the evaluation of student poems, I wanted to comment on her poem using the New Criticism. In offering this text-based analysis, I simply read the poem as I told the students in class that I would. But the New Criticism offers a method of reading that is clearly dispassionate and objective, a method inappropriate both to Penney's poem and to Penney, who had written an emotional poem about her relationship with her mother. Penney required less authoritative intrusion on my part than my New Critical tools permitted, and her poem told me so. I should have noted from her exploration of very serious issues that she needed less control from her reader and more shared authority in determining which gaps, silences, or contradictions she might decide to attend to.

By contrast, Lee (see chapter 5) needed more involvement on my part than I gave him. Again, his poem should have been a clear signal to me that he needed more "hands-on" instruction than deconstruction would permit. I will probably never know for sure why Lee felt he had to respond to my every observation when I deconstructed his poem, but I believe I am correct, in retrospect, to say that I should have responded to Lee's poem with text-based commentary, perhaps offering to him the kind of guidance on basic elements of poetry writing that I mistakenly gave to Penney: that a poem should show rather than tell, that it should avoid clichés, and that it should consolidate language and avoid wordiness. I was not able to help Lee understand that deconstruction asks us to give up our investment in meaning and the authority of the text, that it returns authority, ultimately, to the author. In fact, in its obedient attention to my remarks, Lee's revision is similar to the one John made in response to my New Critical comments in chapter 3. I can only guess that I simply did not know these two students well enough at the time to respond more appropriately to them, and that in learning how to employ various critical methods, I did not recognize in Lee's poem a need for firmer guidance on my part.

To take another example, I believe Mickie and I profited from our interaction through reader-response methodology in chapter 4. Though Mickie wrote his poem for an introductory class, I had seen several of his poems before the class began. He had also taken a contemporary poetry class with me. As a result of these previous interactions, I was able to share authority with Mickie in using reader-response methods to evaluate his poem. Fortunately, these methods enabled me to respond sympathetically to his poem about his father's death. Such sympathetic and cooperative efforts seem to be a feature of reader-response methodology as I have adapted it for use in chapter 4.

I was similarly fortunate in my use of deconstruction in examining Deb's poem (see chapter 5). I had read a short collection of Deb's poems prior to ever evaluating her work. This prior experience as a reader of her poetry enabled me to employ a method of reading and evaluation that resulted in satisfying interactions. Deb was able to accept responsibility for revising her poem and, in one skilled movement, return authority to me. Perhaps the second letter I asked her to author enabled her to feel ownership and control over her text, an ownership Lee did not exert over his poem.

Reconsidering the Strengths and Weaknesses of Literary-Critical Theories

What these experiences showed me is that to be truly flexible in reading and evaluating student poems, a teacher must be conscious of the strengths and limitations of the methods employed. Adaptations of the New Criticism to the evaluation of student poems are limited by the dispassionate nature of the method. While the New Criticism enables a teacher to provide students with large amounts of information in a short time, students are usually overwhelmed by the teacher's authority. In fact, in the end, most poems evaluated through New Critical methods are appropriated by the teacher. And appropriation is something even our most famous living poets claim to have had difficulty overcoming.

One advantage of New Critical commentary, though, is that it is familiar to students. Throughout their educational careers, most students have seen their texts filled with the teacher's comments. In those instances when they have been invited to revise after the teacher has marked up their papers, students knew that their success (their grade) would depend on how nearly their revision conformed to their teacher's expectations.

By contrast, students are unfamiliar with other methods for evaluating writing, which is hardly surprising since few models for those readings and evaluations exist. In experimenting with the models offered here, teachers should thus know that if the text is not filled with the teacher's corrections, some students will assume that the teacher has not done a conscientious job. Nonetheless, it should be clear that parallel and detached texts can be usefully employed with students if the teacher has clarified how these methods of reading will be used. Of course, this means that the writing teacher must become a reading teacher who teaches through example and demonstration. And the teacher must be willing to give up a portion of authority, both over students' poems as well as in the classroom. Only by a teacher's willingness to change can change occur in students. The teacher must signal to students that new roles can be played in the classroom, roles that the students have never played before. More importantly, students must be encouraged to negotiate new identities as readers and writers, both during the workshop and in future writing courses.

And so must their teachers.

References

Adams, Hazard, and Leroy Searle, eds. 1986. *Critical Theory Since 1965.* Tallahassee: Florida State University Press.

Ammons, A. R. 1982. "A Poem Is a Walk." In *Claims for Poetry,* edited by Donald Hall, 1–8. Ann Arbor: University of Michigan Press.

Anson, Chris M., ed. 1989. *Writing and Response: Theory, Practice, and Research.* Urbana, IL: National Council of Teachers of English.

Atkins, G. Douglas, and Michael L. Johnson, eds. 1985. *Writing and Reading Differently: Deconstruction and the Teaching of Composition and Literature.* Lawrence: University Press of Kansas.

Bakhtin, Mikhail M. 1986. "From *Discourse in the Novel.*" In *Critical Theory Since 1965,* edited by Hazard Adams and Leroy Searle, 665–79. Tallahassee: Florida State University Press.

Bauer, Dale. 1990. "The Other 'F' Word: The Feminist in the Classroom." *College English* 52.4: 385–96.

Beach, Richard. 1989. "Showing Students How to Assess: Demonstrating Techniques for Response in the Writing Conference." In *Writing and Response: Theory, Practice, and Research,* edited by Chris M. Anson, 127–48. Urbana, IL: National Council of Teachers of English.

Beach, Richard, and Lillian S. Bridwell, eds. 1984. *New Directions in Composition Research.* New York: Guilford Press.

Bishop, Wendy. 1990. *Released into Language: Options for Teaching Creative Writing.* Urbana, IL: National Council of Teachers of English.

Bizzaro, Patrick. 1992. "Some Applications of Literary Critical Theory to the Reading and Evaluation of Student Poetry Writing." In *Poets' Perspectives: Reading, Writing, and Teaching Poetry,* edited by Charles R. Duke and Sally A. Jacobsen, 154–74. Portsmouth, NH: Boynton/Cook.

———. 1990. "Evaluating Student Poetry Writing: A Primary Trait Scoring Model." *Teaching English in the Two-Year College* 17.1: 54–61.

———. 1990. "Interaction and Assessment: Some Applications of Reader-Response Criticism to the Evaluation of Student Writing in a Poetry Writing Class." In *The Writing Teacher as Researcher,* edited by Donald A. Daiker and Max Morenberg, 256–65. Portsmouth, NH: Boynton/Cook.

———. 1988. "Poetry and Audience: Ten Recent Books." *Raccoon* 28: 72–93.

———. 1983. "Teacher as Writer and Researcher: The Poetry Dilemma." *Language Arts* 60.7: 851–59.

Bizzell, Patricia. 1987. "What Can We Know, What Must We Do, What May We Hope: Writing Assessment." *College English* 49.5: 575–84.

Bolker, Joan. 1979. "Teaching Griselda to Write." *College English* 40.8: 906–8.

Boone, Joseph Allen. 1989. "Of Me(n) and Feminism: Who(se) Is the Sex that Writes?" In *Gender and Theory: Dialogues on Feminist Criticism*, edited by Linda Kauffman, 158–80. New York: Basil Blackwell.

Brannon, Lil, and C. H. Knoblauch. 1982. "On Students' Rights to Their Own Texts: A Model of Teacher Response." *College Composition and Communication* 33.2: 157–66.

Brooke, Robert E. 1991. *Writing and Sense of Self: Identity Negotiation in Writing Workshops*. Urbana, IL: National Council of Teachers of English.

Cahalan, James M., and David B. Downing, eds. 1991. *Practicing Theory in Introductory College Literature Courses*. Urbana, IL: National Council of Teachers of English.

Cain, William. 1984. *The Crisis in Criticism: Theory, Literature, and Reform in English Studies*. Baltimore: Johns Hopkins University Press.

Catano, James V. 1990. "The Rhetoric of Masculinity: Origins, Institutions, and the Myth of the Self-Made Man." *College English* 52.4: 421–36.

Caywood, Cynthia L., and Gillian R. Overing, eds. 1987. *Teaching Writing: Pedagogy, Gender, and Equity*. Albany: State University of New York Press.

Clifford, John, and John Schlib. 1985. "Composition Theory and Literary Theory." In *Perspectives on Research and Scholarship in Composition*, edited by Ben W. McClelland and Timothy R. Donovan, 45–67. New York: Modern Language Association.

Cooper, Charles R. 1977. "Holistic Evaluation of Writing." In *Evaluating Writing: Describing, Measuring, Judging*, edited by Charles R. Cooper and Lee Odell, 3–31. Urbana, IL: National Council of Teachers of English.

Cooper, Charles R., and Lee Odell. 1977. *Evaluating Writing: Describing, Measuring, Judging*. Urbana, IL: National Council of Teachers of English.

Crowley, Sharon. 1989. *A Teacher's Introduction to Deconstruction*. Urbana, IL: National Council of Teachers of English.

Culler, Jonathan. 1982. *On Deconstruction: Theory and Criticism after Structuralism*. Ithaca, NY: Cornell University Press.

Culley, Margo, and Catherine Portuges, eds. 1985. *Gendered Subjects: The Dynamics of Feminist Teaching*. London: Routledge and Kegan Paul.

Daiker, Donald A., and Max Morenberg, eds. 1990. *The Writing Teacher as Researcher: Essays in the Theory and Practice of Class-Based Research*. Portsmouth, NH: Boynton/Cook.

Daumer, Elisabeth, and Sandra Runzo. 1987. "Transforming the Composition Classroom." In *Teaching Writing: Pedagogy, Gender, and Equity*, edited by Cynthia L. Caywood and Gillian R. Overing, 45–63. Albany: State University of New York Press.

Donahue, Patricia, and Ellen Quandahl, eds. 1989. *Reclaiming Pedagogy: The Rhetoric of the Classroom.* Carbondale: Southern Illinois University Press.

Duke, Charles R., and Sally A. Jacobsen, eds. 1992. *Poets' Perspectives: Reading, Writing, and Teaching Poetry.* Portsmouth, NH: Boynton/Cook.

Duyfhuizen, Bernard. 1988. "Textual Harassment of Marvell's Coy Mistress: The Institutionalization of Masculine Criticism." *College English* 50.4: 411–23.

Ebert, Teresa L. 1991. "The 'Difference' of Postmodern Feminism." *College English* 53.8: 886–904.

Ede, Lisa, and Andrea Lunsford. 1988. "Audience Addressed/Audience Invoked: The Role of Audience in Composition Theory and Pedagogy." In *The Writing Teacher's Sourcebook,* edited by Gary Tate and Edward P. J. Corbett, 169–82. New York: Oxford University Press.

Faigley, Lester. 1989. "Judging Writing, Judging Selves." *College Composition and Communication* 40.4: 395–412.

Fetterley, Judith. 1978. *The Resisting Reader: A Feminist Approach to American Fiction.* Bloomington: Indiana University Press.

Flynn, Elizabeth. 1990. "Composing 'Composing as a Woman': A Perspective on Research." *College Composition and Communication* 41.1: 83–91.

———. 1989. "Learning to Read Student Papers from a Feminine Perspective, I." In *Encountering Student Texts,* edited by Bruce Lawson, Susan Sterr Ryan, and W. Ross Winterowd, 49–58. Urbana, IL: National Council of Teachers of English.

———. 1988. "Composing as a Woman." *College Composition and Communication* 39.4: 423–35.

Flynn, John. 1989. "Learning to Read Student Papers from a Feminine Perspective, II." In *Encountering Student Texts,* edited by Bruce Lawson, Susan Sterr Ryan, and W. Ross Winterowd, 131–37. Urbana, IL: National Council of Teachers of English.

Frey, Olivia. 1990. "Beyond Literary Darwinism: Women's Voices and Critical Discourse." *College English* 52.5: 507–26.

Friebert, Stuart. 1980. "Group I." In *Poets Teaching: The Creative Process,* edited by Alberta T. Turner, 25–30. New York: Longman.

Giroux, Henry A. 1988. *Teachers as Intellectuals: Toward a Critical Pedagogy of Learning.* Granby, MA: Bergin and Garvey.

Goldman, Irene C. 1990. "Feminism, Deconstruction, and the Universal: A Case Study on *Walden.*" In *Conversations: Contemporary Critical Theory and the Teaching of Literature,* edited by Charles Moran and Elizabeth F. Penfield, 120–31. Urbana, IL: National Council of Teachers of English.

Goulston, Wendy. 1987. "Women Writing." In *Teaching Writing: Pedagogy, Gender, and Equity,* edited by Cynthia L. Caywood and Gillian R. Overing, 19–30. Albany: State University of New York Press.

Graff, Gerald. 1990. "Determinacy/Indeterminacy." In *Critical Terms for Literary Study,* edited by Frank Lentricchia and Thomas McLaughlin, 163–76. Chicago: University of Chicago Press.

Harker, W. John. 1987. "Literary Theory and the Reading Process: A Meeting of Perspectives." *Written Communication* 9.3: 235–52.

Harris, Joseph. 1989. "The Idea of Community in the Study of Writing." *College Composition and Communication* 40.1: 11–22.

Heath, Stephen. 1987. "Male Feminism." In *Men in Feminism,* edited by Alice Jardine and Paul Smith, 1–32. New York: Methuen.

Hugo, Richard. 1979. *The Triggering Town: Lectures and Essays on Poetry and Writing.* New York: Norton.

Iser, Wolfgang. 1974. *The Implied Reader: Patterns of Communication in Prose Fiction from Bunyan to Beckett.* Baltimore: Johns Hopkins University Press.

Jacobs, Lucky. 1977. "Three Approaches to the Teaching of Poetry Writing." *English Education* 8.2: 161–66.

Jardine, Alice. 1987. "Men in Feminism: Odor di Uomo or Compagnons de Route?" In *Men in Feminism,* edited by Alice Jardine and Paul Smith, 54–61. New York: Methuen.

Jardine, Alice, and Paul Smith, eds. 1987. *Men in Feminism.* New York: Methuen.

Jehlen, Myra. 1990. "Gender." In *Critical Terms for Literary Study,* edited by Frank Lentricchia and Thomas McLaughlin, 263–73. Chicago: University of Chicago Press.

———. 1983. "Archimedes and the Paradox of Feminist Criticism." In *The "Signs" Reader: Women, Gender, and Scholarship,* edited by Elizabeth Abel and Emily K. Abel, 69–96. Chicago: University of Chicago Press.

Jerome, Judson. 1990. *1990 Poet's Market: Where and How to Publish Your Poetry.* Cincinnati: Writer's Digest Books.

Johnson, Barbara. 1985. "Teaching Deconstructively." In *Writing and Reading Differently: Deconstruction and the Teaching of Composition and Literature,* edited by G. Douglas Atkins and Michael L. Johnson, 140–48. Lawrence: University Press of Kansas.

Juncker, Clara. 1988. "Writing (with) Cixous." *College English* 50.4: 424–36.

Kaufer, David, and Gary Waller. 1985. "To Write Is to Read Is to Write, Right?" In *Writing and Reading Differently: Deconstruction and the Teaching of Composition and Literature,* edited by G. Douglas Atkins and Michael L. Johnson, 66–92. Lawrence: University Press of Kansas.

Kauffman, Linda, ed. 1989. *Gender and Theory: Dialogues on Feminist Criticism.* New York: Basil Blackwell.

Knoblauch, C. H., and Lil Brannon. 1981. "Teacher Commentary on Student Writing: The State of the Art." *Freshman English News* 10 (Fall): 1–4.

Knoper, Randall. 1989. "Deconstruction, Process, Writing." In *Reclaiming Pedagogy: The Rhetoric of the Classroom,* edited by Patricia Donahue and Ellen Quandahl, 128–43. Carbondale: Southern Illinois University Press.

Koch, Kenneth. 1970. *Wishes, Lies, and Dreams: Teaching Children to Write Poetry.* New York: Harper and Row.

Kolodny, Annette. [1980] 1991. "Dancing Through the Minefield: Some Observations on the Theory, Practice, and Politics of a Feminist Literary Criticism." In *Feminisms: An Anthology of Literary Theory and Criticism,* edited by Robyn R. Warhol and Diane Price Herndl, 97–116. New Brunswick, NJ: Rutgers University Press.

Lawson, Bruce, and Susan Sterr Ryan. 1989. "Introduction: Interpretive Issues in Student Writing." In *Encountering Student Texts,* edited by Bruce Lawson, Susan Sterr Ryan, and W. Ross Winterowd, vii–xvii. Urbana, IL: National Council of Teachers of English.

Lawson, Bruce, Susan Sterr Ryan, and W. Ross Winterowd, eds. 1989. *Encountering Student Texts: Interpretive Issues in Reading Student Writing.* Urbana, IL: National Council of Teachers of English.

Levertov, Denise. 1987. "Interview." In *The Poet's Craft: Interviews from* The New York Quarterly, edited by William Packard, 52–69. New York: Paragon House.

Lentricchia, Frank, and Thomas McLaughlin, eds. 1990. *Critical Terms for Literary Study.* Chicago: University of Chicago Press.

Lloyd-Jones, Richard. 1977. "Primary Trait Scoring." In *Evaluating Writing: Describing, Measuring, Judging,* edited by Charles R. Cooper and Lee Odell, 33–66. Urbana, IL: National Council of Teachers of English.

Lynn, Steven. 1990. "A Passage into Critical Theory." In *Conversations: Contemporary Critical Theory and the Teaching of Literature,* edited by Charles Moran and Elizabeth F. Penfield, 99–113. Urbana, IL: National Council of Teachers of English.

MacDonald, John D. 1989. "Guidelines and Exercises for Teaching Creative Writing." In *Creative Writing in America: Theory and Pedagogy,* edited by Joseph M. Moxley, 83–87. Urbana, IL: National Council of Teachers of English.

Miller, J. Hillis. 1983. "Composition and Decomposition: Deconstruction and the Teaching of Writing." In *Composition and Literature: Bridging the Gap,* edited by Winifred Bryan Horner, 38–56. Chicago: University of Chicago Press.

Minot, Stephen. 1989. "How a Writer Reads." In *Creative Writing in America: Theory and Pedagogy,* edited by Joseph M. Moxley, 89–95. Urbana, IL: National Council of Teachers of English.

Moi, Toril. 1989. "Men Against Patriarchy." In *Gender and Theory: Dialogues on Feminist Criticism,* edited by Linda Kauffman, 181–88. New York: Basil Blackwell.

Moran, Charles, and Elizabeth F. Penfield, eds. 1990. *Conversations: Contemporary Critical Theory and the Teaching of Literature.* Urbana, IL: National Council of Teachers of English.

Moxley, Joseph M. 1989. *Creative Writing in America: Theory and Pedagogy.* Urbana, IL: National Council of Teachers of English.

Murphy, Patrick D. 1991. "Coyote Midwife in the Classroom: Introducing Literature with Feminist Dialogics." In *Practicing Theory in Introductory College Literature Courses,* edited by James M. Cahalan and David B. Downing, 161–76. Urbana, IL: National Council of Teachers of English.

Murray, Donald. 1982. "Teaching the Other Self: The Writer's First Reader." *College Composition and Communication* 33.2: 140–47.

———. 1968. *A Writer Teaches Writing.* Boston: Houghton Mifflin.

Ong, W. J. 1975. "The Writer's Audience Is Always a Fiction." *PMLA* 90: 9–21.

Onore, Cynthia. 1989. "The Student, the Teacher, and the Text: Negotiating Meanings through Response and Revision." In *Writing and Response: Theory, Practice, and Research,* edited by Chris M. Anson, 231–60. Urbana, IL: National Council of Teachers of English.

Packard, William, ed. 1987. *The Poet's Craft: Interviews from* The New York Quarterly. New York: Paragon House.

———, ed. 1974. *The Craft of Poetry: Interviews from* The New York Quarterly. Garden City, NY: Doubleday.

Peterson, Linda H. 1991. "Gender and the Autobiographical Essay: Research Perspectives, Pedagogical Practices." *College Composition and Communication* 42.2: 170–83.

Petrosky, Anthony. 1989. "Imagining the Past and Teaching Essay and Poetry Writing." In *Encountering Student Texts,* edited by Bruce Lawson, Susan Sterr Ryan, and W. Ross Winterowd, 199–219. Urbana, IL: National Council of Teachers of English.

Reynolds, Nedra. 1992. "Ethos as Location: New Sites for Understanding Discursive Authority." Unpublished essay.

Rich, Adrienne. [1979] 1985. "Taking Women Students Seriously." In *Gendered Subjects: The Dynamics of Feminist Teaching,* edited by Margo Culley and Catherine Portuges, 21–28. London: Routledge and Kegan Paul.

Ross, Andrew. 1987. "Demonstrating Sexual Difference." In *Men in Feminism,* edited by Alice Jardine and Paul Smith, 47–53. New York: Methuen.

———. 1987. "No Question of Silence." In *Men and Feminism,* edited by Alice Jardine and Paul Smith, 85–92. New York: Methuen.

Schorer, Mark. 1948. "Technique as Discovery." *Hudson Review* 1: 67–87.

Shaw, Margaret L. 1991. "What Students Don't Say: An Approach to the Student Text." *College Composition and Communication* 42.1: 45–54.

Shelnutt, Eve. 1989. "Notes from a Cell: Creative Writing Programs in Isolation." In *Creative Writing in America: Theory and Pedagogy,* edited by Joseph M. Moxley, 3–24. Urbana, IL: National Council of Teachers of English.

Showalter, Elaine. [1982] 1987. "Critical Cross-Dressing: Male Feminists and the Woman of the Year." In *Men in Feminism,* edited by Alice Jardine and Paul Smith, 116–32. New York: Methuen.

———, ed. 1985. *The New Feminist Criticism: Essays on Women, Literature, and Theory.* New York: Pantheon Books.

Smith, Dave. 1980. "Passion, Possibility, and Poetry." In *Poets Teaching: The Creative Process,* edited by Alberta T. Turner, 173–90. New York: Longman.

Smith, Dave, and David Bottoms, eds. 1985. *The Morrow Anthology of Younger American Poets.* New York: Quill.

Sommers, Nancy I. 1982. "Responding to Student Writing." *College Composition and Communication* 33.2: 148–56.

Stafford, William. 1978. *Writing the Australian Crawl: Views on the Writer's Vocation.* Ann Arbor: University of Michigan Press.

Stanger, Carol. 1987. "The Sexual Politics of the One-to-One Tutorial Approach and Collaborative Learning." In *Teaching Writing: Pedagogy, Gender, and Equity,* edited by Cynthia L. Caywood and Gillian R. Overing, 31–44. Albany: State University of New York Press.

St. John, David. 1989. "Teaching Poetry Writing Workshops for Undergraduates." In *Creative Writing in America: Theory and Pedagogy,* edited by Joseph M. Moxley, 189–93. Urbana, IL: National Council of Teachers of English.

Summers, Hollis. 1980. "Shaking and Carving." In *Poets Teaching: The Creative Process,* edited by Alberta T. Turner, 87–92. New York: Longman.

Swarts, Heidi, Linda S. Flower, and John R. Hayes. 1984. "Designing Protocol Studies of the Writing Process: An Introduction." In *New Directions in Composition Research,* edited by Richard Beach and Lillian S. Bridwell, 53–71. New York: Guilford Press.

Tate, Gary, and Edward P. J. Corbett, eds. 1988. *The Writing Teacher's Sourcebook.* New York: Oxford University Press.

Todd, Janet. 1988. *Feminist Literary History.* New York: Routledge and Kegan Paul.

Tompkins, Jane. 1990. "A Short Course in Post-Structuralism." In *Conversations: Contemporary Critical Theory and the Teaching of Literature,* edited by Charles Moran and Elizabeth F. Penfield, 19–37. Urbana, IL: National Council of Teachers of English.

Trimbur, John. 1989. "Consensus and Difference in Collaborative Learning." *College English* 51.6: 602–16.

Tsujimoto, Joseph I. 1988. *Teaching Poetry Writing to Adolescents.* Urbana, IL: National Council of Teachers of English.

Turner, Alberta T., ed. 1980. *Poets Teaching: The Creative Process.* New York: Longman.

———, ed. 1977. *Fifty Contemporary Poets: The Creative Process.* New York: Longman.

Warhol, Robyn R., and Diane Price Herndl, eds. 1991. *Feminisms: An Anthology of Literary Theory and Criticism.* New Brunswick, NJ: Rutgers University Press.

Warnock, Tilly. 1989. "An Analysis of Response: Dream, Prayer, and Chart." In *Encountering Student Texts,* edited by Bruce Lawson, Susan Sterr Ryan, and W. Ross Winterowd, 59–72. Urbana, IL: National Council of Teachers of English.

———. 1983. "Preface 5: The Dreadful Has Already Happened; or, What Is a Rhetorician's Role in an English Department?" *Pre/Text* 4: 165–78.

Waxman, Barbara Frey. 1991. "Feminist Theory, Literary Canons, and the Construction of Textual Meanings." In *Practicing Theory in Introductory College Literature Courses,* edited by James M. Cahalan and David B. Downing, 149–60. Urbana, IL: National Council of Teachers of English.

———. 1989. "Politics of the Survey Course: Feminist Challenges." *Teaching English in the Two-Year College* 16.1: 17–22.

Wellek, Rene. 1949. *Theory of Literature.* New York: Harcourt, Brace, and World.

White, Edward. 1985. *Teaching and Assessing Writing.* San Francisco: Jossey-Bass.

Wolcott, Willa. 1987. "Writing Instruction and Assessment: The Need for Interplay between Process and Product." *College Composition and Communication* 38.1: 40–46.

Young, David. 1980. "Group I." In *Poets Teaching: The Creative Process,* edited by Alberta T. Turner, 20–25. New York: Longman.

Ziegler, Alan. 1989. " 'Midwifing the Craft'—Teaching Revision and Editing." In *Creative Writing in America: Theory and Pedagogy,* edited by Joseph M. Moxley, 209–25. Urbana, IL: National Council of Teachers of English.

———. 1984. *The Writing Workshop, Vol. 2.* New York: Teachers and Writers Collaborative.

———. 1981. *The Writing Workshop, Vol. 1.* New York: Teachers and Writers Collaborative.

Author

Patrick Bizzaro's poetry, which has appeared in six chapbooks and over one hundred magazines, has been awarded the Madeline Sadin Award from the *New York Quarterly* and the *Four Quarters* Poetry Prize from La Salle University. In addition, he has published articles on composition and the teaching of writing in *College Composition and Communication, Language Arts,* and *Teaching English in the Two-Year College,* as well as essays in numerous other NCTE affiliate journals. He is co-author of *Writing with Confidence: A Modern College Rhetoric* and the *Concise English Workbook.* His literary scholarship includes articles on Jane Austen, William Blake, and Percy Shelley, as well as a book on contemporary author Fred Chappell and over three dozen articles and book reviews on contemporary poets and poetry. He teaches at East Carolina University, where he serves as director of Writing Across the Curriculum and co-director of the Coastal Plains Writing Project. Marley, his dog, slept on a chair beside his desk throughout the writing of this book.

Grateful acknowledgment is made for permission to reprint or adapt Patrick Bizzaro's previously published poems and articles:

"Imagining the Bees" is reprinted with the permission of *Tar River Poetry*, where the poem originally appeared (Fall 1981).

"Collard Fields" was originally published in *Leaves of Green: The Collard Poems,* edited by Alex Albright and Luke Whisnant (Ayden, North Carolina, Collard Festival, 1984). Copyright © 1984 by Alex Albright and Luke Whisnant. Reprinted with their permission.

Excerpts from "Some Applications of Literary Critical Theory to the Reading and Evaluation of Student Poetry Writing" by Patrick Bizzaro originally appeared in *Poets' Perspectives: Reading, Writing, and Teaching Poetry,* edited by Charles R. Duke and Sally A. Jacobsen (Boynton/Cook Publishers, Portsmouth, NH, 1992). Reprinted by permission of the publisher.

Excerpts from "Interaction and Assessment: Some Applications of Reader-Response Criticism to the Evaluation of Student Writing in a Poetry Writing Class" by Patrick Bizzaro originally appeared in *The Writing Teacher as Researcher: Essays in the Theory and Practice of Class-Based Research,* edited by Donald A. Daiker and Max Morenberg (Boynton/Cook Publishers, Portsmouth, NH, 1990). Reprinted by permission of the publisher.

Grateful acknowledgment is also made for permission to reprint "Everything: Eloy, Arizona, 1956" from *Cruelty* by Ai. Copyright © 1970, 1973 by Ai. Reprinted by permission of Houghton Mifflin Co. All rights reserved.